Counseling

Problem

Gamblers

D0517690

A Self-Regulation Manual for Individual and Family Therapy

Counseling Problem Gamblers

A Self-Regulation Manual for Individual and Family Therapy

Joseph W. Ciarrocchi, PhD

Graduate Programs in Pastoral Counseling
Loyola College
Baltimore, Maryland

Academic Press

San Diego   New York   Boston   London   Sydney   Tokyo   Toronto

This book is printed on acid-free paper. ∞

Copyright © 2002 by ACADEMIC PRESS

All Rights Reserved

No part of this publication may be reproduced or transmitted in any form or by any means, electronic or mechanical, including photocopy, recording, or any information storage and retrieval system, without permission in writing from the Publisher.

Requests for permission to make copies of any part of the work should be mailed to the following address: Permissions Department, Harcourt, Inc., 6277 Sea Harbor Drive, Orlando, Florida 32887-66777

Academic Press
a division of Harcourt, Inc.
525 B Street, Suite 1900, San Diego, California 92101-4495
http://www.academicpress.com

Academic Press
Harcourt Place, 32 Jamestown Road, London NW1 7BY, UK
http://www.academicpress.com

Library of Congress Control Number: 2001094257

International Standard Book Number: 0-12-174653-4

PRINTED IN UNITED STATES OF AMERICA
01 02 03 04 05 06 SB 9 8 7 6 5 4 3 2 1

Dedicated to my parents, Louis and Carmella Ciarrocchi;

my sister Lucia Lawrence

and to the memory of my mother, Lina Ciarrocchi,

and my sister Maria Barnaby Greenwald

CONTENTS

CHAPTER **6 Overview of Clinical Interventions: A Plea for Family Involvement**

CHAPTER **7 Motivational Enhancement, Stages of Change, and Goal-Setting**

ACKNOWLEDGMENTS

My deepest gratitude goes first and foremost to my friend, colleague, and chairperson of Loyola College's Pastoral Counseling Department, Robert Wicks, for insisting for the past ten years that I should write this book. He and Loyola College have supported this project materially with a sabbatical as well as through other forms too numerous to mention. I am grateful to all my colleagues in the Pastoral Counseling Department for their friendship and intellectual stimulation. I especially thank Ralph Piedmont for his tutoring in the benefits of personality assessment with addicted populations, and Sharon Cheston for her model of unifying counseling approaches.

The book could not have been written without the opportunity given me by Taylor Manor Hospital, Ellicott City, Maryland, where I was Director of Addiction Services for eight years. Bruce Taylor, MD, and Irving Taylor, MD, believed in an integrated program for dual diagnosis and provided us with ample resources for quality treatment of pathological gambling, and encouraged our research efforts. Neil Kirschner, PhD, Director of Psychology, was a gracious ally, mentor, and co-researcher. The Gambling Program staff were my first and most able teachers: Robert Custer, Susan Darvas, Joanna Franklin, Sandra Leavey, Dick Richardson, and Jean Richardson. The entire gambling treatment field owes an enormous debt to Robert Custer, MD, for his clinical and political leadership in obtaining recognition of pathological gambling as a mental disorder within the mental health community, particularly through its inclusion in the DSM.

The Delaware Council on Problem Gambling, through workshops on treating gambling disorders, offered a forum to organize the book's main themes with a broad array of mental health professionals. Barbara Barr, Linda Graves, and

Executive Director Elizabeth Pertzoff have encouraged me with their positive feedback and inspired me with their commitment to improving the lives of pathological gamblers and their families.

Once again I must thank Loyola College in Maryland's reference librarians, Susan Cooperstein and her able staff, for their tenacity in tracking down research articles and their patience with my many requests. Katherine Ciarrocchi was invaluable in typing and proofreading. Words are inadequate to express appreciation to my graduate assistant of the last two years, Shannon Wise. Not only did she keep the academic side of my life organized; she typed the bulk of the manuscript, including tables, worksheets, and appendices. My wife, Anna Marie Ciarrocchi, was long-suffering with my time away from the family and gracious in reading every draft.

Readers should know that the publisher and author grant permission to copy the worksheets in this book for use with individual clients.

I am grateful to the South Oaks Foundation and its Board of Trustees for permission to reprint the South Oaks Gambling Screen. The sample psychological report in Chapter 5 of the NEO Personality Inventory–Revised is reproduced by special permission of the Publisher, Psychological Assessment Resources Inc., 16204 North Florida Avenue, Lutz, Florida 33549. It is from the NEO Personality Inventory–Revised, by Paul Costa, and Robert McCrae, © 1978, 1985, 1989, and 1992 by PAR Inc. Further reproduction is prohibited without permission of PAR Inc. The NEO–PI–R test materials can be purchased from PAR (800-331-8378).

LIST OF WORKSHEETS

The Twenty Percent Difference

A CLINICIAN'S EXPERIENCE

Clinical research on gambling is quite primitive in comparison with research on other addictions or mental disorders. Almost no controlled clinical outcome studies exist, nor does most research have even a comparison group to give the reader a sense of how problem gamblers differ from other distressed groups. With next to no government research funding and little interest from the academic community, what was learned in the first twenty years came mostly from clinical insights of practitioners or preliminary data collection from clinicians with an empirical bent. However, following the seminal work of Robert Custer (Custer & Milt, 1985), clinicians working in the hospital programs with gamblers published descriptive research on problem gambler characteristics, family environments, spouse relationships, personality patterns, and dual addiction issues (Ciarrocchi, 1987; Ciarrocchi & Hohmann, 1989; Ciarrocchi & Richardson, 1989; Ciarrocchi *et al.*, 1991; Ciarrocchi, 1993; Ciarrocchi & Reinert, 1993; Russo *et al.*, 1984; Taber *et al.*, 1987). Lacking the necessary funding for rigorously controlled studies, gambling research has made slow progress. A recent U.S. congressional initiative to study the impact of problem gambling may change this picture. The commission's recently released report (National Gambling Impact Study Commission, 1999 [online at http://www.ngisc.gov/]) with its vast literature review (National Academy Press, 1999 [online at http://www.nap.edu]) and new population survey (National Opinion Research Center, 1999 [online at http://www.norc.uchicago.edu/]) may provide an impetus for significant research funding.

In the meantime, we need to rely on clinical wisdom to understand problem gambling and how it differs from other addictions and mental disorders. Custer often remarked that problem gambling was about 80% similar to substance abuse, but he always added that understanding the 20% difference was crucial. The empirical literature (Chapter 4), however, has not identified as yet that 20%, so we are left to ponder clinical experience.

THE OTHER TWENTY PERCENT

If problem gambling is different from substance abuse, what exactly constitutes the difference?

Egotism and Entitlement

Once when staff counselors were on vacation, I substituted as leader for our inpatient gambling therapy group. This group of eight patients let it be known they were eager to meet with the program director to offer feedback on ways to improve treatment.

Their representative was also the Addictions Unit representative. Although pathological gambling patients never comprised more than about one-fourth of the total unit, they invariably served as elected officers. At this particular meeting, limited to gambling patients, the representative began by assuring me that we clearly had the finest program in the world. All concurred that they based this conclusion on extensive investigation prior to hospital admission. They then suggested that, because I was responsible for overall marketing of the program, I would no doubt welcome their suggestions to make the program even more attractive to potential gambling patients. To assist me they wrote out an extensive list of recommendations. Their major request involved setting aside a room on the unit for the exclusive use of gambling inpatients. This room would include: (a) an 800 number toll-free phone line, (b) a fax machine, (c) a copier, and (d) a computer. In this way, the patients could continue their important outside work during their hospital stay.

Moving onto existing services, they brought up our housekeeping department. Surely, they reasoned, it was in my authority to institute needed changes there. Not knowing where they were headed on this issue, I felt my own anger rising. Until now I was merely bemused at their outrageousness. Housekeeping personnel on our unit were on the low end of the wage scale, yet these women went above and beyond job descriptions to create a family atmosphere for the patients. When patients came from out of state, staff would bring them special items on holidays or birthdays and mended patient's clothing at home without compensation. So what exactly did the patients expect from housekeeping? This time the spokesperson was a parish priest in treatment. His complaint was that housekeeping neglected to pick up items from the floor of patients' rooms. After all, he pointed out, in his rectory room the housekeepers willingly picked up his dirty underwear off the floor.

The cumulative effect of hearing these requests was to render me speechless. Only readers who understand something about the culture of inpatient psychiatric treatment have a sense of the grandiosity behind such requests. This discussion took place on a locked unit that, for safety reasons and the nature of addictions treated, required body searches of patients coming in and out. The representative making the requests had embezzled half a million dollars from client stock accounts and kept his job only because the company feared multiple lawsuits if it went public with his behavior. He would probably never again make an unsupervised trade.

The first major difference, as this episode illustrates, relates to issues around egotism and entitlement. Not that other addicted populations totally lack these features, but a much larger number of gamblers exhibit these features. These attributes make standard treatment a tremendous challenge. As therapists, we know how to help persons with low self-esteem much more readily than egotistical or grandiose ones. Egotism leads to such an inflated sense of the self that beating the odds becomes a normal expectation. Later chapters (4 and 11) will explore whether entitlement also relates to types of gambling or even gender. We will also discuss self-esteem issues in relationship to spirituality and recovery in Chapter 15.

A Purely Psychological Addiction

The second major difference between problem gambling and substance abuse pertains to the nature of the addiction in each case. Compulsive behaviors ranging from alcohol and drug abuse through overeating require ingesting some external substance. The peculiarity of problem gambling is that it is a "pure" psychological compulsion. Problem gamblers lose control through repeated behavioral acts that do not, by their nature, trigger intense biological systems. Even "love addiction," which it resembles, has an instinctual affinity to the drive for species survival.

Nevertheless, even social gambling provides an emotional high when it is linked in the person's mind to risk taking. This psychological and physical experience captivates millions of people annually, resulting in their spending many billions of dollars on this activity (see the next chapter). We do not understand, however, what leads a small percentage of gamblers to cross the line to problem gambling when anyone can experience this excitement. This is not surprising given that we still have little understanding of crossing the line to alcoholism—an extremely well researched addiction.

NEED FOR A COMPREHENSIVE CLINICAL MIND

These experiences, therefore, left me with little doubt that problem gambling differed from alcoholism or drug addiction. This book is about understanding and coping with that 20% difference. It is intended for clinicians who tend to fall into two groups. The first group, small but growing rapidly, has extensive experience treating pathological gambling patients. The second consists of therapists whose work with pathological gambling patients represents a smaller portion of their clinical practice but who wish to broaden their understanding and treatment skills.

The health care system historically has not met the therapeutic needs of pathological gambling patients. For example, the main diagnostic system of mental disorders (American Psychiatric Association, 1994) classifies pathological gambling in the section "Impulse Disorders Not Otherwise Classified." As such, gambling disorders take their place next to conditions such as kleptomania and pyromania. Not only is this a kind of diagnostic wasteland, but many insurance companies refused to reimburse services for these conditions. Second, gamblers seeking treatment are tapped out financially and cannot procure mental health treatment, nor do many public treatment programs exist. In the end, therefore, most clinicians have little experience working with problem gambling.

General mental health practitioners, specialists in addiction, or clinical trainees can use this book to develop a broad-based working knowledge of the condition. In the typical first interview, therapists hear much that sounds familiar, particularly if they have addiction experience. These features include compulsive behavior, loss of control, serious impact on family, mental preoccupation, plus large doses of denial. Yet other aspects may be unfamiliar: the sheer amount of debt; needing to decide who gets paid off first—bookies or the car loan; 12-step meetings that can last 2 to 3 hours; symptoms that look like withdrawal in the absence of substance abuse; and the sense of entitlement noted above.

This book intends to be a practical guide for clinicians under all these conditions. As a treatment guide, it is written for qualified mental health professionals (psychologists, psychiatrists, clinical social workers, psychiatric nurses, certified/licensed professional counselors, pastoral counselors, and others) who are searching for a clinical overview of this debilitating problem. It intends to be thorough without being exhaustive.

Mental health professionals who are interested in certification as counselors or supervisors through the National Council on Problem Gambling (see Appendix A) may also find the book helpful as an orientation and review. Clinicians experienced in treating problem gambling may find it a useful summary and update of clinical practice.

THE CASE FOR A PRAGMATIC APPROACH

At this time, we have few well-controlled or long-term studies of problem gambling treatment. This leaves clinicians in a dilemma. A person or family in distress is expecting guidance, but the empirical literature is far from definitive. To remedy this I suggest a model that offers a pragmatic approach suitable to our current knowledge base.

Not wedded to a single theoretical base, it borrows heavily from current work in self-regulation theory, addiction treatment, and abnormal psychology. Important influences include the stages of change model, 12-step approaches, motivational enhancement, relapse prevention models, and recent research on self-esteem. I have tried to walk a tightrope between consensus-empirical models of addiction and clinical wisdom gained in treating an extensive number of problem gamblers and their families.

In addition to these more or less traditional clinical strategies, I have included in this pragmatic approach methods to incorporate clients' spiritual resources in their recovery. Most Americans believe in God, 90% pray at least occasionally, and many pray frequently (Gallup Organization, 1993). Cultural sensitivity as demanded by codes of professional ethics has signaled a bellwether change in the openness of clinical psychology and addiction treatment to spiritual and religious issues (Miller, 1999; Shafranske, 1996).

In keeping, then, with a pragmatic approach, the book emphasizes the case study method (Fishman, 1999). Drawing from a clinical bank of over 400 inpatients and half as many outpatients, the book uses composite, anonymous stories to illustrate a broad array of problem gambling issues. Readers will encounter prototypical cases as well as fuzzy, borderline situations that create diagnostic and treatment puzzles. In a spirit of helpfulness as well as truth-in-advertising, treatment failures are acknowledged so that clinicians may learn what leads to failure as well as success.

COUNTERTRANSFERENCE AND THE THREE WAYS

To serve its purpose, this book needs to help therapists deal with two critical aspects of treating problem gambling. The first relates to helping clinicians in their initial experience of seeing problem gamblers in the acute throes of the disorder. Therapists no doubt experience this in the same way William James describes the infant's view coming out of the womb as "a blooming, buzzing confusion."

The second clinical dimension relates to countertransference issues. Countertransference is used throughout in a broad sense to refer to clinician thoughts, feelings, and behavioral tendencies that arise during the course of treatment. I am not limiting its use to the traditional psychoanalytic meaning that analyzes the therapist's emotional attachment to the patient (Chaplin, 1975, p. 120). Reflection on my own typical countertransference reactions to problem gamblers reveals at least the following:

- Toward problem gamblers and their families—feelings of anger, rage, jealousy, fear, admiration, sympathy, and sadness.

- Feeling within myself—overwhelmed, helpless, hopeless, and flattered.

Not only have I experienced each of these emotions, over time a single client could instigate all of them.

To cope with both these dimensions, the book is organized around a model we have found successful in training professional counselors in our graduate program. Proposed by our colleague, Dr. Sharon Cheston (2000), it divides the clinical experience into three dimensions. Cheston refers to these dimensions as (a) way of being, (b) way of understanding, and (c) way of intervening.

Way of being refers to the therapist's interpersonal style and encompasses the relational aspects of the therapeutic experience. This could relate to a generalized, pervasive style, for example, a client-centered approach. Alternatively, it could refer to a specific style required either for a certain disorder (e.g., borderline personality), or for selective moments in the therapeutic relationship (e.g., crisis intervention). Most therapists are aware that the so-called Rogerian triad of accurate empathy, nonpossessive warmth, and acceptance is critical to establishing the therapeutic alliance. As we will repeat in the chapter on motivational enhancement (Chapter 7), we know empirically that this style has the best outcome in working with addictions (Miller & Rollnick, 1991). We will suggest, further, that the context in which many problem gamblers enter treatment is a crisis-centered one (Chapter 8). This context requires some degree of direction from the therapist, at least with regard to helping clients and families set agendas and mobilize them out of a state of shock.

Way of understanding points to the conceptual underpinnings around the clinical condition. It tries to answer questions about diagnosis, etiology, process, and the relationship between variables such as personality or family background to treatment outcomes. The way of understanding may consist of a broad-based single-theory approach (e.g., psychoanalysis, cognitive-behavioral), an eclectic, multimodal model, or a model specific to certain disorders (e.g., disease model with schizophrenia). Conceptual models help clinicians orient themselves in the longitude and latitude of the therapeutic experience. Clinicians often view models pragmatically, tending to discard or amend what does not work.

Way of intervening describes what therapists actually do in the way of specific treatment strategies with a particular individual. The distinction between way of understanding and intervention is important in several ways. First, it implies that there is no necessary connection between the two. Some may believe that interventions follow logically and deterministically from conceptual models that clinicians use. In reality, clinicians often conceptualize what is happening in the therapeutic experience according to one model, yet intervene using approaches from different systems. For instance, some psychoanalytic colleagues have readily allowed me to implement behavioral toilet training with their strong-willed toddlers.

Second, with no absolute connection between understanding and intervention, therapists must further assess what interventions are likely to be useful. In effect, the emperor has no clothes in many cases, meaning we have little conceptual understanding of many mental disorders. This often means therapists are on their own in making the best case for a specific intervention. It should come as no surprise that this situation is amplified in the case of problem gambling, a disorder officially recognized just twenty years ago.

Finally, and this is a difficult point to grasp for beginning counselors, *there is no requirement to bring the client on board with the professional's way of understanding*. As Bandura (1969) pointed out more than thirty years ago, the goal of psychotherapy is behavior change, not converting clients to our language system. Evidence abounds that clients construe the reasons for therapeutic growth in quite different terms from their therapists. Therefore, in this day of brief treatment we cannot afford to waste valuable time and energy in persuading clients as to the "truth" of our conceptual models—a shaky position at best.

Given this state of affairs, we will stick to a pragmatic course guided by empirical and clinical wisdom and structure this material in the following manner:

1. For a *way of being*, we endorse a motivational enhancement style that is based on the stages-of-change model. In our opinion, this style establishes rapport with clients and facilitates the self-awareness and insight required for effective change.

2. For a *way of understanding*, we advocate a self-regulation model that views pathological gambling as a failure to exert control over feelings, beliefs, behavior, and motivation.

3. For a *way of intervening*, we describe cognitive processing, behavioral, and relationship enhancement strategies from various applied and research traditions.

I hope this will reduce the blooming, buzzing confusion we all encounter as we treat clients with this intriguing and debilitating disorder.

The Scope of Social and Problem Gambling

SOCIAL AND RECREATIONAL GAMBLING

The following scenario in some form occurs hundreds of thousands of times daily around the world.

Aunt Tess, a 73-year-old widow, lives comfortably in her own home in a retirement villa. Occasionally lonely, nonetheless, she surrounds herself with many friends she has made in the senior citizen center. In addition to the planned social events at the center, she enjoys the twice-weekly evening card games there. Some try to teach her the finer points of Mah-Jongg, but she has not quite mastered it.

Living in southern New Jersey enables the center to organize monthly bus trips to the Atlantic City casinos. Aunt Tess looks forward to these trips more than any the Center provides. She and her friends talk about them for several days in advance. The discussion revolves around past trips, how much money each person is taking, her fantasies about hitting the jackpot, and mutual teasing. Some discuss their lucky charms and other superstitions about the trip such as their favorite bus drivers, routes, and clothes that guarantee a win.

The casino sponsoring the trip provides free transportation and $20 in quarters to each senior citizen so there is considerable merriment on the trip down. Some warn their comrades not to horn in on their favorite slot machines while others are silently contemplative like baseball pitchers before a big game.

Today Aunt Tess has a fairly typical day. Shortly after the group arrives, she hits on the nickel slots for $100. This allows her to switch for a while to the quarter slots. Fairly soon, however, she loses her winnings and needs to dip into the $100 she has set aside for the trip. Before doing so, she meets up with her friends for lunch—a sumptuous buffet at the casino, where they eat heartily for a few dollars with the help of their discount coupons.

After lunch Aunt Tess strolls down the boardwalk to the casino next door to see if her luck will be any better there. She hardly notices her arthritis as she navigates the 50 yards or so in the spring sunshine. After several ups and downs, she eventually loses her $100. Aunt Tess briefly considers getting more cash from the automatic teller machine within a few yards of her slot machine but glancing at her watch she realizes the bus leaves soon.

Back on the bus, her friends commiserate with her failure since most are in the same boat. Gladys is the lucky one today, coming home with over $400 in winnings. For a time Tess's friends fill her in about the jackpot win they witnessed after she switched casinos. A patron won the convertible sitting under the center row of slot machines, and the commotion that resulted was incredible. The casino took publicity photos, and the winner talked about driving the car back to New York.

Today gambling represents an enormous recreational growth industry. For the majority of people like Aunt Tess, gambling represents entertainment, excitement, and pleasant distraction from the vagaries of daily existence. Problem gambling can only be understood in the context of various gambling cultures. Awareness of the facts about gambling behavior can help clinicians in at least three ways:

1. Distinguishing social or recreational gambling from problem gambling.

2. Understanding the social climate of recreational gambling provides useful information about the environments that problem gamblers need to cope with, if they are to maintain recovery.

3. Awareness of the political conflicts that gambling growth causes in the culture may assist clinicians in avoiding needless disputes, yet make informed judgements about any number of thorny questions. Should clinicians be for, against, or neutral about the proliferation of gambling in their locales? Should this stance be directed toward all forms of gambling? Should they align themselves with organizations around gambling issues? Which organizations? As private citizens? As clinicians?

Who Gambles?

In the United States, 86% of the population gambles over a lifetime (all statistics are from the National Gambling Impact Study Commission report [NGISC, 1999] unless otherwise noted). In any given year 68% gamble. The proportion of people gambling represents an increase of 18% over the past 25 years, indicating tremendous growth. During this same time frame, the rates of women gambling have doubled men's. Absolute rates of men and women gambling now are roughly equal, although gender differences exist for different forms of gambling. For example, two thirds of adult bingo players are female, whereas men constitute the majority of horse race gamblers.

How Much Money Is Gambled?

In 1998, people in the United States lost a staggering $50 billion in legal wagering, "a figure that has increased every year for over two decades, and often at double digit rates" (NGISC, 1999, p. 1-1). This represents rapid geographic expansion in terms of access to legalized gambling. Forty-eight states have some form of legal gambling (all but Utah and Hawaii). Lotteries exist in 37 states, 40 have parimutuel racetracks, and casinos operate in every region following the advent of Indian gaming on tribal land and riverboat casinos.

Types of Gambling

Lotteries

At the founding of the American republic, all 13 original colonies had lotteries. Harvard and Yale in that same century grew through lottery funds. Outlawed in the 1890s by the federal government following massive scandals, they revived in 1964. In 1997 state governments collected $34 billion from lotteries and per-capita annual spending was $150. Lotteries exist in several formats.

1. Instant games or scratch tickets that reveal winning numbers, or daily three- and four-digit number games.

2. Lotto games that involve bigger numbers and greater jackpots.

3. Video keno in which bettors choose a few numbers out of a larger group and several drawings daily are displayed on video screens.

4. Electronic gaming devices that involve individual computer terminals linked to many games (e.g., video poker) and provide instant results.

Convenience Gambling

These gambling forms are found in convenience food stores, bars, airports, or even laundromats, as opposed to casinos, whose entire purpose is to attract gambling. They include stand-alone slot machines and other electronic gaming devices such as video poker. These forms are characterized by requiring little overhead, make little economic contribution to the communities served, and have potential for rapid earnings for the owners. For example, an adept gambler can play 12 hands of video poker in a minute.

Casinos

Legal in 28 states, these include over 100 "riverboats" (some are unfloatable buildings set in a manmade pool of water), and 260 Indian casinos. Las Vegas and Atlantic City have 30 and 34 million visitors a year, respectively. Gamblers wager $8 billion annually in Nevada, $4 billion in Atlantic City, and $2 billion in Mississippi. Native American tribal gambling collects an estimated $6.7 billion annually, though two-thirds of tribes do not operate casinos.

Horse Racing

This gambling form is legal in 48 states but is in considerable decline in terms of number of people attending and betting at the racetracks. The industry is attempting to attract gamblers through off-track betting (OTB). Thirty-eight states simulcast interstate racing from other tracks, either at a racetrack or in betting parlors. Bettors now wager more money off-site for horse racing than on-site. At this time, eight states allow gamblers to establish off-track accounts and place bets by telephone. As that trend continues, the only restrictions to horse race betting will be access to a phone and credit card. To compensate for lost revenue, racetracks increasingly lobby state governments for permission to install slot machines and other electronic gaming devices to attract customers. A single track may have as many as 1000 slot machines and draw as many gamblers as major casinos. The industry does not see itself surviving without these additional revenue services, and many states support the industry's requests.

Sports Wagering

Only Nevada and Oregon have legal sports wagering. Though illegal, this is the most widespread and popular form of gambling in the United States. Estimates of the amount wagered illegally vary from $80 to 340 billion annually. Sports betting is a problem for organized sports since it provides incentives for altering outcomes. Professional sports in the United States have managed to remain immune from this problem, with select exceptions. Even athletes who have been sanctioned for gambling usually deny betting on their own teams.

The same is not the case in amateur or college sports, where scandals related to attempted game fixing emerge periodically. The popularity of college sports has led to major problems among some big-time sports universities with the discovery of large-scale illegal gambling operations run by students. Naturally, these operations cause concern not just for their legal consequences but also with their proximity to players and the potential to influence game outcomes.

Internet and Related Forms

Online gambling is proliferating in ways still too new to foresee all eventualities. Cable lines now link horse racing feeds directly to living room televisions with interactive ability to place bets with your remote control. Online wagering doubled from 1997 to 1998. The commission reported 250 online casinos, 64 lotteries, 20 bingo games, and 139 sportsbooks. Bettors access these forms with their credit card numbers.

Major concerns around fraud with these operations have probably hindered an even more rapid expansion. Are the people taking your credit card number reputable? In cyberspace, locating an operator to complain to may be futile. To remedy these concerns, two countries, Australia and Antigua, have licensed Internet gambling operations, with more sure to follow. Once bettors realize that operations have sufficient oversight, we predict widespread online gambling. If competition among states in the United States is a guide, we can expect that many countries will realize the potential financial bonanza from worldwide online gambling and market new, attractive forms. Developing countries in particular would have a hard time resisting luring bettors from wealthier nations that proscribe online wagering. Congress has put forth several proposals to ban Internet gambling. Even if these laws pass, it will be difficult to enforce them against minors or to prosecute offshore or foreign government operations.

Both the privacy and convenience of online services may contribute to decreased self-control. Many have worried about generic "Internet addiction," without considering that the content of the Internet activity (gambling) has addiction potential in and of itself. Minors can have access to forms of gambling not easily achieved outside cyberspace.

Governments and Mixed Messages

State governments typically give mixed messages about gambling to their citizens. On the one hand, they regulate gambling by not allowing it to function as a free enterprise, thereby recognizing its potential for abuse. On the other hand, they have a virtual monopoly on the most popular form of legal gambling—state lotteries. Lotteries have the worst odds but the highest payoffs (see Table 2.1). In addition, the lower socioeconomic groups play the lottery in disproportionately larger numbers. States market these games aggressively, something that would be unthinkable for tobacco or alcohol. States now are dependent on lottery income despite the fact that it contributes modestly to overall general revenues (ranging from 0.41 to 4.0%; NGISC, 1999).

TABLE 2.1 Probabilities of Selected Life Events

Winning the Powerball Jackpot	1 in 80,000,000
Dying from drinking detergent	1 in 23,000,000
Being struck by lightning in a given year	1 in 750,000
Dying in a job-related accident in 1994	40 in 1,000,000
The planet being destroyed by an asteroid, meteor, or comet in the coming year	1 in 20,000
Being murdered in the next year	1 in 11,000

Source: *The Wager*, August 4, 1998, Vol. 3, issue 31.

The NGISC recommended that governments take a step back from the rapid proliferation of gambling in their jurisdictions and purposely slow it down. It suggested that governments put more work into assessing the full impact of gambling on citizens: "But overall, all agree that the country has gone very far very fast regarding an activity the consequences of which, frankly, no one really knows much about" (pp. 1–7). They advise governments to consider a pause in gambling expansion. While recognizing that research always trails behind new developments they further suggest, "this recommended pause is to encourage governments to do today what few if any have done: to survey the results of their decisions and to determine if they have chosen wisely" (pp. 1–7).

Whether governments will heed this warning is unknown, particularly because such decisions are intricately connected to competing political interests. If recent history is our guide, legalized gambling will continue its rapid expansion. With or without further expansion, gambling is now firmly established throughout the fabric of social life. Given the unlikelihood of governments eliminating existing forms of gambling, people interested in not gambling must contend with its presence, allure, and acceptability. In the next section we describe those who cross the line from social or recreational gambling into problem gambling and its considerable impact on themselves and society.

SCOPE OF PROBLEM GAMBLING

We will examine the nature and extent of problem gambling through population surveys. However, we will also consider clinical studies of gamblers in treatment to derive a common profile that therapists can recognize. We will also examine issues related to risk management, particularly the troublesome concern over suicide and parasuicide. Among other studies, we make extensive use of the recent congressionally funded National Gambling Impact Study Commission's population survey of gambling problems in the United States (NGISC, 1999).

Prevalence of Gambling Problems

The report defines *pathological gambling* using the same criteria as the DSM-IV (see Chapter 5)—namely, a person with five or more symptoms. United States *lifetime* rates—that is, the number of people likely to meet criteria for the disorder over the course of their lifetime—range from 1.2 to 1.5%. This translates into 2.5 to 3 million people. To put this in perspective, these numbers are higher than the rates for schizophrenia or bipolar disorder. Epidemiology looks not just at lifetime rates for disorders but also asks about the current rate. At this moment, how many people have the condition? The current rates (or point prevalence) of pathological gambling range from 0.6 to 0.9%, or 1.2 to 1.8 million people.

Problem Gambling

Problem gambling is defined as people who meet three or four DSM-IV criteria. Lifetime problem gambling rates range from 1.5 to 3.7% (3 to 7.8 million persons). Current problem gambling rates are 0.7 to 2.0%, or roughly 1.4 to 4 million people. *At-risk gambling*, defined as those meeting one or two DSM-IV criteria, numbers about 15 million.

At the conservative end of these estimates, 4 million people in the United States meet the criteria for problem or pathological gambling. At the liberal end, 10.8 million meet the criteria for problem or pathological gambling, with another 15 million at-risk. Whether looking at the low- or high-end estimates, these numbers speak about a condition that affects a considerable number of people directly and, as we shall see, an even larger number indirectly.

Gender

Table 2.2 provides a demographic breakdown for the disorder. No statistical differences exist between men and women for either problem or pathological gambling. More men fall into the at-risk category (9.6 vs. 6.3%), but not at the level of statistical significance.

This equality of gender is important because nearly every published survey of gamblers in treatment reveals that women are underserved. Despite existing in the general population in the same proportion as men, they are up to ten times *less* likely to enter treatment (Ciarrocchi & Richardson, 1989; Lesieur & Blume, 1991). A variety of reasons could exist for this difference.

1. Social stigma, similar to what exists for substance abuse, may prevent women from admitting to a problem.

2. The absolute amounts of money that women traditionally have had access to are typically smaller than men's, so that financial losses of women do not get the same attention.

3. Existing programs may not meet the treatment needs of women. Some hints at the relevance of this issue will come in the chapter on self-esteem issues.

A large Australian study (*n* = 1,520) with a considerable number of female participants (46%) found that the characteristics for women pathological gambling patients were considerably different from men's (Crisp *et al.*, 2000). Women were more likely to be older, be married, to live with their family, and to have dependent children. Even though women's annual income was similar to men's, their average indebtedness was less than half. Patterns of betting were also different. Women were more likely to bet on electronic gaming devices and bingo, whereas men were more likely to gamble at off-track racing parlors, racetracks, and card games.

Interesting differences emerged on DSM criteria. Men were more likely to report gambling preoccupation, jeopardizing or losing a significant relationship, job, or educational opportunity. They also were more likely to commit illegal acts. Women, on the other hand, were more likely to report gambling as a way of escaping problems. Women viewed treatment as successful more frequently than male pathological gambling patients. Men made more use of legal services and women made more use of family counseling.

TABLE **2.2** Prevalence of Gambling Problems among Demographic Groups

Demographic characteristic	At-risk (n = 267)		Problem (n = 56)		Pathological (n = 67)	
	Life-time	Past year	Life-time	Past year	Life-time	Past year
Gender						
Male	9.6	3.9	2.0	0.9	1.7	0.8
Female	6.0	2.0	1.1	0.6	0.8	0.3
Race						
White	6.8	2.7	1.4	0.6	1.0	0.5
Black	9.2	4.2	2.7	1.7	3.2	1.5
Hispanic	12.7	3.7	0.9	0.7	0.5	0.1
Other	8.8	1.8	1.2	0.5	0.9	0.4
Age						
18–29	10.1	3.9	2.1	1.0	1.3	0.3
30–39	6.9	2.1	1.5	0.8	1.0	0.6
40–49	8.9	3.3	1.9	0.7	1.4	0.8
50–64	6.1	3.6	1.2	0.3	2.2	0.9
65+	6.1	1.7	0.7	0.6	0.4	0.2
Education						
Less than high school	10.0	2.4	1.7	1.2	2.1	1.0
High school graduate	8.0	3.5	2.2	1.1	1.9	1.1
Some college	7.9	3.5	1.5	0.8	1.1	0.3
College graduate	6.4	2.0	0.8	0.2	0.5	0.1
Income						
<$24,000	7.3	2.6	1.6	0.7	1.7	0.9
$24,000–$49,999	6.9	3.2	1.8	0.9	1.4	0.6
$50,000–$99,999	8.0	2.5	1.3	0.7	0.9	0.2
>$100,000	13.4	4.9	1.4	0.4	0.7	0.2

Source: National Opinion Research Center, 1999, Table 7, p. 26.

Surveying population research epidemiologist Rachel Volberg (2000) concluded that, when gambling is legally available, women gamble just as frequently as men. However, they demonstrate a significant relationship between their gambling and risky sexual behavior and eating disorders. In addition, there is a strong correlation between women with gambling behavior and their fathers having drinking problems. Nearly 60% of female problem gamblers report hazardous alcohol use.

Ethnic Differences

African-Americans constitute a higher percentage of at-risk, problem, and pathological gamblers. The numbers of Native Americans surveyed were too small for accurate estimates, but reviews indicate that there may be a slightly higher incidence among tribal members who operate casinos.

Age

Lower rates of gambling problems occur in people older than 65, those making more than $100,000 annually, and college graduates. Higher rates exist in the young, the less educated, the poor, and perhaps those who are employed in the gambling industry.

A disturbing feature of the study is the identification of 2% of adolescents as at-risk (150,000) and 1.5% as problem or pathological gamblers (100,000). These rates are striking when one considers: (a) the relatively small amounts of money adolescents have in relationship to adults, (b) that gambling is illegal for the total age group, and (c) the presence of significant negative effects from gambling in the very young.

The *Journal of Gambling Studies* devoted an entire recent issue (Volume 16, 2000) to youth gambling in which several surveys agree with the high prevalence rates found in the NORC study. One reviewer (Jacobs, 2000) concluded that, "In the United States and Canada, as many as 15.3 million 12 year olds have been gambling with or without adult awareness or approval, and 2.2 million of these are experiencing serious gambling-related problems" (p. 119). Furthermore, the proportion of juveniles gambling and experiencing gambling problems has increased in the previous 15 years.

College surveys found that 23% of students gamble once a week, with 6 to 8% identified as problem or pathological gamblers (Lesieur *et al.*, 1991). Although these rates are much higher than in the general population, only longitudinal studies can determine whether this is a disturbing new trend or whether college-age problem gamblers mature out in ways similar to alcohol misuse. Suggestive evidence for the latter comes from the data cited above which note that problem gambling is lower in college graduates but others are less sanguine about long-term outcomes (Jacobs, 2000).

Social Costs of Gambling Problems

Employment

Problem and pathological gamblers are more likely to have lost a job in the past year. We can get a sense of the economic impact when, on average, it costs $320 in retraining costs for each gambler who loses a job.

Financial losses. Studies of Gamblers Anonymous (GA) report that between 18 and 28% of men and about 8% of women members have declared bankruptcy. In the national survey, 19% of pathological and 10% of problem gamblers declared bankruptcy. Bankruptcy figures are useful when considering an argument sometimes made for the positive effects of gambling. Economists speak in terms of "zero-sum" gains whereby someone's economic loss is someone else's gain. When applied to gambling, this argument goes, gambling losses are transferred to some segment of society that experiences a net gain. In the case of bankruptcy, the argument falters. Each bankruptcy costs creditors on average $39,000 in losses.

Problem gambling also raises household debt. On average, pathological gamblers have $48,000 in household debt compared to $22,000 for nongamblers. Table 2.3 summarizes financial characteristics and impact by type of gambler.

TABLE 2.3 Financial Characteristics and Impact

Characteristic	Lifetime gambling behavior			
	Low-risk	At-risk	Problem gambler	Pathological gambler
Any unemployment benefits, 12 months	4.0	10.9	10.9	15.0%
Received welfare benefits, 12 months	1.3	2.7	7.3	4.6%
Household income, 12 months	$47,000	$48,000	$45,000	$40,000
Household debt, current	$38,000	$37,000	$14,000	$48,000
Filed bankruptcy, ever	5.5	4.7	10.3	19.2%

Source: National Opinion Research Center, 1994, p. 44

Gamblers in treatment have considerably higher amounts of debt. One study found that 18% had debts higher than $100,000 (Ciarrocchi & Richardson, 1989).

Criminal Justice Issues

Problem and pathological gamblers in the community have higher rates of arrest and incarceration (Table 2.4). The corrections costs for each pathological gambler in the population is estimated at $1700, and $670 for each problem gambler. Gamblers in treatment have even greater legal problems. An inpatient study found 40% had been arrested, 19% incarcerated, 20% had criminal charges, and 31% had civil charges pending (Ciarrocchi & Richardson, 1989).

Divorce

Community sampling indicates higher divorce rates for pathological gamblers (54 versus 18% for nongamblers Table 2.5). We will discuss family issues in more detail in Chapter 14.

TABLE 2.4   Occurrence of Criminal Justice Consequences, by Type of Gambler

Type of consequence	Lifetime gambling behavior				
	Non-gambler	Low-risk	At-risk	Problem gambler	Pathological gambler
Arrested	4.5	11.1	20.7	36.3	32.3
Incarcerated	0.4	3.7	7.8	10.4	21.4

Source: National Opinion Research Center, 1999, p. 46.

TABLE 2.5   Marital and Health Status

Status	Lifetime gambling behavior				
	Non-gambler	Low-risk	At-risk	Problem gambler	Pathological gambler
Divorced	18.2	29.8	36.3	39.5	53.5
Poor/fair health	21.8	13.9	16.0	16.4	31.1
Mental health treatment	6.9	6.5	5.8	12.8	13.3

Source: National Opinion Research Center, 1999, p. 47.

Health

The NGISC survey estimated that increased physical problems in people with gambling disorders cost an additional $750 annually per problem gambler, and increased mental health problems cost about $330 per person (Table 2.5). In a study that compared inpatient pathological gamblers to inpatient substance abusers, pathological gamblers had a *higher incidence* of physical problems, especially those related to stress-influenced conditions (Ciarrocchi, 1987).

Conclusions

It is instructive to examine quantification of the financial burden of gambling disorders on society. The NGISC study does so as follows.

> The costs of problem and pathological gambling minus transfers [the cost to others aside from the gamblers] are $1050 and $560 per year, and $10,550 and $5130 per lifetime, respectively. When these sums are multiplied by the estimated prevalence of pathological and problem gamblers ... they translate into annual costs of about $4 billion per year, and $28 billion on a lifetime basis. If transfers to the gambler from creditors and other taxpayers are included, the costs rise to about $5 billion per year and $40 billion per lifetime. (National Opinion Research Center, 1999, p. 49)

Comorbidity

Sometimes referred to as dual diagnosis, the more precise term *comorbidity* refers to *the occurrence of two or more disorders simultaneously in a person.* An appreciation of comorbidity is especially important for the clinical management of gambling disorders due to:

1. High rates of suicidality and mood disorders.

2. Need for referral and medication management when relevant.

3. High rates of comorbid addiction and compulsive behaviors: for example, alcohol and other drug abuse, overspending, and compulsive sexual behaviors.

Table 2.6 presents the rates of psychological disorders in gamblers from the Epidemiological Catchment Area Survey. Although this study used a comprehensive diagnostic instrument, its results are limited to one geographical area (St. Louis).

Surveys indicate quite high rates of pathological gambling in substance-abusing patients in treatment (5–16%). Table 2.7 combines data from a previously

TABLE **2.6**   Prevalence of Psychiatric and Substance Abuse
Disorders in Problem Gamblers

	Percentage problem cases
Psychiatric disorder	
Manic Episode	3.1
Manic Depression	8.8
Dysthymia	4.2
Schizophrenia	3.9
Obsessive-Compulsive Disorder	0.9
Panic Disorder	23.3
Generalized Anxiety Disorder	7.7
Phobias	14.6
Somatization	8.6
Antisocial Personality	35.0
Substance use disorders	
Alcohol Abuse/Dependence	44.4
Drug Use/Dependence	39.9

Source: Cunningham-Williams *et al.*, 1998.

TABLE **2.7**   Pathological Gambling in Substance Abusers: Combined
Data from Three Programs ($n = 917$)

SOGS	Male	Female	Total
>5	626 (93%)	220 (91%)	846 (92%)
5+	48 (7%)	23 (9%)	71 (8%)
Total	674 (74%)	243 (26%)	917 (100%)

Note: 5 or more = pathological gambler

Source: Ciarrocchi *et al.*, 1998.

published study (Ciarrocchi, 1993) of substance abusers in a publicly funded outpatient program with additional samples from public and private programs totaling over 900 patients. This study (Ciarrocchi *et al.*, 1998) found that 8% met criteria for probable pathological gambler, with little difference between men and women (9 and 7%, respectively).

Not only do substance abusers in treatment have high rates of pathological gambling, but drug users recruited in community population surveys have equally high rates (Cunningham-Williams *et al.*, 2000). Drug users with Antisocial Personality Disorder were also twice as likely to be pathological gamblers than those who were not antisocial.

Taken together, studies of substance abusers are strikingly similar in demonstrating that current prevalence of pathological and problem gambling is ten times higher among substance abusers than in the general population. We now have abundant evidence from a multiplicity of research suggesting that it is unconscionable *not* to screen for gambling problems in substance abusers. One can only speculate as to what percentage of substance-abuse treatment failure results from undiagnosed and untreated problem gambling.

Finally, no discussion of comorbidity is complete without emphasizing the high rates of suicide attempts found in studies of problem gamblers. Once again, the data are amazingly consistent, whether using inpatient, outpatient, or GA samples. Taken together, about 15–20% of pathological gamblers report a significant suicide attempt. These facts provide still one more basis for employing a crisis intervention model in the initial treatment focus.

Now that we have examined the scope and nature of gambling problems, the next chapter reviews research findings on causes and treatment of pathological gambling.

Research on Causes and Treatment of Pathological Gambling

INTRODUCTION

For purposes of clinical efficiency and relevance, this review does not intend to summarize all categories of empirical work linked to pathological gambling. Rather, it focuses on the findings that are most salient for the practicing clinician. Nor does it cover population research, comorbidity, family issues, or legal issues, which are covered in the relevant chapters.

Practically speaking, then, this review addresses two main topics. The first addresses Rachlin's oft-quoted question, "Why do people gamble and keep gambling despite heavy losses?" (1990, p. 294). This will take us into the literature on risk factors and individual differences in gambling behavior. The second major topic that is relevant to clinicians, of course, is the treatment literature. As we shall see, this literature is quite sparse, and likely to remain so without adequate funding for controlled-outcome research.

RISK FACTORS

This section critically examines survey literature on age, gender, ethnicity, and family background factors as risk factors for pathological gambling.

Age

In modern industrial societies, on average, people gamble at an early age. Male pathological gamblers start gambling much earlier than the general population and earlier than female pathological gamblers. In a study of 892 11th- and 12th-grade students in three public and one Catholic school in New Jersey, 86% reported they gambled within the past year (Lesieur & Klein, 1987). Overall, 5.7% met criteria for pathological gambling based on DSM-III criteria. Among the significant problems caused by gambling, 11% reported family disruption, 15% lied to cover up gambling, and 10% committed a gambling-related illegal act. Although proximity to Atlantic City was not related to problem gambling, it is interesting that 46% of all students, despite their underage status, claim to have gambled in casinos. These results are typical of several investigations of adolescent gambling in the United States and elsewhere (Jacobs, 1989).

College students showed similar gambling patterns and consequences. A survey of more than 1,700 college students in five states found that 85% gambled (Lesieur et al., 1991), and 23% once a week or more. On the basis of the SOGS, 15% fell into the problem gambling range and 5.5% in the pathological gambling range. As expected, schools and states with more legal gambling venues had significantly greater rates of pathological gambling.

In Minnesota, 88% of 1,361 undergraduate students sampled at two colleges gambled in the past year (Winters *et al.*, 1998). Using the SOGS, 4.4 and 2.9% fell in the potential and probable pathological gambling categories, respectively, compared to the 1.1% pathological gambling rate in that state's general population.

In the most extensive U.S. national population survey to date (NORC, 1999), youth problematic gambling was lower than for adults. Among 16–17 year olds interviewed, 2% fell in the at-risk group and 1.5% in the problem or pathological gambling range. This compares to 7.95 at-risk and 2.1% problem and pathological gamblers among adults in the same survey. A third of adolescents never gambled, compared to a seventh of adults.

Young people also demonstrated different betting patterns. They wagered considerably less money in absolute amounts, with only 2% (vs. 22% of adults) losing more than $100.00 in a single day. Adolescents also bet differently from adults, with private betting on games of skill as the most popular (40 vs. 10% for adults). Lotteries are the most popular for adults (50%), but only one in eight teenagers played them. The report noted the difficulty of determining what represents pathological gambling among the young. When the researchers adjusted for the smaller amounts of money at stake, rates of pathological and problem gambling matched adult rates and at-risk gambling was twice the adult rate.

Interpreting this study in light of previous surveys is puzzling. High school and college surveys consistently find that pathological gambling is *greater* among the young. NORC data state the opposite, unless spending is adjusted, in which case problem and pathological gambling are equal to adult rates. School surveys may inflate gambling rates due to the potential social contagion effect of recruiting students in classroom settings. Alternatively, the random phone interviews NORC conducted that required first obtaining parental consent may have screened out a greater percentage of youngsters likely to have a problem.

Many studies have found pathological gambling patients report gambling at an early age. The breakdown of age first gambled for 186 pathological gamblers in treatment at a private psychiatric hospital was as follows: 8% before age 10; 46% between 10 and 13 years old; and 27% between 14 and 17 (Ciarrocchi & Richardson, 1989). Over half gambled by age 13 and 81% before 18 years of age. Adolescents classified as pathological gamblers reported gambling significantly earlier (9.2 years old) than the age (11.3) reported by those without problems (Griffiths, 1990a,b).

From cross-sectional survey literature we can draw two conclusions: people in the general population gamble at a fairly young age, and problem gamblers begin even earlier, with many exhibiting problems in their adolescence.

Interpretation of these facts is less clear. Without longitudinal studies, we are left with two opposing theories. The "slippery-slope" hypothesis suggests that pathological gambling patterns in a young person is the template for that individual's future career in gambling—one likely to lead to adult status pathological gambling. This model suggests that educators and mental health specialists should aggressively identify and intervene with adolescent and college-age problem gambling. The "sow-their-wild-oats" theory suggests that problem gambling is a developmental phase for a small number of young people prone to excitement-seeking—a pattern that will "mature out" for the majority, as occurs with alcohol and drug abuse.

As this book maintains throughout, however, therapists cannot wait for definitive research. Under these opposing viewpoints, what makes the most sense clinically? Adolescent behavior is fluid, and even those scoring high on the SOGS in these samples do not resemble scores of adult pathological gamblers in treatment. Therefore, one should be tentative about diagnostic labels for several reasons. Adolescents spend considerably less money gambling than adults, have less access to gambling venues, and resist describing themselves as addicted. Furthermore, the research evidence as yet does not support believing that problem gambling patterns in adolescence continue into adulthood. What may be more salient in the clinical evaluation of young people is inability to control gambling and its negative consequences.

Nevertheless, individual adolescents can cause significant damage to their lives even if they do not meet diagnostic criteria for pathological gambling. For example, although many high school and college age drinkers will cease abusing alcohol as they grow up, the behavior itself is linked to many personal and social problems. These problems include overdose potential, unsafe sex practices, aggressive behavior, and operating motor vehicles under the influence, to name a few. Many a promising student has derailed his or her education due to alcohol-related infractions, even though their problem was "only" one of abuse. Similarly, problem gambling in a high school senior that leads to getting caught in a "sting" operation could end his or her chances of going to a military academy, joining the police force, or obtaining a computer job that requires security clearance.

Until we have a diagnostic distinction between gambling abuse and pathological gambling, it seems wise for the clinician to interpret the diagnostic entities in adolescent gambling behavior cautiously. Using the Adjustment Disorder category or Impulse Control Disorder, Not Otherwise Specified when gambling is causing problems in school or with family permits addressing gambling problems without fitting youngsters into an adult-based addiction model.

At the other end of the age spectrum is concern about the popularity of gambling as entertainment for the elderly and those in retirement. Is this population more susceptible to gambling problems due to increased leisure, health concerns, personal loss, or social-status shift? Are they vulnerable, moreover, to financial devastation from excessive gambling with little opportunity to recoup lost income? Despite evidence that casinos market aggressively to retirees and the notable presence of the elderly in gambling establishments, survey research does not point to any great wave of pathological gambling in the elderly. The recent survey conducted for a U.S. Congress gambling impact study found low rates of pathological gambling in those 65 and older as has other research (Mok & Hraba, 1991). It classified 1.3 and 0.8% as problem and pathological gamblers, respectively, in the general population, with the respective rates in the 65-and-older group 0.2 and 0.1%. Elderly patrons at gambling venues, however, had significantly higher rates of problem and pathological gambling than community controls (McNeilly & Burke, 2000). These results may support clinical concerns that elderly gamblers exhibit a more rapid progression toward pathological gambling than is developmentally typical for younger cohorts, but presently those concerns are speculative.

Gender

A literature review for the DSM-IV Task Force reported that pathological gambling is two times more common in males than females in population surveys (Lesieur & Rosenthal, 1991). Furthermore, women were highly underrepresented in treatment programs and Gamblers Anonymous. The National Opinion Research Center population survey (1999) found that rates of problem and pathological gambling for men and women were comparable: problem gambling 1.6% for men, 1% for women, pathological gambling 0.9 and 0.7 for men and women, respectively. This report, however, makes a misleading statement in interpreting gender differences. It states, "Both the NRC [National Research Council] and NORC studies found that men are more likely to be pathological, problem, or at-risk gamblers than women" (NGISC, 2000, p. 4-11), but only the at-risk group reached statistical significance in the NORC study (9.6 vs. 6.3%, men vs. women).

Various explanations could account for the discrepant findings on gender difference in gambling problems. NORC's data may be correct in that they signal women catching up to men in terms of gambling problems nationwide. On the other hand, they may mean that the telephone sampling technique undersampled male pathological gamblers but not female ones. Evidence exists for this interpretation in the patron survey data of the NORC report. Researchers interviewed patrons of gambling establishments, and these data demonstrated the typical 2:1 male:female ratio for pathological gambling. This reasoning itself may be faulty as well in that most previous population surveys were telephone interviews.

The NORC study does not report gender results for its sample of 16–17 year olds, except for noting that two-thirds of those who gambled $100 or more in a single day were male. The early adolescent and college-age studies reviewed above, however, uniformly report higher gambling involvement in young males and rates about twice as high for problem–pathological gambling.

Ethnicity and Socioeconomic Status

The NRC review states that "studies have also generally failed to disentangle race and ethnicity from issues of poverty and socio-demographic status" (National Academy Press, 1999, p. 116). It concluded that problem but not pathological gambling was more likely to affect whites than African-Americans. The NORC study rates can be found in Table 2.2 in the previous chapter. Only the higher rate of pathological gambling for blacks reached statistical significance. Once again, the patron survey changed the results so that blacks were significantly higher for the at-risk, problem, and pathological categories as well.

Few studies have addressed pathological gambling among Native American populations in the United States. One survey (Volberg & Abbott, 1997) found more gambling involvement and gambling-related problems in a Native American population than for a comparable white population. Similarly, adolescent Native Americans had significantly greater gambling-related problems than their non-Indian peers did (Zitrow, 1996).

Family Influences

A study of over 400 Canadian children indicates how prevalent gambling is within the family setting (Gupta & Derevensky, 1997). Overall, 81% of the students gambled; 52% of those who gambled did so weekly, and 81% who gambled did so with family members. The family breakdown was as follows: 40% gambled with their parents, 53% with siblings, and 46% with other relatives. Only 18% reported gambling alone, but 75% gambled with friends. This validates previous research that implicates social learning in the development of gambling behavior. In Minnesota, 72% of adolescents surveyed reported receiving lottery tickets from their parents (Gupta & Derevensky, 1997).

A meaningful clinical question is the degree to which pathological gambling in parents influences its development among offspring. Methodological limitations prevent a direct answer to that question at present. However, several studies noted high rates of perceived problem gambling in the parents of pathological gamblers (Ciarrocchi & Richardson, 1989; National Academy Press, 1999), ranging from three to eight times higher than population surveys. The same research also found high rates of alcoholism and substance abuse in the parents of pathological gamblers. Such findings support the general theory of addictions discussed later.

Hereditary Influences

Pathological gamblers were more likely than controls to have an allele of the dopamine 2 receptor, a gene implicated in substance abuse transmission (Comings *et al.*, 1996). Not only was the gene found in a greater percentage of pathological gamblers, but the percentage increased with degree of severity of the disorder.

Jews had considerably lower rates of the gene, suggesting an alternative predisposition to pathological gambling. Surprisingly, major depression was *less* likely to occur in pathological gamblers with the gene, and this was particularly notable in women (83 vs. 9% in controls). For women, then, major depression may provide a different route from genetics to developing pathological gambling (Zuckerman, 1999, pp. 308–309).

INDIVIDUAL DIFFERENCES: MODELS AND RESEARCH

Preliminary Considerations

Disentangling the causes of pathological gambling is fraught with scientific and practical complexity. At one level, why people gamble is exceedingly easy to answer. They gamble for the same reason bank robber Willie Sutton gave for robbing banks: "That's where the money is." Those who study pathological gambling are curious as to why some *persist* in behavior that causes such negative consequences. The scientific understanding of pathological gambling, therefore, has to contend with several questions:

1. What leads *anyone* to gamble?

2. What leads gamblers to *persist* when losing?

3. What leads *this* gambler to persist when losing?

Answering these questions requires fairly rigorous research that unfortunately is lacking. Social psychologists and the gaming industry have a particular interest in question 1. Clinicians are interested in 2 and 3.

Much confusion occurs, however, when answers to the first question are applied indiscriminately to the other two. The review on individual differences is not meant to be an exhaustive survey (for reviews, see Walker, 1992, and Zuckerman, 1999). Early on in their treatment of pathological gamblers, clinicians were quick to comment on how pathological gamblers as a group seem unique in terms of their personality structure. Psychoanalysts noted their entitlement, and others pointed to excitement-seeking as a common trait. As we shall see, however, the use of personality tests to measure these individual differences is a promise unfulfilled. Often the studies do not include adequate comparison groups, or they use measures that have limited predictability for specific behaviors (Bandura, 1986). Nevertheless, researchers have examined several plausible individual differences that have clinical relevance.

Sensation-Seeking

Casual observation suggests people gamble for excitement. Theorists interested in the personality trait of sensation-seeking suggested its link to pathological gambling. Since the majority of people in the population gamble, this theory predicts that pathological gamblers would be higher on sensation-seeking relative to nonpathological gamblers. This also follows from assuming that sensation-seeking represents a normally distributed personality feature.

An early study of 30 pathological gamblers found this group significantly higher on all four subscales of a standard sensation-measuring instrument (Zuckerman, 1979). The GA 20, a measure that GA members use to screen potential members but whose psychometric properties have received scant attention, was used to determine pathological gambling status. More studies have found sensation-seeking was either lower in pathological gamblers (Blaszczynski *et al.*, 1986; Coventry & Brown, 1993) or not related to gambling problems (Dickerson *et al.*, 1990b; Langewisch & Frisch, 1998). Some research found sensation-seeking was linked to greater gambling involvement as well as problematic gambling styles, for example, chasing (Dickerson *et al.*, 1987), but others have not found a relationship between sensation-seeking and chasing behavior (Breen & Zuckerman, 1999).

Some evidence has emerged linking sensation-seeking to different forms of gambling. Although off-track bettors were *lower* on sensation-seeking than the general population, casino and racetrack gamblers scored *higher* (Coventry & Brown, 1993). However, problem poker machine players were no different from problem horse-race gamblers on proneness to boredom (Cocco *et al.*, 1995). Other work has failed to find sensation-seeking differences between pathological gamblers and substance abusers (Castellani & Rugle, 1995), or between men and women college students relative to gambling involvement (Wolfgang, 1988).

In summary, sensation-seeking received little support for its strong form, which suggests it is a core underlying personality trait predisposing one to develop pathological gambling. There may be a relationship in high school students, for certain types of gamblers, or as a predisposition to more problematic wagering. Pathological gamblers as a group are not cortically underaroused, excitement-seeking individuals.

Arousal Theories

Arousal theories attempt to link the psychophysiological underpinnings in pathological gambling to the subjectively experienced excitement that occurs during the enterprise itself. To date, the findings are complex and inconclusive. What appears undisputed at this time is that gambling does indeed increase physiological arousal (Anderson & Brown, 1984; Brown, 1986; Leary &

Dickerson, 1985), and that arousal is greater in the real gambling situation than in the laboratory (Anderson & Brown, 1984).

Other relationships are equivocal at this point. Regular gamblers report greater arousal than less regular gamblers (Dickerson & Adcock, 1987; Dickerson *et al.*, 1987). In other research, problem gamblers reported higher arousal than potential problem gamblers and nonproblem gamblers, but no differences existed between potential problem gamblers and nonproblem gamblers (Ladouceur *et al.*, 1997). On psychophysiological measures, no differences in heart rate occurred between these groups when actually gambling (Griffiths, 1993). Level of preferred arousal appears to differentiate types of gambling. Problem horse-race gamblers preferred higher levels of arousal than did problem poker-machine players (Cocco *et. al.*, 1995). When multiple measures of physical arousal are included, the relationships become highly complex. Heart rate changes did not occur when pathological gamblers were compared to high- and low-frequency social gamblers. However, skin conductance measures did differentiate pathological gamblers from social gamblers, but not low- and high-frequency gamblers from each other (Sharpe *et al.*, 1995). This suggests that arousal as a phenomenon in pathological gambling is multidimensional and that the relationships among the measures are asynchronous. The same study also found evidence that arousal may be cognitively mediated but did not study specific cognitions.

The theories attempting to explore the link between arousal and gambling behavior are thus flat out contradictory. Some view arousal as reinforcing and thus sought after, some as aversive, thereby motivating people to escape it via gambling, and still others view arousal as driving people to an optimal resting state. In summary, arousal theories, whether emphasizing sensation-seeking, excitement-seeking, proneness to boredom, or physiological arousal set, have weak empirical support. This may be related to inconsistency in population samples, method variance, or simply lack of a relationship.

Impulsivity

Impulsivity has obvious prima facie validity in its relationship to pathological gambling. For clarity, however, it is important to distinguish impulsivity from similar variables. Eysenck, for example, whose impulsivity scale is often used in gambling research, sees sensation-seeking as one aspect of impulsivity. Furthermore, he sees impulsivity as part of extroversion (Eysenck & Eysenck, 1977), whereas the leading sensation-seeking researcher maintains that impulsivity is independent of extroversion (Zuckerman, 1994). This latter position has strong empirical support from research on the five-factor model (FFM) of personality (Piedmont, 1998) and is the view shared in this review. Impulsivity, therefore, is conceptualized as giving in to one's impulses or desires even though they have negative consequences. Excitement-seeking and/or sensation-seeking, however, are part of the broader dimension of extroversion.

Empirical support also exists for this distinction from gambling research. Eysenck's Impulsivity Scale has four subscales: Impulsivity, Risk-Taking, Nonplanning, and Liveliness. Impulsivity and Nonplanning consistently separate out pathological gamblers from nonpathological gamblers, whereas the other two do not (Steel & Blaszczynski, 1998). In addition, impulsivity measured in 13-year-old boys predicted pathological gambling at age 17 (Vitaro *et al.*, 1997). This represents the only long-term longitudinal study of a personality variable in pathological gambling research. Impulsivity also discriminated chasers from non-chasers in a laboratory gambling study (Breen & Zuckerman, 1999). Several aspects of impulsivity—including craving, motor impulsivity, and nonplanning—distinguished pathological gamblers from alcoholics and cocaine addicts in treatment (Castellani & Rugle, 1995).

In summary, the consistency of this research supports the conclusion that impulsivity plays a key role in understanding pathological gamblers (Steel & Blaszczynski, 1998). Future research needs to replicate the greater degree of impulsivity in pathological gamblers compared to other addictive disorders and to understand its development through developmental, motivational, affective, and cognitive antecedents. The FFM may provide greater heuristic benefit, for it orients impulsivity within the broader factor of neuroticism, that is, the tendency to experience negative emotions. Researchers may also gain a greater understanding of pathological gambling by anchoring pathological gambling behavior under the motivation to reduce emotional distress. In discussing self-regulation theory, we shall examine research linking emotional distress to self-control failure. Another hypothesis relates sensation-seeking and impulsivity to different points in pathological gambling development (Zuckerman, 1999). Sensation-seeking may predispose people to start gambling, whereas impulsivity may influence self-control, a position that also fits in with the self-regulation model discussed in the next chapter.

GENERAL PERSONALITY CHARACTERISTICS

Research on personality variables associated with problem gambling has mostly focused on specific lower-order traits such as sensation-seeking, arousal, and impulsivity. This next section looks at the relatively little research that has examined broad personality features in pathological gambling.

MMPI Studies

In terms of sheer numbers, MMPI studies have dominated the field of pathological gambling. The MMPI is a frequently used measure of psychological symptoms with a long history of clinical and experimental use. In a study of 100 male pathological gamblers in a Veteran's Administration (VA) hospital treatment program, four scales were in the elevated range: 4, 2, 7, and 8 (Graham & Lowenfeld, 1986). The major symptom patterns for these scales are impulsive acting out, depression, severe tension, and alienation respectively (Butcher, 1990). The predominance of scale 4 elevation reflects a population on the whole that has "disregard for social customs and mores, inability to profit from experience, and immature, aggressive, and shallow personalities" (Graham & Lowenfeld, 1986, p. 65). Cluster analysis revealed four predominant patterns accounting for 89% of the cases. The most common cluster (scales 4 and 9 elevation) represents a personality disorder characterized by rebellion, immaturity, and acting out. Cluster 2 (elevations on scales 8, 7, 2, and 4) typifies persons who tend to be suspicious, rigid, irritable, and withdrawn. Cluster 3 (very elevated scale 2 and moderate elevations on 3, 4, and 7) typifies passive-aggressive personalities, who often have problems with alcoholism. Cluster 4 (highly elevated scale 4) characterizes immature, moody, tense individuals with extremely low frustration tolerance. VA patients with this profile typically have histories of substance abuse as well. Smaller MMPI studies have found similar patterns, particularly scale 2 and 4 elevations (Moravec & Munley, 1983), which represent the prototypical substance-abuse treatment profile (Butcher, 1990).

The similarity between pathological gambling and substance abuse on the MMPI is interesting both clinically and theoretically. How do the two groups compare on the MMPI? Unpublished work (Lowenfeld, 1978) reported that alcoholics and pathological gamblers in a VA hospital treatment program did not differ on any individual MMPI scale. They did differ on 35 MMPI items, an unimpressive 6% of the total test. Such studies have a major confound in that they have not systematically eliminated pathological gambling from substance-abuse problems. Rates of alcoholism in pathological gamblers are exceedingly high, so the similarity in profiles may be an artefact of both groups' alcohol dependence.

To address this methodological concern, a study of pathological gamblers and alcoholics in a private psychiatric hospital compared 96 alcoholics to 81 pathological gamblers with substance dependence and 55 without substance dependence (Ciarrocchi *et al.*, 1991). No differences emerged when alcoholics were compared to the entire pathological gambling sample or when nonalcoholic gamblers were compared either to alcoholic gamblers or alcoholics alone. Once again, the familiar 2–4-scale pattern stood out as the only ones in the elevated range.

Tests of Normal Personality

Tests of normal personality have not fared much better in terms of finding differences between pathological gamblers and alcoholics. Gamblers and alcoholics differed from medical controls on several scales of the California Personality

Inventory (McCormick *et al.*, 1987) but did not differ from each other. Even when the analysis split gamblers into substance-abusing and nonsubstance-abusing groups, no major differences emerged.

In summary, the burden of proof clearly lies with those maintaining some unique personality configuration for pathological gamblers. The only differences to date occurred on scales related to impulsivity but these differences lack consistency across studies. Given that the MMPI represents a limited dimension of personality (neuroticism), it is not surprising that researchers have found few differences. It is perhaps noteworthy that the best controlled study that found differences between alcoholics and pathological gamblers (Castellani & Rugel, 1995) used subscales from a five-factor model of personality (NEO–PI–R). This may represent a wiser choice for finding distinguishing characteristics of pathological gamblers from substance abusers (Piedmont, 1998). Answering this theoretical question remains important, for it may determine whether clinicians should approach treating pathological gamblers in the same way they approach treating alcoholics.

AFFECTIVE–MOTIVATIONAL VARIABLES

Depression

In this section we examine negative mood states in relationship to motivation to gamble. Positive findings would suggest some form of escape mechanism. Arousal and sensation-seeking are motivational variables as well, but this section considers only negative emotional states.

Despite the obvious clinical interest in depression, few studies have addressed depressed mood as an antecedent to gambling. As noted above in the MMPI review, pathological gamblers clearly report high levels of depression relative to nontreatment groups. We cannot determine from this research whether depression is the cause or the effect of pathological gambling. Research into depressed mood as an antecedent to gambling is inconclusive. Some studies found that depression in adults is higher in probable pathological gamblers than in potential or nonproblem gamblers (Ladouceur *et al.*, 1997). Others found similar results for high school students (Gupta & Derevensky, 1998). Mood states, however, did not predict level of gambling involvement, duration of gambling session, or persistence when losing for poker machine players (Dickerson *et al.*, 1990a). Similarly, in general surveys asking people their reasons for gambling, as few as 1% report "forgetting troubles" as a major reason (Dickerson *et al.*, 1990b). A comparison of heavy gamblers with light gamblers and nongamblers found that heavy gambling was negatively correlated with depression and anxiety (Kusyszyn & Rutter, 1985), suggesting that negative moods might *decrease* with heavy gambling.

The results for anxiety as a negative state are similar. Some have found pathological gamblers higher in state anxiety than high- or low-frequency gamblers (Sharpe *et al.*, 1995), while others measuring the same variable found no differences (Ladouceur *et al.*, 1997). Although pathological gambling high school students were higher on apprehension than their nonproblem gambling peers, their scores were not above normal for the standardized sample (Gupta & Derevensky, 1998).

A potentially fruitful area for exploring meaningful new differences in pathological gambling may relate to the distinction between skill and luck gambling. Some gambling activities are purely chance enterprises (e.g., lotteries, slot machines), whereas skill enhances the probability of winning some types (horseracing, poker, and sports betting). We saw earlier that arousal levels differ for types of gamblers, and this pattern may hold for negative mood states as well. A study of VA inpatients found that predominantly luck pathological gamblers scored significantly higher on scales 2 and 0, but significantly lower on scale 9 than predominantly skill pathological gamblers (Adkins *et al.*, 1988). Scale 2 relates to depression, scale 0 is a measure of social introversion, and scale 9 relates to psychological and physical energy (Graham, 1990). Similarly, poker machine players (luck) scored higher on trait anxiety than horse-race players (skill) (Cocco *et al.*, 1995). Drawbacks in the former study include the use of social gamblers and a small sample of luck gamblers (133 skill, 21 luck).

In summary, the role played by negative mood states in either the onset or persistence of problem gambling is not known at this time, although depression as a consequence of pathological gambling is well established.

Escape

Jacobs (1986) has proposed a motivational model based on the centrality of escape and its similarity across addictions. Gambling, like alcohol and drug abuse, begins with intensely negative childhood experiences that predispose the person to high levels of negative affect. This, in turn, leads to various escape routes, some of which include addictive behaviors. In a study of 30 GA members and 30 social gamblers, the former endorsed four dissociative items more frequently (Kuley & Jacobs, 1988). These items referred to feeling like a different person while gambling, feeling in a trance after a period of gambling, feeling outside oneself while gambling, and experiencing memory blackouts after a period of gambling. Similar dissociative items discriminated problem gambling from social gambling in a sample of French-Canadian high school students (Gupta & Derevensky, 1998). Pathological gamblers differed from other gamblers on a series of reasons given for gambling. Nevertheless, only 20% of pathological gamblers reported "escape problems" as a reason for gambling in contrast, for example, to "enjoyment" (92.3%), excitement (92.3%) or "make money" (87.7%). This suggests that escape, as a conscious motivation, is not foremost in adolescents with pathological gambling problems.

COGNITIVE DISTORTIONS

Research on cognitive errors and their relationship to gambling has special importance for the pathological gambling field. First, this research has generated promising treatment strategies. Second, the model flows organically from some of the best research in social-cognitive psychology, arguably the major paradigm in social psychology today (Bandura, 1986; Barrone *et al.*, 1997). Before reviewing the gambling-related literature, it seems useful to anchor that research within the broader domain of social-cognitive theory, particularly for those less familiar with academic social psychology.

To simplify enormously, social-cognitive theory developed three separate insights as to how people engage in the process of social knowing. These views are not necessarily in opposition to each other, and many findings support one or the other. The first insight is seeing people as "naive scientists." In this view, people approach planning and other cognitive tasks in a similar way to how scientists problem-solve. They define the problem, analyze solutions, select the most adequate one, implement it, and then evaluate it.

The second insight challenged this view through research that found people regularly take mental shortcuts in the rush of everyday life. We operate on a series of implicit, highly personal rules that guide our judgment. For example, people probably use a few simple rules when deciding which breakfast cereal to purchase from the hundreds of different brands in the grocery store aisle. The rules may range from familiarity, past experience, advertising, cost, nutritional advantage, or simply what the children are most likely to eat. Researchers dubbed this insight the "cognitive miser" approach, meaning that we tend to make our mental efforts as least taxing as possible.

The third insight represents a swing of the pendulum between these positions. It suggests that people operate both as naive scientists *and* cognitive misers, but that context is all important. Purchasing a new home usually elicits a much broader range of cognitive strategies than choosing cereal—ones that more closely resemble the naive scientist. This insight, then, sees people as "motivated tacticians"—using more elaborate cognitive strategies when facing situations where there is much to lose.

Early Findings

One of the earliest aspects of social knowing that interested psychologists was the central role that a belief in control played in people's lives. This belief is essential for nearly every action, from getting out of bed in the morning to building a tunnel under the English Channel. So strong is the necessity of this belief that research discovered we sometimes maintain that belief even when it is illusory. In a series of elegant studies using chance gambling situations Ellen Langer (1975; Langer & Roth, 1975) found that several factors influence this illusion of control.

1. *Personal choice*. People believe their lottery ticket is worth more if they personally select it rather than when randomly distributed.

2. *Practice*. People believe they have a greater chance of winning a totally random game when they are given a chance to practice with the apparatus.

3. *Early wins*. People who correctly predict heads or tails early in a sequence of coin tossing believe more strongly in their control than those who do not.

4. *Familiarity*. People who are familiar with the situation believe more strongly in their sense of control than people who are less familiar with it, even though chance determines the outcome.

5. *Type of competitor*. People wager more against a seemingly incompetent bettor than a seemingly competent one, even though, once again, the outcome is totally determined by chance.

A second major insight on cognitive distortions in gambling came from studying biased evaluations of gambling outcomes (Gilovich, 1983; Gilovich & Douglas, 1986; Gilovich *et al.*, 1985). This work addresses the paradox that "many gamblers have, or acquire, a belief that they will be successful, and this belief tends to persist despite seemingly convincing evidence to the contrary" (Gilovich, 1983, p. 1111). They hypothesized that people's *interpretations* of gambling might be biased and thus influence their gambling persistence. For example, a well-known bias in social cognitive theory is the so-called self-serving bias. This is the tendency for people to explain positive outcomes in their life as a result of their own skill or character, but to explain negative outcomes as caused by the situation, chance, or some other external cause. These studies found similar tendencies when people explained gambling outcomes. People thought about their losses longer and remembered them better than their wins. Consistent with the self-serving bias, they explained away their losses but saw wins as bolstering their own skills. When people perceived a "fluke" in the wagering situation, they expressed confidence in their ability to predict outcomes even though they actually lost that wager. This was also the case in betting situations that were totally chance-determined.

The third source of insight into distortions came from research on predicting outcomes. Imagine a fair coin that has turned up ten heads in a row. Many people predict that the chance of a tail coming up next is significantly higher than 50% even though probability states each outcome is totally independent of the previous one. Cognitive psychology, which studies both the effectiveness and ineffectiveness of our thinking strategies, labeled this error the *gambler's fallacy*. Linking events to their antecedents is quite functional for survival. If I turn the ignition key, the car starts; hit the nail with the hammer, it goes into the wood; red sky in the morning, sailor's warning, and so on. Random events, however, represent a part of reality where linking antecedents to consequences tricks us into making erroneous conclusions. Staying with that slot machine because it hasn't paid off all day is a prime example of the gambler's fallacy, as is repeatedly playing my lottery number because "it's bound to hit." On a recent television documentary about Las Vegas, a gambling instructor pointed out that the number 15 is very popular in Keno wagering. This is remarkable, given its low statistical probability, combined with the fact that the number has never hit in the entire history of Keno there.

In summary, social cognitive theory states that people have a variety of cognitive schemas or relatively persistent ways of looking at the universe that work very well for us most of the time. However, just because they are our "default" mechanisms does not make them error-free. Just as a mirage can fool depth perception into thinking there is water ahead, so too our schemas can distort reality.

A social cognitive perspective would see at least three reasons for persistence in gambling:

1. Our illusions of control lead us to persist because we have unrealistic confidence in our ability to influence even random outcomes.

2. Our tendency to interpret outcomes in a self-serving way leads to our not using outcome data effectively. We view success as related to our ability but failure as external. Once again, this contributes to excessive confidence in our ability to succeed at gambling.

3. The very way our minds work to organize cause–effect relationships leads us to believe random events are actually related. Bolstered by this (mis)belief, we again assume an unwarranted confidence in our ability to predict and control future outcomes and wager unrealistically.

Recent Research

Recent research on gambling and pathological gambling attempts to link these three avenues under the rubric of "cognitive distortions." As we examine this literature, it is useful to keep in mind the distinctions between initiating gambling, persisting at gambling, and becoming a pathological gambler.

The studies reviewed earlier in this section provide good support for the relationship between gambling persistence and cognitive distortions. More recent work has validated the familiarity effect with longer-term gambling in a laboratory gambling situation (Breen & Frank, 1993), although no evidence of increased wagering during winning or losing streaks emerged. Off-track bettors in Australia reported a high degree of exaggerated beliefs (Dickerson et al., 1990b), with 80% believing they would be successful on their next bet. Confirming earlier lab research (Langer, 1975) and clinical observations (Custer & Milt, 1985), the same study found that 83% of those surveyed reported a "big win," 25% of them early in their gambling careers. Contrary to social cognitive theory, however, gambling beliefs were not related to level of gambling involvement. French-Canadian potential pathological gamblers reported higher levels of erroneous gambling perceptions than nonproblem gamblers (Ladouceur et al., 1997). However, of five gambling types surveyed, this finding held only for bingo and roulette. Potential pathological gamblers also had higher levels of nongambling-related superstitious beliefs than nonproblem gamblers.

Chasing is associated with problem gambling and represents one DSM criterion for pathological gambling (Chapter 5). In a laboratory simulation, the gambling beliefs of university students discriminated between those who chased and those who did not (Breen & Zuckerman, 1999). Frequency of gambling, however, was not related to chasing, suggesting that pathological gamblers might require the presence of both frequent gambling *and* cognitive distortions. One limitation of the study is that about half of the items in the gambling beliefs questionnaire related to issues other than illusion of control (e.g., "I usually don't get very excited when I gamble"). To further complicate the interpretation, factor analysis extracted only one factor in the questionnaire that the authors term "gambling affinity." Therefore, it is difficult to determine precisely which beliefs were related to chasing.

When the focus shifts to the relationship between cognitive distortions and pathological gambling, the results are similarly inconclusive. In a laboratory gambling simulation, pathological gamblers did not wager more on trials than social gamblers, thus not supporting the overconfidence hypothesis (Breen & Frank, 1993). Erroneous gambling beliefs discriminated problem pathological gamblers from nonpathological gamblers, but only for two of five types of gamblers (Ladouceur et al., 1997). Internal locus of control was not related to extent of abstinence in GA members (Johnson et al., 1992) or to SOGS scores in Australian university undergraduates (Kweitel & Allen, 1998). In the latter study, belief in powerful others was related to increased SOGS scores, suggesting that interpersonal externality was related to increased gambling behavior. The historically equivocal results using Rotter's I–E scale in gambling studies may result from locus of control being a generalized expectancy variable that traditionally has weak predictive outcomes (Bandura, 1986). As the next two studies suggest, using specific expectancy measures should be more heuristic.

The strongest empirical support available today emerges not from studies of adult pathological gamblers but from studies of adolescents. Viewing winning at

slot machines as "all or mostly skilled" versus "all or mostly chance" discriminated pathological gambling from nonpathological gambling youth in England
(Griffiths, 1990a,b). Illusions of control were significantly related to both frequency of gambling and problem gambling in a large study of Australian high
school and undergraduate students (Moore & Ohtsuka, 1999). Regression analysis
revealed that the need for money and belief in the system accounted for most of
the variance in predicting pathological gambling in males; for females, each of
these variables plus a cynical attitude about winning (negative relationship) predicted pathological gambling. Illusions of control, belief in one's ability to control
gambling, and cynicism about winning (males only) predicted gambling frequency.

Summary

Strong support exists for the tendency of people to engage in cognitive distortions about gambling outcomes. These distortions take various forms, but, taken
together, they increase people's expectancies about their probabilities of success
in future gambling. These distortions seem to hold whether the gambling involves
games having a degree of skill (e.g., sports betting) or those involving purely
random outcomes (lotteries).

Despite this evidence, much about these tendencies to distort remains unclear.
The research is overwhelmingly correlational in outcome, so the causal direction
is entirely ambiguous. This renders all sorts of interaction scenarios plausible. For
example, "frequent gambling contributes to inadequate perceptions of causality
which in turn contributes to maintenance of gambling behavior in a mutually
reinforcing way" (Ladouceur *et al.*, 1997, p. 81). Naturally, the reverse sequence
is equally plausible, assuming the biased evaluations of outcomes hypothesis.

No doubt, methodological issues have contributed to the inconclusiveness of
the findings regarding cognitive distortions, as they have for most studies of
pathological gambling. In addition to the correlational nature of most studies, no
measure of gambling beliefs has emerged with sufficient psychometric robustness
to use with different populations in different settings. As a result, conclusions from
different studies are exceedingly difficult to compare. Few have compared social
with pathological gamblers. Many have studied "heavy gamblers," but the gener-
alizability of these findings to pathological gamblers is unknown at this time. In
no case am I aware of cognitive distortion studies controlling for the presence of
depression. A huge and controversial literature exists on the nature of depression's
influence on attributions of control (Taylor *et al.*, 1993). Indeed, some of the most
pertinent research relating to this issue involved people's estimates of their control
over chance outcomes (Alloy & Abramson, 1979).

Finding no differences in cognitive distortions between heavy (or social)
gamblers and pathological gamblers indicates that the precise effect of these

distortions is unclear. Given that the gambler's fallacy and other error-prone schemas create huge profits for the gaming industry, their existence does not explain how most people overcome these distortions and end up behaving more or less rationally. In the language of social cognitive theory, what are the circumstances that prevent cognitive misers from seeing the error of their ways and immigrating into the land of motivated tacticians? To follow through on the optical illusion example above, most of us can resist trying to drink asphalt when we realize the mirage on the road is just a mirage. According to social cognitive theory, pathological gamblers remain locked in their cognitive distortions. But who is likely to do so, under what circumstances, and for which types of gambling is totally unknown at this time.

Despite these shortcomings, social cognitive theory still appears to have significant potential for future research. The findings for adolescents and young adults suggest that certain developmental processes may operate in the nature and degree of controlled beliefs. Only longitudinal research can uncover these fundamental cognitive-developmental processes. Although the inconsistent findings for cognitive distortions among gambling types may be disheartening, they also represent a challenge. The equivocal results in these studies fits a gambling-type by cognitive-distortion interaction: "[T]o assume that the same psychological models will explain impaired control in all forms of gambling is not only naive but runs the risk of not fully exploiting the significant differences between different forms to develop a far richer and informative vein of research" (Dickerson, 1993, p. 243).

TREATMENT APPROACHES

Preliminary Considerations

We review data about so-called "natural recovery" in Chapter 7 under the discussion about Motivational Enhancement. Readers interested in comprehensive reviews of gambling treatment effectiveness may wish to consult more detailed analyses (Lopez Viets & Miller, 1997; NORC, 1999; Walker, 1992).

Several guidelines frame the approach to this section. First, a spirit of constructive, but relatively mild criticism shapes it. This flows from the fact that, from a rigorous scientific standpoint, the entire section could begin and end with one sentence: to date, no one has conducted a controlled, random assignment, comparative outcome study of the effectiveness of psychological treatment with a credible placebo. At the time of this writing, the best-controlled-outcome study investigated telephone-contact-only interventions. For those who maintain that only controlled-outcome studies provide meaningful information about treatment effectiveness, then skepticism is the only justified conclusion. The goal of this book, however, is to be useful to the clinician, so it requires a middle ground between total skepticism and unquestioning acceptance of treatment research. Second, this review highlights conceptual views that may not have weighty empirical support but fit well into the general model of self-regulation that this book suggests. This, too, is consistent with the clinical thrust of this book. Third, we make the assumption that most clinicians are eclectic in their approaches to psychotherapy and have little interest in the exclusive use of one strategy.

Psychoanalytic Approaches

Sigmund Freud made the earliest clinical observations about pathological gambling. Consistent with his overall formulation of the etiology of behavioral disorders, he viewed pathological gambling as a symptom of a *neurotic* conflict. Although few would today adhere to his view that pathological gambling represents the individual's attempt to cope with masturbatory conflicts (Freud, 1974), he anticipated modern treatment by categorizing the behavior as an addictive disorder. Others in the psychoanalytic tradition emphasize different conflicts. Some saw excessive gambling deriving from a bipolar motivational dynamic. Gambling could be a manic reaction against helplessness or driven by depression for those suffering loss (Boyd & Bolen, 1970). The obvious self-defeating consequences of pathological gambling no doubt encouraged the theory that pathological gamblers have an unconscious wish to lose (Bergler, 1970). From this perspective, pathological gambling represents the person's unconscious rebellion against social and moral standards.

Contemporary formulations integrated the methodology of traditional psychodynamic treatment with the insights from recent advances in understanding the disorder. The proponents of this approach (Rosenthal & Rugle, 1994) make a strong case for introducing traditional psychodynamic techniques early in the therapeutic process. The purpose is to help individuals understand the function and meaning of gambling in their lives. Therapeutic experience suggested pathological gambling patients offered at least six explanations for their behavior, and the therapeutic task is to address these explanations via confrontation, clarification, and interpretation.

These explanations include the following (Rosenthal & Rugle, 1994):

1. To achieve a spectacular success.
2. To rebel against authority.
3. To attain freedom from various forms of constraining dependencies (e.g., emotional or financial dependency).
4. To gain social acceptance and a sense of belonging with gambling peers.
5. To escape from painful or intolerable affect.
6. To compete against others.

Psychodynamic clinicians were the first to highlight the central role narcissism and grandiosity play in the personality structure of many pathological gamblers. So central a role are these characteristics that "omnipotence may be the most important concept for understanding the pathological gambler" (Rosenthal & Rugle, 1994, p. 31). The gambler's underlying character structure thereby creates the breeding ground for the self-defeating gambling style known as chasing. If I feel omnipotent (unconsciously), then expecting to win is a logical expression of my narcissistic entitlement or my excessive competitiveness. This model has several useful features. It links personality structure in a coherent way to behavioral expressions of a gambling disorder. It emphasizes the importance of a functional analysis of the meaning of the person's behavior and the importance of that understanding early in the treatment process. Finally, it proposes a model that is inclusive and cooperative with client participation in Gambler's Anonymous.

No controlled-outcome studies of psychodynamically oriented treatment for pathological gambling exist. The only extensive review consists of a detailed description of about 60 cases involving psychoanalysis of pathological gamblers by a single therapist (Bergler, 1970). About 50% of those entering treatment were rated as cured. This conclusion is difficult to interpret given that objective criteria for cure are not given and follow-up is neither specified nor described (Walker, 1992). Given these limitations, a 50% recovery rate would still provide evidence that some pathological gambling patients benefited from this treatment approach. This conclusion requires caution, however, given that the author reported having one or two consultation sessions with approximately 100 other pathological gamblers who did not enter treatment. Some of these did not because of cost or distance, but most because they were unmotivated. A totally conservative estimate, then, would put the recovery rate at close to 20%. With these limitations in mind, some pathological gamblers apparently improved with a psychoanalytic approach.

Behavioral Approaches

Behavioral treatments encompass a range of strategies involving classical as well as operant conditioning methods.

Aversion Therapy

Aversion therapy involves the pairing of some unpleasant stimulus (e.g., electric shock, nausea) with some enticing gambling-related activity. A summary of seven studies involving case reports with a total of 53 pathological gamblers (Walker, 1992) found a low rate of abstinence (23%). From the standpoint of methodology, the studies varied in terms of length of treatment, number of shocks given, situations that were paired with shock, and other adjunctive treatments available. Thus, aversion therapy does not appear promising, and clinicians today are reluctant to use strategies that involve delivery of physical pain.

Exposure–Extinction Strategies

These strategies involve presenting some aspect of gambling to the person but preventing the person from engaging in the desired gambling behavior. The logic behind this is similar to desensitization models of anxiety. In the case of pathological gambling, however, instead of extinguishing anxiety it is hoped that the desire to gamble extinguishes. Therapists can employ different types of exposure as well. Some may use *in vivo* forms whereby the client enters the gambling situation and, after a period of staying there without gambling, leaves. More often, therapists present the gambling stimuli imaginarily until the person reports gambling interest has waned. Another variant is to have the client engage in deep-muscle relaxation while imagining the gambling scene.

In a comparative behavior therapy outcome study 120 pathological gamblers received imaginal exposure, *in vivo* exposure, relaxation therapy alone, or aversion therapy (Blaszczynski, 1988). About half the participants were followed up after 2 years. Rates of abstinence were 10 out of 33 for imaginal exposure, 2 out of 10 for *in-vivo* exposure, 6 out of 14 for relaxation therapy, and 0 out of 6 for aversion therapy (Walker, 1992). The study did not have a waiting-list control group, so it is impossible to know how these recovery rates compare to natural rates. For example, is the relaxation group a "control" or a "treatment" group? If a control group, does that mean aversion therapy harms pathological gamblers given the high loss to follow-up and the low abstinence? It is also difficult to interpret the results given the loss of 57 of the original 120 participants at follow-up. A totally conservative approach is to label them as treatment failures, thereby reducing treatment effectiveness considerably.

A more rigorous investigation employed a control group to determine the effectiveness of relapse prevention behavioral methods following an initial program of stimulus control and exposure to all participants (Echeburua *et al.*, 2000). The study treated slot-machine gamblers first with stimulus control and exposure strategies. On completion of this phase, all participants were assigned to a control group or a treatment component. Each treatment component involved relapse-prevention strategies, with one occurring in a group setting and the other in individual sessions. At 12-month follow-up, neither treatment group was more effective. Both treatments, however, were more successful than the control group. In the treatment groups, 83% in the individual and 78% in the group modality achieved abstinence after 1 year versus 52% in the control group. The treatment groups also fared better in terms of lower failure and relapse rates than the control group. On self-report measures, treatment was significantly better in reducing anxiety and depression as well as improving family member ratings of relationship satisfaction. Using the control group as a benchmark, we can conclude that booster treatments such as relapse prevention significantly added to the efficacy of stimulus control and exposure. The design has two limitations, however. The lack of a control group at the initial phase of treatment prevents us from drawing conclusions as to how effective the first treatment was. This may not be critical given the low rates of natural recovery among pathological gamblers. The second is more substantial in that the relapse prevention modality involved a wide collection of behavioral and cognitive strategies. Technically we cannot know which components of the many used led to the greater effectiveness of relapse prevention. On the positive side, this study is important for achieving higher rates of abstinence than is customary. Second, it demonstrated that additional treatment could arrest the normal therapeutic decay that takes place following standard treatments of pathological gambling (see the section on multimodal treatments).

Behavioral approaches, specifically exposure–extinction treatment, have benefited pathological gambling patients. With the exception of the last study, we cannot determine whether they are more effective than no treatment, and no study yet exists that compares behavioral treatments to other modalities. A secondary contribution of behavior therapy research is that follow-up data confirm the existence of controlled gambling for some pathological gamblers. An imaginal exposure study, for example, found that 16 of 33 followed up were controlled gamblers (Blaszczynski, 1988). The researcher categorized the person as a controlled gambler only after obtaining validation from family members who knew the person well. Further follow-up that averaged 5.5 years found that 25 of the total group were controlled gamblers (Blaszczynski *et al.*, 1991).

Cognitive Approaches

Cognitive therapy has wide acceptance as a treatment strategy for emotional and behavioral problems as well as extensive empirical support for its effectiveness. This fact, as well as the seminal research in social-cognitive models of gambling persistence, led to the application of cognitive therapy to pathological gambling treatment. Consistent with the social-cognitive model, cognitive therapy attempts to make gamblers aware of the various cognitive distortions that influence problematic gambling (Ladouceur & Walker, 1996). It has much in common with standard cognitive approaches that rely heavily on identifying distortions, analyzing their impact, and then challenging them with the goal of developing alternative beliefs. At the same time, its starting point is the distortions specific to gambling, for example, the gambler's fallacy, biased evaluation of outcomes, and exaggerated estimates of personal control. Cognitive therapy with pathological gambling represents a creative integration of cognitive techniques with an understanding of gambling-specific schemas.

A well-designed outcome study that employed cognitive therapy strategies combined those techniques with social skills training, problem-solving, and relapse prevention (Sylvain *et al.*, 1997). The researchers randomly assigned 15 pathological gamblers into a treatment group and 15 into a waiting-list control group, measuring outcome at the end of treatment, as well as at 6- and 12-month follow-ups. The treatment group improved more than the control group with regard to hours spent gambling, number of gambling episodes, SOGS scores (mean = 2.7 vs. 13.0, treatment vs. control, respectively), perception of control, desire to gamble, and perception of self-efficacy. From a clinical standpoint, "12 of the 14 participants in the treatment group improved by 50% or more on three of the five variables in comparison to 1 of 15 participants in the control group" (p. 730). Equally impressive was the fact that 8 of the 12 maintained these gains at 12-month follow-up.

The design of the study, however, does not allow any conclusions as to the effectiveness of cognitive therapy alone, involving as it did three other distinct treatment interventions, each of which has significant empirical support. From the standpoint of demonstrating the effectiveness of treatment for pathological gambling, it is a strong study and one that should generate considerable optimism in the treatment field. From the standpoint of demonstrating the effectiveness of cognitive therapy alone, it remains promising, but future research requires a dismantling strategy to disentangle the effects of the various treatment components.

Multimodal Approaches

In the United States, relatively long-term residential treatment (approximately 30 days) was common for addictive disorders at one time in both private and publicly funded settings. These programs developed multimodal treatment strategies influenced primarily by the so-called "American disease model" of addictions (Hester & Miller, 1995). Multimodal approaches used the following components with varying emphasis: individual therapy, group therapy, didactic lectures, audiovisual education, family therapy, pharmacotherapy, vocational counseling, recreational therapy, and mandatory participation in 12-step mutual-help groups. Gambling treatment either was integrated into already existing programs for alcoholism and substance abuse problems (Russo *et al.*, 1984), or developed separate residential programs (Franklin & Ciarrocchi, 1987). Gambling-specific programs may have included financial and legal counseling in addition to the other modalities. Cost-cutting measures have largely eliminated such programs over the past 10 years in private treatment programs and also significantly reduced their availability in publicly funded ones as well. Nevertheless, a series of follow-up studies from these programs can give us some indication of treatment effectiveness with pathological gambling patients. It is possible to summarize these various studies partly because their outcomes are remarkably consistent. With little in the way of research budgets and relying on fairly global assessment instruments, they nonetheless point to similar rates of abstinence at follow-up ranging from 6 months to several years.

A VA hospital mail survey (60 returns out of 124) at 1-year follow-up reported 55% were abstinent since treatment (Russo *et al.*, 1984), whereas a 6-month follow-up with a different subset of patients from the same program (Taber *et al.*, 1987) indicated a 56% abstinence rate (out of 57 interviewed). This latter study confirmed abstinence through direct contact with collaterals. A private inpatient program at 1-year follow-up ($n = 77$) reported 46% abstinence (Franklin & Richardson, 1988), a result evaluated at the time as "the best published results reported for psychotherapy [with pathological gambling]" (Walker, 1992, p. 201). In the United States, similar results were found at follow-up with 72 patients (63.9% abstinence; Lesieur & Blume, 1991), and in Germany two-thirds of 58 gamblers were abstinent at 1-year follow-up (Schwarz & Lindner, 1992).

In terms of sheer number of participants, these outcome studies of multimodal treatment represent the largest single source of outcome data for pathological gambling. Although they represent substantive confirmation of treatment effectiveness, they are less than empirically rigorous. As noted above, so many treatment components make it impossible to disentangle the relative influence of each. This is especially important given the huge range of cost variation in the different components. Some are extremely costly (e.g., inpatient residential programs), while others are essentially free (Gamblers Anonymous). Indeed, the VA studies provide some support for the notion that Gamblers Anonymous was perhaps the most relevant component. Even if Gamblers Anonymous has the greatest influence on recovery, without a control group we cannot know whether inpatient treatment is essential to motivate attendance at GA. Other methodological problems include the absence of independent raters, the lack of a control group, predominantly male participants, and almost exclusive reliance on self-report measures.

Pharmacotherapy

Pharmacotherapy is a regular component of inpatient treatment in multimodal treatment. Today it represents a common element in outpatient treatment as well. Controlled pharmacotherapy group treatment studies of pathological gambling are rarer than psychological treatment research. One study using a single-blind treatment with fluvoxamine found that 7 of 10 gamblers were rated as treatment responders (Hollander *et al.*, 2000). Although these results are certainly encouraging and should lead to larger investigations, the brief (4-week) time-frame is too short to have extended confidence in the findings. Such results highlight the necessity of careful research. For example, fluoxetine was prescribed for the majority of patients treated in one of the successful multimodal treatment studies described above (Franklin & Richardson, 1988, Franklin & Ciarrocchi, 1987). It may be that the medication played a key role in the good results, but it is impossible to know without controlled research.

A Self-Regulation Model for Understanding Pathological Gambling

This book uses a self-regulation model throughout to frame both a conceptual understanding and clinical interventions for pathological gambling. Building on the empirical review in the previous chapter, we present an overview of self-regulation theory as applied to pathological gambling. Self-regulation theory then serves as the approach to organize into a coherent framework the interventions proposed in the remaining chapters for treating pathological gamblers.

ADVANTAGES OF SELF-REGULATION THEORY

Research evidence is mounting that self-regulation is critically important for psychological functioning. Longitudinal studies of children starting at age 4 demonstrated that the capacity for self-regulation predicts increased competence, social skill development, and even higher Scholastic Aptitude Test scores in adolescents 10 or more years later (Mischel *et al.*, 1988; Shoda *et al.*, 1990). Youngsters with greater self-regulatory capabilities coped better in a variety of situations and handled frustration more adequately.

It requires no leap of logic to see the importance of self-regulation for addictive behaviors. Any reflective observer knows that problem gambling and other addictions involve loss of self-control. Nevertheless, the addictions field has remained ambivalent about the concept of self-control. The disease model and its mutual-help groups put a strong emphasis on the need for recovering people to acknowledge their *inability to control* their behavior. In fact, the disease model encourages "surrender" as the appropriate perspective toward one's addiction as well the trait required for recovery (Reinert, 1998). Yet at the same time, the disease model insists on the personal responsibility of the individual, emphasizing the differences between pathological overcontrol and responsible control (Kurtz, 1999). Sometimes this is framed as suggesting that the individual is not responsible for their condition, that is, having the tendency to lose control over alcohol, but being responsible for the behavior itself. Yet even this approach does not always fully resolve the problem. For example, when people take a long time to develop a dependency on alcohol, drugs, or gambling, are they responsible for their end state? Within the framework of the 12-step tradition, "control" means that the person engages in a futile attempt to exercise restraint directly over behavior that one is unable to manage. Alcoholics ought not to start drinking, drug addicts take a drug, or pathological gamblers bet on a race, because, *once begun*, self-control is impossible. "Control" as used in self-regulation theory has a different meaning. For self-regulation theory, control means not engaging in the targeted behavior at all. Self-regulation theory, therefore, has no inherent conflict with a disease model around the concept of control. At minimum, therapists who wish to make use of a self-regulation model need to acknowledge that people are not totally helpless around their addiction. To use the model, a therapist would have to agree that people could exercise some degree of self-regulation around initiating gambling behavior.

Self-regulation theory in this book falls under the rubric of a working model. Models in psychology are meant to help us understand a disorder and develop interventions. All models are "works in progress." The purpose of this working model, then, is to supplement not supplant existing models. Self-regulation theory has at least three benefits for clinicians working with pathological gambling problems. First, the theory has the ability to harmonize insights from many sources. Clinicians will no doubt sense that many of the therapeutic strategies and interventions suggested sound familiar. Second, self-regulation theory explains the *process* of losing control over gambling more comprehensively than existing models. As such, it can offer targeted interventions at specific points along the continuum when individuals lose control. Third, self-regulation theory directs much energy toward explaining *positive* behavioral self-control. In working with addictive behavior, it is as useful to understand how to maintain personal control over positive behaviors that work as substitutes for the addictive behavior as it is to control negative behavior. Finally, choosing a theory that is a work in progress is a logical response to every clinician's dilemma at this historical moment in treating pathological gambling. Understanding the causes or development of pathological gambling is in its infancy. As one expert has noted, "the answers to such questions [causes and development of problem gambling] can only be answered by research, but the amount of research in this area is minuscule compared to the millions of dollars spent on alcohol and drug research" (Zuckerman, 1999, p. 300). No single model dominates by sheer weight of evidence or efficacy. Clinicians, however, cannot wait for definitive answers when they are ethically charged with providing treatment. Self-regulation theory draws on evidence-based approaches for understanding the management of a wide range of compulsive behaviors and therefore is broadly applicable for treating pathological gambling.

SELF-REGULATION THEORY: GENERAL FEATURES

Basic Premises

Self-regulation theory is embedded within a broad-based theoretical movement in psychology known as social-cognitive psychology. Described by its adherents as a "hybrid," social-cognitive psychology "refers to recent approaches in personality and social psychology that emphasize cognition in the context of social interaction and behavioral adaptation" (Barrone, *et al.*, 1997, p. 24). Although much of its research originated in social and personality psychology, many studies focused on clinical phenomena (e.g., Bandura, 1986). Furthermore, social-cognitive psychology considers the boundaries between social and clinical psychology permeable, meaning that cognitive–social interaction processes have clinical relevance, and clinical data shed light on social-cognitive processes. Furthermore, much cross-fertilization occurs between the insights of social-cognitive psychology and cognitive-behavior therapy. In this chapter, we are mainly interested in those aspects of social-cognitive psychology that directly relate to the self-regulatory processes involved in managing compulsive behaviors similar to pathological gambling. This overview should make clear how self-regulatory theory could help clinicians move beyond cafeteria interventions in treating problem gambling.

The first basic premise of self-regulation theory is that *human behavior is adaptive because people organize their behavior around goals* (Carver & Scheier, 1998). Development of higher-order thinking meant that human beings have an added dimension to enhance survival over other animals in that they can establish goals, monitor their progress, and adjust their activities accordingly. Goal setting influences self-regulation failure in multiple ways:

1. People fail to set goals that are essential to well-being.
2. People set attainable goals but fail to achieve them.
3. People set unattainable goals.
4. People set goals that are too easily attained and then experience boredom or emptiness.
5. People get frustrated at the delay or effort involved in achieving goals.
6. People identify core aspects of their identity with goals that may be peripheral to more long-lasting sources of self-worth.
7. Painful emotions result when people notice the discrepancy between their goals and their actual accomplishments.

The foundation of self-regulation theory is the centrality of personal control in human functioning. Personal control is a critical component in psychological well-being. The corollary of this is that much human misery occurs when people fail to exercise personal control. Among the many paradoxes of modern life is that wealthy, advantaged societies have high rates of eating disorders, suicide among their young, alcohol, drug, and tobacco addiction, along with increasing amounts of depression for each succeeding generation (Seligman, 1991). Even a cursory look at these phenomena indicates how they relate to failures in self-regulation. Despite unparalleled material goods and individual freedom, many today cannot control either their behavior or their emotions.

The second basic premise in self-regulation theory is that *expectancies are powerful motivators*. As Henry Ford reportedly said, "Whether you think you can or think you can't, in either case you're right." Levels of optimism and belief in our own ability predict such widely divergent efforts as cold-calling persistence in insurance sales, length of stay following open-heart surgery, coping with breast cancer, and academic performance (Carver & Sheier, 1998; Seligman, 1991). In the field of education, researchers have dubbed this the "Pygmalion effect." Researchers identified elementary school children as "late bloomers." Late bloomers were children who were not performing as well as expected and who required more time to develop their talents than other children their age. In other words, they worked at a different developmental pace but were just as intelligent as higher-achieving students. By the end of the school year, late bloomers significantly improved their academic performance. The striking aspect of the experiment, however, was that the test identifying late bloomers was bogus. Children who improved did so because teachers, believing that their efforts would bear fruit, gave special attention to the "late bloomers" who responded positively.

The expectations of substance-abuse counselors were also found to have a similar effect. An intake assessment identified a group of substance-abusing patients as highly motivated and likely to benefit from treatment. This group not only did significantly better in treatment than patients not so identified, but also had greater abstinence 2 years following discharge. In addition to longer abstinence, these individuals had better work records as well as family and psychological functioning. Once again, the evaluation test was bogus and the patients were randomly assigned.

SELF-REGULATION THEORY: SPECIFIC MECHANISMS

Self-regulation theory tries to explain mechanisms of self-regulation failure. This understanding can ultimately serve two clinical goals. First, it can assist clinicians in *assessing* the process by which an individual fails to exercise self-control. Second, clinicians can help clients *develop skills* to enhance personal control.

Underregulation Failures

Underregulation "refers to a failure to exert control over oneself" (Baumeister *et al.*, 1994, p. 14). This failure relates to the standards one sets, the monitoring of those standards, and the ability to change one's behavior to achieve the desired standards. People can thus fail to self-regulate for multiple reasons. Regarding the standards themselves, people can either fail to set goals (e.g., a monetary limit when visiting the casino) or have conflicting standards (a desire for easy money versus not risking one's savings). Social gamblers differ from pathological gamblers in that they typically set gambling limits for themselves prior to betting. This is similar to an individual going to a party and setting a limit on the number of beers she will have to drink if she has to drive home. Using credit cards for cash advances may indicate an overall lack of financial planning as well as momentary impulsiveness.

Sometimes the problem is not that the individual has goals but that the goals are in conflict with each other. A desire to relax versus a desire to maintain a good impression with the boss may conflict in a high-pressure work setting. The lure of easy money entices people to engage in behavior that conflicts with basic goals, for example, honesty. The case histories used throughout this book exemplify how gambling interferes with goals related to personal and social integrity.

People also fail to self-regulate not because they lack clear standards but because they fail to attend to them. This phenomenon is at the heart of one of the great puzzles in psychology—namely, attitude–behavior inconsistency. Advertisers find it hard to predict which vehicle you will purchase on the basis of an attitude test. Similarly, it is difficult to understand how seemingly religious individuals violate their moral principles so easily. The explanation for these anomalies appears rooted in the fact that people frequently act without *awareness* of their attitudes or goals. Behavior that appears to be hypocritical or inconsistent emanates from people who do not *intend* to be hypocritical or inconsistent. In similar fashion, the person who is wagering his daughter's college tuition money may be doing so because he is not attending to the standard of being a responsible parent.

The second way that people fail to attend to their standards occurs through loss of self-awareness. Getting lost in the crowd is a well-known phenomenon that leads to abandoning personal standards. A classic example occurs in the novel and movie *To Kill a Mockingbird*. Scout, the storyteller, a kindergarten-aged girl, disperses an angry mob about to lynch a black man falsely accused of rape when she starts to address participants individually by name. One by one, the group breaks up as each person's identity emerges from the faceless crowd through this simple human encounter. The link between alcohol use and moral disengagement is also well known. This effect, dubbed "alcohol myopia" (Steele & Josephs, 1990), refers to the tunnel vision that occurs when under the influence. Gambling has the potential to cause loss of self-awareness in at least two ways. The gambling activity itself is highly engaging, and the gaming industry produces machines that are especially marketed for their stimulus value and attention-riveting effects. There is evidence that people who engage in forms of gambling using machines develop problem gambling more rapidly than forms that rely less on sensory-perceptual salience (Breen & Zuckerman, 2001). Second, gambling has a strong correlation with drinking alcohol. Whether the neighborhood poker game with its bottle of whisky or the modern casino and its free alcohol provided by attractive attendants, alcohol-induced myopia leads to the loss of individuality and attention to standards. The gaming industry creates a multitude of environmental structures to enhance loss of self-awareness among its clientele. Casinos are notorious for their absence of clocks and windows, features that would create awareness of space and time. Additionally, mirrors are absent in casinos, further diminishing self-awareness. Experiments on cheating, for example, have demonstrated that seeing oneself in a mirror inhibits dishonest behavior (Baumeister *et al.*, 1994).

A third way in which people fail to attend to their standards is through what has been called *transcendence failure* (Baumeister *et al.*, 1994). In this instance, the person focuses on the immediacy of the experience at a low level of meaning but fails to attend to goals with broader meaning. An example of this is the gambler who is caught up with creating a "system" for picking winning horses but fails to attend to personal standards related to being a caring spouse or parent. Although this term is used in a psychological sense, we shall extend this concept to incorporate spiritual goals (Chapter 15).

More and more evidence supports the idea that self-regulation works like a muscle and that underregulation failure involves loss of strength. From this perspective, our ability to self-regulate is a limited resource and even gets "used up" when dealing with stressors (Baumeister *et al.*, 1998; Muraven *et al.*, 1998; Baumeister & Exline, 1999). Substance-abuse treatment programs, for example, seldom ask clients to cease smoking at the same time they are withdrawing from drugs or alcohol. The 12-step programs have a long tradition of alerting members to high-risk situations that tax personal resources. Members use the mnemonic HALT to warn recovering persons of four likely high-risk situations: being hungry, being angry, being lonely, and being tired. Self-control failures increase when we are tired—for example, most violations of diets occur late at night, not early in the morning.

How loss of strength works against recovery from pathological gambling is readily evident. As one's gambling career advances, the stressors arising from financial desperation, family conflict, and occupational disarray are hardly conducive to developing the "muscle" of self-regulation. Further contributing to underregulation failure is *inertia failure*, or the inability to interrupt a problem behavior once it has gained momentum. People who experience loss of control describe it as inevitable. In reality, loss of control occurs incrementally the way a snowball starts an avalanche by gathering momentum down a steep mountain. It is much harder to exercise willpower standing at the casino blackjack table than when sitting in your living room 250 miles away. Loss of control begins with the decision "just to take a drive" to the town with the casino. Behavior therapists counter inertia failure through the use of strategies known as stimulus control. We shall explore several of these strategies in Chapter 8.

Underregulation may also result from the *abstinence violation effect* first described in alcoholism research (Marlatt & Gordon, 1985). It refers to the tendency of those exercising restraint to give up once a lapse/slip occurs. Documented also in binge-eaters (Herman & Mack, 1975), people seem to tell themselves that once they've slipped it's permissible to fail grandly. In clinical work, I call this the "oh-what-the-hell" effect. It also represents a form of dichotomous thinking that can work against an individual who desires to recover from a slip. For this reason, it is important that members of 12-step programs be aware of a tendency towards all-or-nothing thinking regarding the recovery process.

The last source of underregulation is *acquiescence*. In acquiescence people contribute to their self-regulation failures by intentionally placing themselves in high-risk situations or through creating environments that make self-regulation difficult. If we can use the analogy of a snowballing avalanche to describe inertia failure, we can use the metaphor of rolling the snowball to describe acquiescence. In other words, if losing control is a momentum-gathering process, people sometimes start the avalanche themselves by rolling the snowball down the side of the mountain. The heroin addict who wants to see "old friends," the alcoholic desiring to check out the decor of a new bar, and the dieter who buys an oversize bag of potato chips "for the family" are all examples of acquiescence, or rolling the snowball. The staff of our gambling treatment program often noted the incongruity of pathological gambling patients detouring several hundred miles through Atlantic City to get to the hospital.

Misregulation

Misregulation refers to those attempts at self-regulation that fail as a result of an inept strategy. Paying attention to one's behavior provides an example of misregulation. Ordinarily, this is an effective strategy for self-regulation. However, excessive focus on motor acts often has a negative affect. This is evident in the sports concept known as "choking." Choking occurs when people with adequate skill fail to exercise it under pressure. Major league baseball, involving subtle physical prowess, seems especially prone to this phenomenon. Two celebrated examples involve second basemen Steve Sax and Chuck Knoblauch. Both accomplished players, they nonetheless had periods in their professional careers when they seemingly could not make a simple throw of 40 to 70 feet accurately to first base. Test anxiety is another example of ineffective attention to a task. People fail to perform to their potential because their excessive worry leads to mental distraction from the task itself.

Thought misregulation creates numerous problems for people dealing with addictive behavior. A gambler fighting the idea of returning to the racetrack will try to suppress such thoughts, yet a large body of research demonstrated that this is ineffective. Attempts to suppress thinking lead to *increased* thoughts about the subject (Wegner, 1994). Wegner dubbed this the "white bear" phenomenon from the story of Leo Tolstoy, whose older brother refused to play with him as a child until Leo could stand in a corner and *not* think about white bears. Research has discovered that attempts to suppress thoughts leads to a rebound in their frequency and intensity. Twelve-step approaches to recovery intuitively understood this phenomenon and advised members to "surrender" rather than combat their thoughts. Practical experience combined with thought suppression research form the basis for the newer acceptance strategies in thought regulation discussed in Chapter 9 for managing gambling urges.

People not only misregulate their thinking; they also misregulate feelings and moods. Controlling a bad mood by distraction is common, but people are prone to engage in risky behaviors in such cases, potentially creating negative consequences (Leith & Baumeister, 1996). Other people work at "figuring things out" when they get in a bad mood. Although this strategy may have value for low-level emotional arousal, a tendency to ruminate over negative experiences is linked to depression (Nolen-Hoeksema, 1990). In a misregulation scenario, a person who has a setback ruminates and becomes depressed. She then gambles to distract herself but ends up in worse shape because her depression leads to risky bets.

Expectations

Beliefs and expectations lead to both misregulation and underregulation strategies. "Everybody drinks" is a common expectation and misperception that counselors in the substance-abuse arena face regularly with their clients. I give the homework assignment to alcoholic individuals when attending social functions to count the actual number of people drinking alcohol as a percentage of the total group. Depending on the locale or social situation, clients come back astounded to see that anywhere from 25 to 50% of attendees are teetotalers. Children as young as 7 or 8 years of age in the United States have firm beliefs about the positive effects of alcohol even though they never consumed any. Research shows that people with more positive expectancies drink at an earlier age.

The research reviewed on cognitive distortions suggested that expectations also influence persistent gambling. Ordinarily in life, persistence pays off. Belief in control over low-probability chance events leads to persistence at activities preprogrammed to cause monetary loss. For example, playing slot machines means that a person on average wins 85 cents for every dollar spent. Overly optimistic people sometimes fail to distinguish random outcomes from those that are linked to personal effort (Alloy & Abramson, 1975). Following his Super Bowl victory, a quarterback who had struggled earlier in his career stated that he meditated prior to the game on the biblical verse "All things are possible for those who believe." He attributed his improved play to the newfound belief in himself. Optimism, thus, is adaptive for situations requiring effort. It is dysfunctional when it leads to confidence in predicting outcomes for chance events.

Similarly, early winning creates a belief in personal control that may help explain the "big win" phenomena discussed by Robert Custer. People may also explain their wins and losses differently, seeing wins as confirming personal skill but losses due to uncontrollable factors. We also noted how near-wins inspire more gambling even though slot machines are rigged this way intentionally. Finally, the so-called gambler's fallacy, in which one believes that future chance events can be predicted from knowing the outcome of past ones, encourages chasing and doubling up. Overconfidence, heightened egotism, and an illusion of control, then, are some of the self-variables that could relate to gambling persistence in the face of losing. They may lead people to have inflated views of themselves, make riskier bets, and engage in a vicious cycle of losing and attempting to prove one's control.

In summary, many influences on misregulation exist, all of which have the paradoxical effect of losing control despite intending to self-regulate. The elegance of self-regulation theory in dealing with compulsive behaviors is that it provides a coherent framework for organizing many clinical interventions. Experienced therapists can easily link their various therapeutic techniques to the descriptions outlined above. Many behavioral strategies aim at problems in underregulation, whereas cognitive, experiential, and psychodynamic strategies often target various misregulation strategies. Later chapters will show that many effective addiction treatments including cognitive-behavioral, 12-step, and motivational enhancement approaches also lend themselves to a self-regulation model.

RISK-TAKING: THE MISSING INGREDIENT IN A COMPREHENSIVE UNDERSTANDING OF PATHOLOGICAL GAMBLING

Loss of money is so punishing to the average person, the mystery is how anyone could gamble self-destructively. Cognitive theories are inadequate in themselves to explain gambling persistence because people are not mere information processors. If they were, the optical illusions people bring to gambling should eventually self-correct through experience. Self-regulation theory adds two missing ingredients to cognitive influences that increase our understanding of the affective-motivational components in self-destructive gambling.

The first ingredient is a noncontroversial one: the presence of emotional distress. Emotional pain often leads to self-defeating attempts at distraction. Empirical support is plentiful that emotional pain is highly related to maladaptive behavior such as substance abuse (Piedmont & Ciarrocchi, 1999). Research has also linked emotional distress to an important behavioral response in the etiology of self-regulation failure—risk-taking (Baumeister, 1997a; Leith & Baumeister, 1996). Experiencing negative emotions led people to take risks on longshots, whereas people in neutral or happy moods made low-risk bets. The affective source of self-regulation failure may be attention (Carver & Scheier, 1998). When the experimenters had the angry participants list the pros and cons of their choices, this eliminated high-risk lottery wagering.

Although clinicians certainly see their share of emotionally distraught patho-logical gambling patients, a subgroup appears relatively euthymic, and their negative affect is situational. The NEO–PI–R presented in Chapter 5 represents the typical profile of one such individual. His neuroticism score is in the average range on admission to treatment, but his positive affect is in the high range. Despite serious family and financial problems, his Beck Depression Inventory score was in the nondepressed range.

Other factors, then, aside from negative emotion must account for gambling persistence. The high rate of narcissism among pathological gambling patients, 50% in a large inpatient program (Taber & Chaplin, 1988), is a possible candidate. This feature in pathological gambling patients challenges even experienced clini-cians (see Rugle & Rosenthal, 1994, for managing countertransference arising from gambling patients' narcissism). How then can we understand gambling persistence in people who either do not have dispositional negative affect or have inflated rather than negative self-esteem?

Recent work in social psychology has extended self-regulation theory to the affective, motivational, and behavioral aspects of self-esteem. Social psychologist Roy Baumeister has played a major role empirically and conceptually in examin-ing the link between self-esteem and self-regulation (Baumeister, 1993, 1997a,b, 1998; Baumeister *et al.*, 1993, 1996). Some findings are counterintuitive but compelling in how they shed light on little understood gambling phenomena.

THE DOWNSIDE OF EGOTISM

High self-esteem has several negative aspects. Americans have viewed high self-esteem as an unconditional good related to educational, social, and employ-ment success. So entrenched is this view that the state of California established a Self-Esteem Task Force that reported on ways to enhance self-esteem in its students (California Task Force, 1990). Research suggests, however, that this faith in high self-esteem is unwarranted. High self-esteem is linked only modestly to relevant positive outcomes, but under certain circumstances is linked to violence and aggression. A comprehensive literature review (Baumeister *et al.*, 1996) determined that when self-esteem is threatened people with high self-esteem are more likely to become violent and aggressive than low self-esteem individuals. In laboratory research with particular relevance to gambling (Baumeister *et al.*, 1993), persons with high self-esteem were more likely to engage in risky betting after an insult than were people with low self-esteem.

These findings run counter to the worldview of many. Two psychodynamic formulations are often accepted as truisms. One is that self-destructive motiva-tions lead to self-destructive behavior. The second is that narcissism, or inflated self-esteem, is actually a disguise for low self-worth. The first formulation lacks any substantive empirical support (Baumeister, 1997a; Baumeister & Scher, 1988). "The idea that people are commonly driven by a death wish, urge for punishment or loathing for success has generally been consigned to the scrap heap of social science mythology" (Baumeister, 1997a, p. 145). This chapter has explored multiple alternative pathways to self-regulation failure (e.g., underregulation, misregulation).

The second formulation that narcissism is low self-esteem masquerading as high self-esteem continues to resonate with many clinicians. The problem with this formulation is that understanding a syndrome that involves an inflated sense of self along with "an inordinate need for tribute from others" (Kernberg, 1967, p. 655, as cited in Millon, 1981) requires enormous conceptual stretching. Millon, a leading expert in personality disorders, describes psychoanalytic attempts to explain this condition as "circuitous labyrinths through which their metapsychological assertions wind their way" (Millon, 1981, p. 162).

A second problem relates to explaining violence as a self-esteem deficit. First, low-self-esteem people blame themselves, so when threatened they tend not to take it out on others. High-self-esteem individuals blame external forces (including others) when things go wrong or when threatened, so they react aggressively under challenge. Here the illogic of the traditional formulation becomes evident. Thus, "anyone who wants to salvage the low self-esteem theory has to argue, oddly, that *overt* low self-esteem is nonviolent and only *covert* low self-esteem is violent. In other words, they have to say that low self-esteem is bad only when you can't see it. Aside from the theoretical vacuousness and apparent absurdity of that argument, it begs the question" (Baumeister, 1997b, p. 154, emphasis in original). Narcissistic individuals' entitlement inclines them to project failures rather than internalize them. This tendency, therefore, forms the motivational basis for aggression.

THE PSYCHOLOGICAL FUNCTION OF SELF-ESTEEM

The downside of narcissism tells only one side of the story. If 50% of pathological gamblers are narcissistic and entitled, what about the other 50%? Do the same mechanisms in self-regulation failure operate for them? To answer that question, it is necessary to take a broader look at the role of self-esteem in psychological functioning and apply this understanding to self-regulation failure.

Threatened Egotism Versus Absolute Level of Self-Esteem

A cohesive body of evidence downplays the role of absolute levels of self-esteem (e.g., Baumeister, 1997a; 1998). High self-esteem is not the panacea that some educators propose, nor is low self-esteem the cause of all things evil that some clinicians imagine. Certainly, reliable individual differences exist between people with high and low self-esteem, and these differences predict some interesting psychological variables (Baumeister, 1993). The real culprit in self-regulation failure is neither high nor low self-esteem but *threats* to self-esteem. People's need to belong is so powerful that maintaining a positive view of the self is crucial. In this view, maintaining self-esteem is not a *product* we strive for but a *process* to measure how others see us. Self-esteem is a "sociometer," a social thermometer of our standing in relationship to others (Leary, 1999). To carry the analogy further, our primary concern is the fever, not the mercury reading itself. In social life, the concern is how people view us, not how we rate ourselves on a self-esteem scale.

Baumeister argues that challenges to self-esteem are an impetus for self-defeating behavior. Whether self-esteem is high or low, people strive to maintain favorable views of themselves. Even those with low self-esteem believe they have some qualities that are above average (Baumeister, 1993). Research shows, however, that esteem threats function differently for high- and low-self-esteem individuals. High-self-esteem people, as noted above, tend to engage in more high-risk as well as aggressive or violent behavior. Low-self-esteem persons tend to blame themselves. For high-self-esteem, individuals the link to pathological gambling seems straightforward. I would propose that high-self-esteem gamblers who suffer losses, as every gambler inevitably does, is more likely to maintain biased evaluations (Gilovich, 1983) of their failures, which in turn leads to gambling persistence—a clear failure in self-regulation. In other words, the illusory optimism that researchers have identified among gamblers may play a large role for high-self-esteem gamblers with exaggerated views of their own skills.

If threatened egotism leads to gambling persistence in pathological gamblers with high self-esteem, what about low-self-esteem pathological gamblers? Low-self-esteem people tend to react conservatively in decision-making following ego threats (Baumeister *et al.*, 1993). For these individuals, then, a separate mechanism in self-regulation failure must operate. Here is where emotional distress represents another powerful force in self-regulation failure. Emotional distress leads to self-regulation failure when people try to turn off distress. High-level distress leads to attention failures, taking cognitive shortcuts, or other information processing styles likely to result in losing control, as was found in risky lottery play (Leith & Baumeister, 1996).

SUMMARY

Baumeister's model, then, recognizes that loss of self-esteem rather than its absolute level influences self-defeating behavior. To use an analogy from research on mood variation, some believe that seasonal mood shifts are more related to rapid changes in sunlight rather than its absolute level (Jamison, 1993). People are vulnerable during the shift from long summer days to fall and from short winter days to spring. In similar fashion, having high or low self-esteem is less relevant to self-regulation failure than a perceived threat to one's self-esteem. People may respond somewhat differently depending on their relative levels, for example, high-self-esteem individuals may become aggressive while low-self-esteem persons may internalize and experience emotional distress.

This suggests that the motivations for gambling initiation and persistence differ for high- and low-self-esteem pathological gamblers. High-self-esteem individuals may gamble initially for reasons related to the excitement and challenges of gambling, perhaps as a way to prove themselves or simply have fun. Cognitive distortions allow them to minimize ego threats from losing by seeing the losses as "near wins," by maintaining belief in their "expertise," or viewing luck as a personal attribute. Their persistence may result from trying to maintain inflated views of their prowess. Winning validates these optimistic views, but losing motivates them to prove themselves via high-risk decisions.

Low-self-esteem individuals under emotional distress gamble as a form of escape (Baumeister, 1991a). Recent failure or loss inclines people to believe that they are bad (Janoff-Bulman, 1992), particularly when they cannot externalize explanations for failure (Abramson *et al.*, 1978). Although cognitive distortions also help low-self-esteem individuals protect their self-esteem and provide hope as they incur loss, the primary motivation for initiating gambling in their case is escape from distress. Low-self-esteem people, in this formulation, respond to losses with further decrements to their self-esteem. They persist in gambling after losing as a continuing form of escape, with their self-destructive behavior motivated by emotional distress rather than by a need to prove themselves.

This formulation fits in with clinical experience that identifies narcissism disproportionately in pathological gambling patients who are skill gamblers, that is, in games where knowledge and experience improve predicting outcomes (e.g., sports betting, card games, financial gambling). Alternatively, many pathological gambling patients (perhaps 50% as Taber and Chaplin, 1988, suggest) consist of persons whose deep emotional pain *preceded* their gambling problems. This low-self-esteem group may represent people who experienced significant loss or trauma (Custer & Milt, 1985) or suffer comorbid psychological or physical impairment that preceded the development of pathological gambling.

It is clinically significant that women pathological gamblers are overrepresented in this group, while men are overrepresented in the high-self-esteem group. Research on women pathological gamblers consistently reveals that they have greater histories of trauma and comorbid disorders. In a sample of hospitalized inpatients, 82% of the women versus 24% of the men reported childhood physical or sexual abuse, and 50% of the women attempted suicide compared to 15% of the male pathological gamblers (Ciarrocchi & Richardson, 1989). Research on gender differences in a large sample (1520 pathological gamblers in treatment) also speaks to these differences and supports our formulation (Crisp *et al.*, 2000). Women were more likely to wager on games of chance and less likely to wager on skill games. They were also one and a half times more likely to gamble as a form of escape than men.

This formulation also supports models of pathological gambling that emphasize the central role of dissociative experiences (Jacobs, 1988; Kuley & Jacobs, 1988). Our model, however, proposes that the initial dissociative-like experiences in gambling are more salient for low- than high-self-esteem pathological gamblers. As high-self-esteem gamblers develop problems *related* to gambling, their motivation to seek dissociative experiences increases as well.

We can speculate further as to whether dispositional and genetic models can assimilate a self-regulation formulation. We could hypothesize either a biological-genetic predisposition related to differential neurotransmitter findings among pathological gamblers (Zuckerman, 1999) and/or dispositional factors such as high baseline neuroticism and low conscientiousness (Walsh, 2001). Such factors could lead to emotional distress or other predisposing factors toward underregulation and misregulation. Environmental variables could interact with these diathesis factors, including trauma history and addiction as well as other family backgrounds (Ciarrocchi & Richardson, 1989), further diminishing a person's capacity for self-regulation. These suggestions highlight the potential utility of self-regulation theory in future research with pathological gamblers.

This chapter provides only an outline of self-regulation theory as applied to pathological gambling. The theory's implications are spelled out in the individual clinical chapters. Although self-regulation theory seems to be an efficient model to organize the clinical applications that follow, the reader does not have to accept the theory to implement the clinical strategies. The strategies represent unique extensions of various standard treatments for pathological gambling and should have utility on their own. The model has a further advantage of being a way of understanding (Cheston, 2000) but does not require selling the client on the therapist's language system. It is my opinion, however, that the model is more heuristic for understanding and generating treatment approaches with pathological gambling than currently available ones.

We may have a limited response to Rachlin's (1990) question regarding "Why do people gamble and keep gambling despite heavy losses?" It may be that beliefs that are normally functional and adaptive in enhancing our self-worth—optimism, and sense of control—work against us in gambling situations. Just as we need to correct for optical illusions regarding depth perception (e.g., seeing a mirage on the highway), so too we may need to correct our instinctive expectation that antecedents cause consequences in chance episodes such as dice rolling. Developing strategies to counter these illusions and the behavior patterns they engender is the focus of this book's clinical interventions.

Diagnosis and Assessment of Pathological Gambling

This chapter covers a range of issues in the diagnosis and assessment of gambling problems. First, we examine classification and categorization of pathological gambling. Next we discuss assessment instruments and the relevance of gambling subtypes. Finally, we look at a model for personality assessment of pathological gambling patients.

PATHOLOGICAL GAMBLING AND THE DSM

Pathological gambling became part of official psychiatric nomenclature only with the third edition of the codebook of mental disorders (DSM-III) published by the American Psychiatric Association in 1980 (American Psychiatric Association, 1980). The work of psychiatrist Robert Custer, who established the first residential gambling treatment program in the United States at the Brecksville VA Hospital in Ohio (Custer & Milt, 1985) greatly influenced its inclusion.

In all editions, the DSM placed pathological gambling in the section Impulse-Control Disorders, Not Elsewhere Classified. The definition of an impulse control disorder in its original form was as follows: "Failure to resist an impulse, drive, or temptation to perform some act that is harmful to the individual or others" (APA, 1980, p. 291). Interestingly, whether intentional or not, the original definition of pathological gambling stated the person "is chronically and progressively *unable* to resist impulses to gamble" (p. 292, emphasis added). This created numerous difficulties for forensic psychiatrists and psychologists, an issue explored in Chapter 13. Originally, the DSM listed seven items as indicative of pathological gambling, with three needed to meet the diagnosis. The criteria emphasized the negative effects of gambling. In the next edition (DSM-IV), an important shift occurred in organizing the criteria. The manual arranged criteria in such a way as to mirror symptom patterns in substance abuse and dependence. For example, it included withdrawal and needing to gamble in order to relieve negative emotional states. In this way, the disorder fit neatly into an addictions model even though the manual continued to locate it under Impulse Control Disorders. No field studies existed to examine the reliability or validity of the criteria prior to their first inclusion in the DSM. Recent work has refined these original criteria, and the latest definition includes ten items, of which the person must meet at least five. The ten criteria discussed in what follows represent three dimensions: damage/disruption, loss of control, and dependence.

In its original formulation, antisocial personality disorder (ASP) was an exclusionary diagnosis, but over time the DSM allowed ASP as a comorbid condition. The practical diagnostic task for clinicians is determining whether a pathological gambler's antisocial acts are *a means to an end for a person without ASP*, or that these antisocial acts are *part of an overall antisocial personality lifestyle*. The manual later added the exclusionary situation of a manic episode. Bipolar disorder is a common diagnostic error for clinicians in assessing gambling problems. Gamblers in treatment often report receiving lithium or anti-manic medications despite little evidence of this disorder, even with careful history-taking. These errors are understandable given the hyperactivity of an active problem gambler.

THE CLINICAL PICTURE

The following case history represents a prototypical pathological gambler and will be referred to throughout this section to illustrate diagnostic considerations with the DSM-IV.

Al was a 58-year-old surgeon who voluntarily withdrew from medical practice to handle his legal problems. The federal government had charged him with six counts of failure to pay income tax. Al had a difficult childhood. His alcoholic father physically abused both him and his mother. He recalled once kneeling on cinders for hours as punishment for some childish misdeed. The family lived in a depressed economic area, and Al's father was unemployed as often as he worked. Al himself was a go-getter from an early age and started working before adolescence to help his family. This created serious family conflict, however, because Al's success reinforced his father's own sense of inadequacy. Mom, having her own issues with her husband, would pit the son-hero against the husband-failure. "When you grow up," she would often say, "you'll avenge me and beat him up." Despite these harsh realities, Al was an exemplary student. He interrupted his education to spend four years in the military, then attended college on the G.I. Bill. He completed medical school on a full scholarship, then spent six years on the staff of a prestigious university hospital before going into private practice. Al married Myrna while he was still in school and had seven children over the course of their 40-year marriage. Myrna described him as a responsible family man for the first 15 years of the marriage. The family lived on $30 a week when Al was in medical school, and Myrna managed to pay the bills on time. She described his dedication to her when she was in the late stages of pregnancy with their first child, noting how he would study at home instead of in student groups in case she might need to go to the hospital.

Al's earliest memories of gambling revolved around his father. Al's father would take him to the local playground when he was 5 or 6 years old to watch him play dice. These were the only times in their relationship that Al's father would share anything personal with his son. He recalled his father, often unemployed, stating, "When you win, you look like somebody."

Unfortunately, in Al's memory, his father lost most of the time. When 12 or 13 years old, Al lost all of the money he had earned selling newspapers in a card game. It could only have amounted to ten or twenty dollars; nonetheless, the loss made an impression on him. He avoided all gambling until he entered military service. Once, while in the service, he won $120 at Las Vegas but lost it all the same evening. He did not gamble during medical school, residency training, or through the first years of private practice.

A turn of events occurred about 20 years ago, when he accompanied a friend to the racetrack. He wagered $60 on a 35-to-1 long shot in the ninth race and won about $2000. This win stunned him, since it happened on only his second or third visit ever to a track. He remembered feeling impressed by the large amount won with so little effort. As a solo private practitioner with high overhead costs, the extra cash was exhilarating. Following this win, he couldn't wait to return to the track. Al began to attend the races every evening. At first, he took his wife because it made him feel less guilty. When Al kept losing, Myrna gradually lost interest and stopped attending altogether. He rationalized the amount of time spent away from home by telling her, "It's up to you. I want to take you out, but if you don't want to go, then it's your choice." Within a year, he was "doubleheading"—going to day and night races at different tracks. In these early years of sustained gambling, several features dominated Al's patterns. A flurry of interest in gambling activities overtook him. He believed he had the skills necessary to become a professional gambler, that is, one who makes his living from gambling. In one 3-year period, Al won over $68,000 as a result of three large wins. This led to increasing grandiosity regarding his ability to win. He carried on voluminous correspondence with state racing commissions near and far hoping to learn about various winning combinations.

Over a period of time, this "professional" gambler began wagering in a most irrational manner. He would chase bets, attempting to recoup losses by doubling or tripling his next wager. He made strenuous efforts to minimize his losses yet stay in action. For example, Al would wait outside the track until the fourth race when he could play combinations. As soon as the fourth race was over, he would leave to keep some money for the ninth race. If he couldn't control himself and lost his money before the ninth race, he would get money from the three automatic teller machine accounts he maintained near the track.

Early on, financial problems were a harsh reality. In the first five years, Al took out eight separate loans totaling $114,000. A striking example of his gambling mentality occurred when he won $42,000 three days after receiving a $50,000 loan. He kept the loan, believing he could use his winnings to amass an even larger sum. To pay household debts, he and Myrna sold a small farm they had bought as an investment. Al's medical equipment suppliers brought judgments against him for nonpayment. Eventually, he had to sell the building where he practiced medicine to his own tenants and pay rent for the space he once owned. He described his eventual eviction from his office by his former tenants for nonpayment of rent as the ultimate humiliation.

As gambling took over Al's life, he made many resolutions to stop. Once, he swore on his son's head never to set foot onto the track again. This worked for no more than a few days, and then to keep his vow he resorted to betting from the parking lot through the fence to a friend. Gradually, even this fiction ceased, and he resumed his normal pattern. When Al realized how desperate his situation was, the only solution he could envision was death. Describing himself as "chicken," he entered a phase of learning as much as he could about death and dying. He took a course at the local university to find out what people who cared for the dying knew about it. He read voraciously about near-death experiences to understand what he might experience if he were to commit suicide.

Al was not sure how the shift occurred, but well into his racetrack gambling he shifted to casinos. Casinos intensified his gambling several times over. Replacing the rhythm of the racetrack with a limited number of daily bets and stretches of time in between was a Garden of Eden of continual action. Checks in a single 4-month period totaled over $89,000. Al began driving daily to the casinos, 2 hours each way, often pulling over to the side of the road to sleep in his car. At first, the casinos extended him large lines of credit. Quickly, however, they served him judgments for nonpayment. In a single year, five casinos served judgments for amounts ranging from $3000 to $11,000.

Within the family, financial problems reached disaster level. Myrna declared bankruptcy to save their home from being sold at a sheriff's sale for nonpayment of a second mortgage. All their credit was destroyed, so Al began borrowing from loan sharks. By the time his gambling ended after approximately 16 years, he owed $400,000 to loan sharks. His wife vividly described the impact of his gambling on the family. Al's gambling transformed him from a devoted family man to a completely irresponsible spouse and father. Continual calls from creditors led to unlisted and frequently changed phone numbers. Service companies regularly disconnected the phone and electricity. Myrna had to borrow money from a neighbor once to take a sick child to the hospital. When she was in labor with their last child, Al went to the track, fell asleep on the side of the road, and could not be reached until hours after delivery. Indebtedness severely affected Myrna and the children. Their children became accustomed to the fact that they couldn't afford things. To obtain food, she would write a check for the groceries, threaten to cash it knowing it would bounce, and thereby coerce Al to give her money. The sheriff got to know her children individually from repeated visits to post sheriff sales notices. The entire family dreaded answering the phone because they knew the callers were mainly creditors. Myrna described Al's inexplicable attitude toward needing money for gambling versus paying basic household needs. Once, facing a notice to turn off the electricity, she searched the house and found $5000 in a pair of his pants. She confronted him, saying he told her there was no money. He shot back that he told the truth because the money she found was gambling money. When asked by the therapist why she didn't leave him, she said that she had no place to go with seven children.

In reference to his legal problems, Al maintained that he never willfully failed to pay his taxes. His excuse was that the squeaky wheel gets the oil, and that he was no more thinking about the IRS's money than he was thinking about the bank's. He never thought much about paying anyone; his only focus was thinking up ways to get money to gamble. When asked why he made payments to loan sharks but not the IRS, he made the point that the loan sharks had higher interest rates than the IRS and that they collected their interest in flesh when you failed to pay.

DSM CRITERIA

Focusing on each of the ten DSM-IV items can provide us with a useful, if not exhaustive, diagnostic picture of pathological gambling.

Preoccupation with Gambling

Long periods (e.g., 2 weeks or more) spent thinking about past gambling experiences, handicapping, planning future gambling episodes, or ways to get money to gamble. Al demonstrated this in several ways, including writing racing commissioners in states he had no chance of visiting. Another avid blackjack gambler who served jail time for income tax evasion noted that, even 2 years into abstinence, when he saw car license plates he could not keep himself from making combinations of the number 21 from the digits.

Tolerance

Gambling with increasing amounts to achieve excitement. Tolerance is a relative term. A homemaker betting a day's grocery money may feel the same level of excitement as a high roller wagering 10% of the company's stock portfolio. The task here is to assess whether the person has to bet *increasing* amounts to get the effect. Like heroin use, the absolute magnitude of the quantities it takes to achieve a "high" can be truly prodigious. Al remarked that he didn't care if he won $50 or lost $50? In his mind, gambling "meaningless" amounts was no fun.

Seeking excitement also plays a role *in which forms of gambling a person chooses*. Cross-tolerance, for example, defined as developing tolerance for a similarly acting drug, is a common phenomenon in substance abuse disorders. People tolerant to benzodiazapenes (e.g., valium) frequently are tolerant to alcohol and use it for the same effect. Such crossing over occurs but is not as pronounced in pathological gambling. Although people with gambling problems will dabble in various gambling forms, many will have a clear preference for specific games. They often describe this preference in relationship to excitement. Racetrack bettors may find bingo hopelessly boring and would only go to accompany a family member. When they play a less preferred form such as the lottery, it is with the hope of winning but devoid of any sense of personal excitement. As we saw in Chapter 3, excitement-seeking is a variable posited by some theorists as an explanation for the origins of gambling problems.

Withdrawal

When attempting to reduce or stop gambling, the person becomes restless or irritated. Our inpatient treatment team observed several hundred patients with gambling problems enter the hospital, often direct from a last-ditch binge to solve their problems. We observed a level of restlessness that matched or exceeded alcoholism and drug addiction. The gambler's restlessness was not simply a reaction to confinement because it was distinct from the general psychiatric patients. Attending psychiatrists regularly prescribed medication for the first few days of treatment.

Family members notice this same phenomenon when circumstances impede gambling such as vacation, travel, illness, or bad weather. They describe the gambler as "climbing the walls" with nervous energy. For someone not in recovery this is a good predictor of preparing to gamble. Al's restlessness was so great that he could not handle long stretches without gambling even when he needed to be present at the birth of his child.

Loss of Control

Despite repeated attempts, the person is unsuccessful in stopping, cutting down, or controlling the gambling. This criterion represents the core of compulsive or addictive behavior. It describes a failure in self-regulation following the person's determination to reduce or stop gambling. People react differently to this experience. Some justify that gambling is "just who I am." Out-of-control gambling for them represents a feature of their personality that they claim to accept. They enter therapy, initially maintaining that their behavior is consistent with the profile of a professional gambler, not one with problems. Others sense their helplessness, and this adds one more layer of self-recrimination to an already battered self-efficacy. They enter therapy wondering if they can ever gain control.

Al made an oath to God on his son's head, hoping this would motivate him enough to stop gambling. Many gamblers try similarly inventive methods to gain control. Some shift to a total cash lifestyle in the hope that access to bank accounts and credit cards will dissuade them. Others give financial control over to a family member.

Escape

Gambling in order to escape personal problems or negative emotions (e.g., guilt, anxiety, depression, and helplessness). Clinicians need to distinguish escape behavior that *instigates* gambling from escape behavior that *maintains* it. Escape, in the sense used here, may not motivate gambling originally. As in Al's case, it may provide recreational relief from normal life stress. In one sense, everyone who gambles does so for escape, as do weekend golfers or artists. Escape that instigates problem gambling is more like the example of the clergyman who was close to retirement and gambled to avoid dealing with his unacknowledged homosexuality.

Once problem gambling accelerates, however, stress takes a quantum leap upward. Now gambling is an escape *from the problems it generates*, thus creating a vicious cycle. From a diagnostic standpoint, escape gamblers are ones that are more likely to have comorbid psychiatric or serious life problems that need addressing to maintain recovery. We will cite case examples of escape gambling throughout and shall see that women's problem gambling more often conforms to that pattern.

Chasing

After losing money, the person returns another day to get even. In popular language, this means "throwing good money after bad." Typical recreational gamblers "cut their losses," meaning that after losing they accept it and walk away. When they gamble again it is a new discrete event. They may have learned something from the previous bad experience, but, unlike pathological gamblers, it does not generate a personal vendetta. Gamblers who chase keep an informal tally of their losses. The losses eat at them, and they cannot feel satisfied until they either break even or, better yet, come out ahead. This explains seemingly senseless acts.

> Bill was at an Atlantic City casino and needed $5000 to prevent the bank from repossessing his prized possession, his 1-year-old sport utility vehicle. He was lucky at craps and within 2 hours was up $6000. He was aware that he could save his vehicle and pay off other bills with the surplus. However, he remembered that a month ago in the same casino he lost $10,000 advanced by his employer and borrowed from his parents. In his mind, he was not ahead $6000, he was down $4000. He continued playing and predictably lost his winnings, and even went in the hole by taking the last remaining cash advances on his credit card.

Al reported a similar phenomenon when he kept a substantial loan, even though he had just won an amount nearly equal to his current debt. In his mind, again, he was not really ahead.

Lying

To conceal the extent of gambling, the person lies to family, friends, acquaintances, and therapists. Lying has more subtlety than simply deceiving others about the extent of their gambling. Naturally, gamblers lie about behavior that could lead to others learning about their gambling. In this sense, lying is *reactive*. "Where were you tonight?" asks the spouse. "At the movies," lies the gambler. We saw this in Al's case when he told his wife there was no money for bills when he had ample cash. There is another level of deception that infiltrates problem gambling. To gamble, or "remain in action," an entire persona is required, one based on deception. This deception is *proactive* and geared toward maintaining access to the addiction. Imagine a sports bettor who gambles compulsively. He uses several bookies whom he meets in person. Although hopelessly in debt, not having had a decent meal in weeks, and living off friends, he nevertheless appears in his perfectly tailored suit and speaks with the optimism and bravado of a business tycoon. This deception is essential, because the minute a single bookie discovers the truth he cuts off the gambler's credit. Word spreads that the gambler is a bad risk. Creating this front becomes ingrained as a smoke-and-mirrors act, so that the real person is unknowable—either to others or to the gamblers themselves (Lesieur, 1984).

Developing a deceptive lifestyle is clinically significant since this gambling persona survives well into abstinence and affects what GA refers to as character faults. Putting up this false front impedes trust with families or friends and complicates the therapeutic relationship. The tendency to appear upbeat and in control can fool even the most experienced therapist about the degree of progress. This is one of the many reasons why conjoint therapy sessions with family or friends are essential (see Chapter 14). Self-awareness around this issue often startles pathological gambling patients themselves.

"The strangest thing happened the other night," Mary told her therapist. "John has not questioned me one time about my whereabouts in the past six months since I've been straight. I stayed at the office an extra 45 minutes to catch up on paperwork when no one was around to interrupt. When I got home, John noted I was late as he was cooking dinner. I told him there was a bad accident on the freeway. That was *so* nuts! He would not have batted an eye if I told him the truth." This led to a fruitful discussion of how Mary had programmed herself to deceive others in order to gamble, that it became automatic, and perhaps it was something she might want to work on.

Illegal Acts

Taking money from others in order to finance gambling. "Taking money" covers a huge range of illegal acts, including but not limited to forgery, writing bad checks, fraud, theft, embezzlement, and misappropriation of funds. This category can become fuzzy around the distinction between criminal and civil offenses. Failure to pay a bank loan is illegal but may result in civil rather than criminal proceedings. Either offense, however, should be considered as fitting under this criterion.

A second situation that can lack clarity involves the phrase "in order to finance gambling." In the chaos of an out-of-control existence resulting from pathological gambling, it may be impossible to determine exactly why gamblers commit illegal acts. They may say they embezzled a client's stock account to pay a mortgage in arrears, and this may be literally true. The situation existed because of gambling, and, in my view, this criterion holds when someone commits illegal acts *in a money-deficient context* resulting from gambling, whatever the immediate intention. A good illustration of this is tax crimes. People charged with these offenses do not literally take money from the government in order to finance their gambling. Rather, they lose all their discretionary income and, if self-employed, simply have no money left over to pay their taxes. Again, in my opinion, this behavior meets the illegal-acts criterion.

The range of illegal acts committed in order to finance gambling ranges from commonplace to ingenious. Some gamblers keep several checking accounts and fraudulently write checks without getting caught for many years. They are tireless in moving money around, spending $500 a month in bad check fees, but never having their accounts closed (after all, the banks profited from the service fees). Families fail to prosecute many illegal acts out of sympathy for the gambler or personal embarrassment. The scope of illegal acts associated with gambling is more frequently white-collar crimes than the violent crimes regularly associated with drug abuse. Occasionally violence surfaces in the media around gambling debts, such as killing a family member to obtain life insurance. Illegal acts committed in the gambler's history generates a severe crisis for pathological gambling patients and their families. Addressing this crisis is the focus of Chapters 8 and 13.

Risked Significant Relationship

Jeopardizing or losing a significant relationship, job, educational or career opportunity. Those familiar with substance abuse will note the similarity of this criterion. Amidst such a chaotic life filled with deceit and uncertainty, few can sustain the components of intimacy or friendship. It is a tribute to people's interdependency that both gamblers and those around them work so hard for so long to keep these relationships viable. Research recognizes the central role that supportive relationships play in health maintenance from biological to psychological well-being (see Chapter 14).

Although pathological gambling causes job-related problems and unemployment, job loss is often seen only in the late stages. Common sense suggests that you cannot gamble if you don't have money, so pathological gambling patients hold onto their jobs as long as possible. One feature of employment has clinical significance. Even though they need to work, problem gamblers may need autonomy to pursue gambling. Certain forms of gambling (e.g., horse racing) are difficult within the constraints of a nine-to-five job. Gamblers often adjust their employment to fit in with their preferred gambling activities. For example, horse race bettors will tend to be self-employed or work in sales occupations that permit them when on the road to "drop in" at the track or betting parlors. Job structure needs careful evaluation during treatment.

Al's history saw the wreckage of family, marriage, and occupation due to his gambling. His wife remained only because she could not fathom any other way to feed and clothe her children. She described numerous painful experiences that the family endured from constant financial deprivation. They suffered embarrassment from the sheriff knowing her children on a first-name basis from visits around foreclosures. She described Al's abandoning her at moments of need such as childbirth.

Bailout

Needing money from others to relieve a desperate financial situation caused by gambling. This criterion is critical not just because it identifies pathological gambling but because of its central role in counseling families. Gamblers are effective in persuading others to bail them out financially. Wealthy families may spend millions, and those with less money mortgage the future or give up pensions on behalf of a relative. Again, this highlights the need to work with families as well as the gambler.

In determining whether the person meets the criterion for bailouts, one must pay attention to "loans" in name only. Often family members and friends, as well as the gambler, know there is no chance of repayment, despite using that term for the transaction. If the person is not making regular payments, one must consider the money a bailout. In the same vein, borrowing money from institutions when there is little chance of repayment constitutes a bailout. Declaring bankruptcy functions for many as a form of bailout.

ROBERT CUSTER AND STAGES OF GAMBLING

Although not a diagnostic formulary as such, Robert Custer's description of the stages in the career of pathological gambling is important historically and clinically. From a historical standpoint, Custer was the first to describe from clinical observation what he viewed as a progressive pattern that differentiated pathological gambling from social or recreational gambling. Inspired by Jellinek's famous U-curve depiction of the stages of alcoholism, Custer applied the downward spiral model to gambling addiction. To my knowledge, no longitudinal study has been conducted to validate the progression, but many therapists and clients find it useful.

Custer begins his discussion (Custer & Milt, 1985) of the phases of compulsive gambling with what he calls the preparatory period. Here he combines various personality and family background variables as creating the essential foundation (reviewed in Chapter 3). Custer viewed the stages or phases of the compulsive gambler as representing a progression from milder forms of gambling to compulsive, maladaptive ones.

The first phase begins with social or recreational gambling. Here they exhibit the usual level of interest and excitement as most people. At some point in this phase, the gambler experiences a *big win*. Difficult to describe precisely, a big win could amount to 3 to 6 months' income for a person. Naturally, a big win is a relative concept. It represents significantly more money for a corporate executive with a six-figure salary than a homemaker on a household welfare budget. Custer's point was not to emphasize the actual dollar amount as much as *its psychological significance*. The meaning people place on this event is what leads them further down the road to pathological gambling. In simple terms, the meaning could be described as "this is easy." This was the effect for Al in winning big only the second or third time he bet. In cognitive theory, we might say it sets up an outcome expectancy about how reality operates. Counselors with experience in treating the disorder know that a big win occurs for many with the disorder.

The big win ushers in the *winning phase*. Buoyed by the ease of winning, the person focuses on winning events. Of course, losses happen, but overall the person is ahead of the game. Eventually, the law of averages takes over and the person enters the *losing phase*. This phase is a crossroads. Custer speculates that some gamblers develop insight and either stop gambling or return to social gambling—sadder but wiser. Others, however, are unable to control their gambling, and this stage leads to many of the behaviors outlined in the DSM-IV criteria. Custer was the first to identify *chasing* as diagnostic. Chasing results in fairly rapid financial, psychological, and social deterioration and represents, as we have seen, one of the ten DSM-IV criteria. Chasing leads to the *desperation phase*. Here there are substantial negative effects, with the person on the verge of total ruin and possible suicide. In the U-curve model, the desperation stage marks the bottom of the curve but may also lead upward to recovery. Although there is little empirical support for Custer's stages, the phases fit the clinical features of many pathological gambling patients. Clients are especially intrigued with the model in early stages of treatment. The downside of putting too much emphasis on these stages is that it may hinder intervening with gambling patients who have yet to "hit bottom."

GAMBLING ASSESSMENT INSTRUMENTS

The NORC DSM-IV Screen for Gambling Problems

The NORC report suggested that the field needs to move beyond the South Oaks Gambling Screen (see next section), because it originally was standardized using DSM-III criteria. With the DSM-IV as the current benchmark in diagnosis, the report argues, assessment instruments need to link their criteria to that manual.

Therefore, the researchers developed the NORC DSM-IV Screen for Gambling Problems (NODS) to assess pathological gambling according to DSM-IV criteria. The field study developing it can be found in the NORC report (National Opinion Research Center, 1999), and the instrument itself is reproduced in the appendix to this chapter. The NODS is in the public domain according to communication received from NORC, and clinicians may use it free of charge.

The NODS was originally used as a survey instrument administered by non-clinicians for research purposes. For clinical purposes, however, clinicians will need to supplement any information from the NODS with a full clinical interview.

The NODS questions are divided between lifetime questions and past year questions. This structure emerged from the need of population surveys to provide diagnoses for two different time points: (a) people who have *ever* in their lifetime met criteria for pathological gambling ("lifetime diagnosis"), and (b) those who *currently* meet criteria for the condition ("point prevalence").

The screen's developers believed it could be difficult to determine some criteria with a single question, so it consists of 17 questions instead of just one for each of the ten DSM-IV criteria. Three criteria have two questions to ensure that relevant facts are not missed. These include preoccupation, escape, and risked significant relationship. *Any* affirmative response in these three clusters counts as one point, even if only one is answered positively. Score *only* one point even if two or three questions within a cluster are answered positively.

Three other criteria—withdrawal, loss of control, and lying—also have two questions, *both* of which must be answered "yes" to count as one point in the category. For example, for withdrawal the interviewer first asks, "Have you ever tried to stop, cut down, or control your gambling?" Only if the answer to that question *and* the next question about becoming restless and irritable is "yes" does the client meet criteria for the symptom.

The interviewer asks the first 17 questions as to whether the person has ever over the course of his lifetime experienced the particular problem. After completing the first set of 17 questions, the interviewer selects the appropriate question(s) from the second set of questions about the past year. Notice that the instructions in brackets state "ANSWER ONLY IF [a specific bracket] = YES." For example, only ask question 18 ("In the past year, have there been any periods lasting two weeks or longer when you spent a lot of time thinking about your gambling experiences or planning future gambling ventures or bets?") if the person previously said "yes" to question 1. Question 1 covers the same content but begins, "Have there *ever* been periods, etc." (emphasis added). Zero is low-risk gambler, one or two is at-risk, three or four is problem gambler, and five or more is pathological gambler by DSM-IV criteria.

The South Oaks Gambling Screen

The South Oaks Gambling Screen (SOGS) (Lesieur & Blume, 1993) (included in the appendix of this chapter) is the most frequently cited instrument in published research for assessing gambling problems. It originated in a clinical setting, then spread to survey research for estimating the frequency of pathological gambling in large populations. The authors of the SOGS have generously made it available to clinicians and researchers alike. "The most common question surrounds copyright. The answer to this question is that the SOGS can be used, translated, etc., free of charge so long as the user does not revise the scored items or rename the instrument" (e.g., "The John Doe Gambling Screen") (Lesieur & Blume, 1993, p. 215). The authors note, however, that various national groups may have to change the currency designations to fit the local situation.

The SOGS has many advantages. It is brief and easily administered in interview or paper-and-pencil format, it correlates highly with the DSM (both III-R and IV), it provides useful information on types of gambling, frequency, largest amount spent, and relatives/friends with gambling problems. Clinicians may use it to refine a DSM diagnosis. Customary scoring suggests that zero constitutes no problem, 1–4 is equal to some problem, and 5 indicates a probable pathological gambler. Some have used the scores of 3–4 to designate "problem" gambling in survey research as well as in clinical screening. The questionnaire asks the individual if they have experienced any of these problems in their lifetime. The SOGS may be modified for particular purposes to include other time frames. For example, in follow-up studies one could survey gambling behavior from the time of treatment or during the past year.

Criticisms of the SOGS have mostly centered on its use in epidemiological surveys. The most common criticism is that the SOGS generates an excessive number of false positives. In other words, critics believe the SOGS identifies more people in the population with pathological gambling problems than actually exist.

A recent study (Ladouceur *et al.*, 2000) found that the majority of people misunderstood at least some SOGS items. When researchers clarified items for participants, the rates of pathological gambling diagnosis dropped significantly by 23%. Even larger drops occurred for children (ages 9–12) and adolescents—73 and 44%, respectively—using a modified SOGS. That study raises important concerns regarding use of the SOGS as a survey instrument for population studies, but its relevance for clinical use seems minimal. The items misinterpreted to the largest degree were #5 (lying about gambling), #6 (having a problem with gambling), #15 (lost time from work), and #8 (people have criticized your gambling). Clinicians should follow up these questions to eliminate false endorsement. The article did not address clinical concerns when people *minimize* the consequences of gambling on the SOGS. Although no nonproblem gamblers moved into the pathological gambling range following clarification, some items were endorsed in a *positive* direction at retest. These included #10 (loss of control), #11 (concealed gambling from others), and #12–13 (argued about money). Clinicians need to follow up negative responses on these items to ensure client understanding as well.

Both the SOGS and NODS provide clinicians with straightforward interview tools for clinical practice. Each tool has its critics. The SOGS purportedly overstates the number of pathological gamblers, while the NODS underestimates them (Jacobs, 2000). This suggests that population researchers have not fully resolved basic issues in establishing criteria for pathological gambling. Fortunately, clinicians have a somewhat easier task. We need to be cautious regarding either's use as a screening tool without benefit of follow-up interview where false positives or false negatives could impair clinical decisions. Clinicians can minimize these problems through discussion with those scoring *any* positives, as well as those scoring in the pathological gambling range. This practice represents more typical

clinical procedures and should reduce the methodological complications in diagnosis. Clinicians also need not be slaves to cutoff scores. As pointed out, even
when clients do not meet DSM-IV criteria, a problem with gambling may exist
and require treatment. Such conditions are diagnosed as "impulse control disorder
not otherwise specified" and are treated based on the broader definition of mental
disorder (e.g., emotional stress, impairment).

GAMBLING SUBTYPES

The DSM-IV does not recognize gambling subtypes. Unlike substance-related
disorders, no category equivalent to substance abuse or dependence exists.
Pathological gambling is a straight yes/no decision, even though the ten diagnostic criteria mirror substance-related symptoms. It is crucial to remember that
the whole DSM-IV diagnostic enterprise rests on *determining the existence of
a mental disorder*. It is worth repeating here the DSM-IV's definition of a mental
disorder: "a clinically significant behavioral or psychological syndrome or
pattern that occurs in an individual and that is associated with present distress
(e.g., a painful symptom) or disability (i.e., impairment in one or more important
areas of functioning) or an important loss of freedom" (APA, 1994, p. xxi). It
is easy to forget that *naming the disorder* is of secondary importance in the
diagnostic enterprise. A clinician's first judgment in diagnosis is to determine
whether a disorder is present based on the above definition.

From a practical standpoint, then, even if a person does not meet all five
criteria for pathological gambling, yet meets criteria for a mental disorder, the
person has a gambling problem *and* a mental disorder. When this occurs, the
clinician assigns the diagnostic code of Impulse Control Disorder, Not Otherwise
Specified (APA, 1994, p. 621). The following case highlights some clinical
issues related to subthreshold gambling patterns:

> Louis was a 38-year-old successful neurologist who entered treatment in the
> middle of the summer. He became anxious when he heard that professional
> football training camps were starting up. He described how, after a lifetime
> of purely social gambling, he "got totally carried away" during the last season
> betting on professional football. Louis was especially concerned that he had
> borrowed $60,000 from his pension, a sum he was legally required to pay
> back, and was afraid he could go deeper in the hole if he didn't control his
> gambling. Over the course of five individual therapy sessions, he developed
> an abstinence control and debt reduction plan (Chapters 8 and 13). He
> reported that he had no urges to gamble through the first 2 weeks of football
> season, but agreed with the therapist it would be good to have his wife join

him for at least one session. Phyllis cried continuously for the first 30 minutes of the family session. She worried about the future financial risk for them as a couple and the potential harm to her and the children in that she stayed at home with their three small children. The therapist suggested two strategies. One was for Phyllis to take over Louis's business checks to limit his access to larger sums, and the second was for Louis to spend at least 30 minutes daily with their children. In previous sessions, he stated that he could resist watching football if he had some positive distractions, and he was highly motivated by the idea of being a responsible parent. The couple wanted to try these strategies on their own and agreed to call the therapist for further sessions if they felt needed.

When we view this case in light of DSM-IV criteria, we see that it is a subthreshold case. Louis meets criteria for preoccupation with gambling (limited to one season), chasing, and risking losing a significant relationship. It was questionable in his and his wife's mind whether Louis had actually lied or concealed his gambling, although he had concealed the amount taken from the pension fund. No evidence existed of tolerance, restlessness, loss of control, illegal activities, escape, or bailout. Even though he did not satisfy DSM-IV criteria for pathological gambling, he certainly saw the need for treatment as a function of his distress and fear of potential losses. For practical purposes, the clinician proceeded to engage Louis and his wife in standard pathological gambling treatment with complete success for that football season. We can only speculate if Louis would have been "scared straight" on his own. His therapist certainly saw him as highly motivated to avoid a repeat of the previous season. Nor can we know if Louis represents an instance of catching and arresting the development of pathological gambling. However, he does typify a subtype of problem gambling that clinicians will encounter.

Researchers also have grappled with what it means when someone meets some criteria for pathological gambling but not all five. To address such concerns, researchers categorize people in terms of how many criteria they meet. For example, using the NORC DSM-IV Screen for Gambling Problems (NORC, 1999), an instrument for assessing pathological gambling discussed below, researchers developed the following classification:

1. Nongambler: never gambled.
2. Low-risk gambler: never lost more than $100 in single day or year, or, if they did, reports no DSM-IV criteria.
3. At-risk gambler: one to two DSM-IV criteria.
4. Problem gambler: three to four DSM-IV criteria.
5. Pathological gambler: five or more DSM-IV criteria.

Although intuitively appealing, bear in mind that these categories require validating research as to their usefulness. Presently, we have limited evidence that these categories relate in some meaningful way to clinical issues. In other words, is "problem" gambling truly a problem, or do people in this category have little impairment? Similarly, what are people in the at-risk category at risk for? How often? How much? Answering such questions requires longitudinal studies that so far no one has conducted.

The recent NORC study (1999) indicates that people in these subthreshold categories have more problems than nongamblers or low-risk ones. Pathological and problem gamblers are more likely to have health problems, seek professional help for emotional problems, and feel emotionally troubled. At-risk, problem, and pathological gamblers are more likely to have been alcohol- or drug-dependent, to have used illicit drugs in the past year, and to have been arrested or incarcerated. This study is a promising start to developing useful gambling subtypes, but more clinical studies are needed before the average therapist can make useful distinctions among gambling patterns.

PROBLEM VERSUS NONPROBLEM GAMBLING

We can move even further out on the diagnostic continuum to distinguish nonproblem from problem gambling. Again, the best guideline for this distinction begins with DSM-IV's definition of a mental disorder given above. Any or all of the diagnostic criteria for pathological gambling need to consider whether distress, impairment, or loss of freedom is involved. Only when gambling significantly affects one of those areas does a disorder exist. Clinicians also need to appreciate how *salience* of a criterion can distort our judgment (Barrone *et al.*, 1997). Some gambling symptoms present in a dramatic way, but they need to be taken in context with the definition of a mental disorder *and* the ten diagnostic criteria. Often, for example, the sheer amount of money gambled leads to the presumption of pathological gambling in a client. At other times, the clinician has to weigh the concern of a spouse or family member to determine to what degree the gambling is truly risking the loss of a relationship. Attorneys representing clients in cases involving money management, child custody, or fraud may need an evaluation to determine if the gambling behavior that is linked to the legal issue represents pathological gambling. In each of these situations, clinicians must keep in mind both the definition of a mental disorder and the ten diagnostic criteria.

The following case illustrates how the salience of one criterion raised a question about the diagnosis of pathological gambling with important domestic considerations:

Ted was a 45-year-old divorced man who was evaluated for pathological gambling due to a custody dispute with his former wife. The court wished to determine if the client should have his children for unsupervised visitations given their mother's allegation that he was a pathological gambler. Ted's history revealed an intense interest in horse racing. He kept meticulous betting records indicating a current positive balance over several years of betting. This pattern met criteria for having a preoccupation with gambling. In evaluating the other criteria, except for a brief period in his twenties, Ted bet predetermined amounts and kept religiously to them, win or lose. When asked if keeping records didn't occupy too much time, thus impairing social or family obligations, he was able to recite how it took him precisely ten minutes twice weekly to work out his calculations. Based on an examination of Ted's tax returns and credit reports, there was no evidence of financial difficulties. Nor was there any evidence of large loans, refinancing, bounced checks, or legal problems.

Once it was clear that the gambling behavior did not meet criteria for pathological gambling, it was necessary to contextualize it within a comprehensive clinical assessment. The clinician's final determination was that Ted's gambling behavior was embedded within an Obsessive-Compulsive Personality. His preoccupation with gambling fit into a personality pattern that emphasized orderliness, precision, and attention to detail. If there were issues related to fitness for unsupervised visitation, they would not relate to a gambling disorder. This case illustrates the importance of conducting a comprehensive mental health evaluation when screening for gambling problems.

COMORBIDITY

Comorbidity, the degree to which pathological gambling patients have other diagnosable mental disorders, is not known with much certainty due to the quantity and quality of research on this issue. A review of this area (Crockford & el-Guebaly, 1998) drew three conclusions. First, there are high rates of substance abuse in pathological gambling patients; second, antisocial personality disorder exists as a subset, but far more pathological gambling patients have antisocial personality traits related to their disorder; and third, it appears that there is a high incidence of mood disorders, but the studies attesting to this lack rigor. The high rates of suicidal ideation and attempts in pathological gambling patients also point to an affective component in this population (Ciarrocchi & Richardson, 1989). Clinical experience suggests that males are more likely to have a comorbid antisocial personality disorder than females and that both males and females are likely to have affective disorders, but the rates are unknown.

A history of trauma and loss is common for both men and women pathological gambling patients (Custer & Milt, 1985) but probably occurs more frequently in female pathological gambling patients in a manner similar to this case:

> Reba was a 64-year-old divorced woman who lost $250,000 within 13 months in the slot machines at a casino on a Native American reservation in her midwest state. In the past week, she lost another $5000 and decided to seek treatment. She had a serious kidney disease that was misdiagnosed and resulted in a three-million-dollar malpractice settlement. Similar to stories of lottery winners, however, the money portended nothing but misery in its wake. At the time of the settlement, her husband of 25 years left her for another woman. Over an eight-year period, she had three psychiatric hospitalizations, once following a suicide attempt by gas that was thwarted by an alert letter-carrier. At intake Reba told the outpatient therapist that she could think of no reason for living.
>
> In her family of origin, her father committed suicide in a mental hospital, and two siblings had died of drug overdoses at an early age. Reba was entirely isolated socially because the insurance settlement separated her from her family and friends. At the beginning, she was generous to those she saw in need but began to feel used. Her relatives and acquaintances criticized her for being selfish and ostracized her. In the supermarket, she once overheard shoppers whispering that she had her nerve using manufacturers' coupons to buy groceries.

Reba's case also highlights the concern that we discuss later about the possible rapid development of pathological gambling among the elderly.

PERSONALITY ASSESSMENT OF PATHOLOGICAL GAMBLERS

Chapter 3 reviews the sparse research literature on personality assessment in pathological gambling. Most of the research focuses on characteristics such as sensation-seeking or impulsivity. The MMPI has been the most widely used clinical instrument with pathological gambling patients. Unfortunately, it has two major drawbacks when it comes to pathological gambling. As the review points out, the MMPI cannot differentiate pathological gambling patients from substance-abuse patients. Second, the MMPI measures a relatively narrow band of personality—namely, neuroticism—so that reliance on this scale alone restricts the clinician to a quite limited range of relevant patient dimensions (Piedmont, 1998). Research suggests that the broader dimensions of personality captured by a five-factor model (FFM) of personality has potential to differentiate pathological gambling patients from substance abusers (Castellani & Rugle,

1995) and can predict important treatment response features in chronic addicts (Piedmont & Ciarrocchi, 1999).

The FFM captures five broad dimensions of personality that are consistent across people's lifespan development. Furthermore, it describes a range of personality features that represent positive qualities for coping, in contrast to the pathological emphasis of instruments such as the MMPI or the Millon Clinical Multiaxial Inventory. The Revised NEO Personality Inventory (NEO–PI–R) was constructed specifically to measure these five dimensions (Costa & McCrae, 1992) and has rapidly become the standard instrument for the FFM in clinical practice. Each of the five dimensions is further divided into six lower-order traits that, taken together, provide a comprehensive description of the individual. These five components can be described briefly as:

1. *Neuroticism.* The person's tendency to experience emotional pain such as anxiety, depression, anger, as well as vulnerability to stress. This factor also captures the important feature of impulsiveness, a facet closely linked to addiction (Piedmont & Ciarrocchi, 1999).

2. *Extraversion.* This describes the person's tendency to experience positive emotions, particularly as related to interpersonal energy. As we shall see in a case below, it is not uncommon to find pathological gambling patients high on this factor. In this way they do not resemble the bulk of substance-abusing patients. This scale measures the facet of excitement-seeking as well, so it relates easily to research in the pathological gambling field (Chapter 3).

3. *Openness.* This dimension describes an individual's openness to various kinds of interior and exterior experiences. Such experiences range from one's fantasy life, feelings, and ideas to aesthetics and values.

4. *Agreeableness.* This important factor describes people on the continuum of competitiveness—cooperativeness. It has utility in alerting clinicians to the likely level of compliance in therapy.

5. *Conscientiousness.* "This domain assesses the individual's degree of organization, persistence, and motivation in goal-directed behaviors" (Piedmont, 1998, p. 90). It correlates negatively with substance dependence and separately measures the facet of achievement striving.

From the standpoint of self-regulation theory (Chapter, 4) the NEO–PI–R is a useful tool for describing people who tend to underregulate their behavior through impulsivity and escaping emotional pain (neuroticism) and those who misregulate through avoidance, procrastination, and giving up (conscientiousness). The FFM can also describe the high-energy, outgoing pathological gambling patient who does not have the low self-esteem characteristic of most clinical populations, and this information could prevent strategic errors in treatment planning. At the time of this writing, qualified professionals can purchase software for unlimited administrations, which makes it ideal for clinical practice and research. The following is a case described in detail that illustrates the potential clinical use of the NEO–PI–R for assessment and treatment planning.

> Jake was a 49-year-old video poker player, employed as an emergency medical technician supervisor, who 4 years before had run up $25,000 in debt that he and his wife managed to pay off with considerable difficulty. Now he entered therapy $30,000 in debt from loans and automatic teller machine withdrawals. His NEO–PI–R assessment (see below) indicated low neuroticism, high extraversion, high excitement-seeking, and low self-discipline. His excitement-seeking score suggested he possibly looked to gambling for thrills. As a supervisor, he no longer made runs with the emergency crews and possibly missed this emotionally stirring work in his day-to-day experience. His low self-discipline was characteristic of people who cannot persist at tasks that have long-term benefit but are not intrinsically interesting. His low neuroticism is atypical of both addictive disorders and other clinical conditions presenting for treatment. Low neuroticism combined with high extraversion usually indicates a person who is relatively cheerful and outgoing. Indeed, Jake showed few signs of depression as a trait, although he was quite concerned about the problems his gambling had caused in his marriage.
>
> The therapist saw Jake for twelve sessions, the maximum permitted by his managed-care insurance provider, and four of those were with his wife. Jake gave his wife control over the finances, and one session was used to renegotiate his quite small daily pocket-cash allowance ($3). By the tenth session, his gambling urges had declined from once or twice daily to twice monthly. In the therapist's judgment, Jake's NEO–PI–R suggested that he would bond well with Gamblers Anonymous (GA). Jake benefited greatly from GA, and his wife participated in GamAnon. They saved their last therapy session for a 6-month follow-up visit, and both patient and spouse reported he was abstinent and continuing his GA meetings.

The report below is the computer-generated report for Jake's NEO–PI–R.

Jake (Male)

Scale		Raw score	T score	Range
Factors				
(N)	Neuroticism	—	47	AVERAGE
(E)	Extraversion	—	58	HIGH
(O)	Openness	—	46	AVERAGE
(A)	Agreeableness	—	47	AVERAGE
(C)	Conscientiousness	—	49	AVERAGE
Neuroticism facets				
(N1)	Anxiety	9	41	LOW
(N2)	Angry hostility	9	43	LOW
(N3)	Depression	9	45	AVERAGE
(N4)	Self-Consciousness	15	53	AVERAGE
(N5)	Impulsiveness	21	64	HIGH
(N6)	Vulnerability	8	47	AVERAGE
Extraversion facets				
(E1)	Warmth	22	49	AVERAGE
(E2)	Gregariousness	20	58	HIGH
(E3)	Assertiveness	19	56	HIGH
(E4)	Activity	21	59	HIGH
(E5)	Excitement-seeking	20	56	HIGH
(E6)	Positive Emotions	23	58	HIGH
Openness facets				
(O1)	Fantasy	15	46	AVERAGE
(O2)	Aesthetics	19	54	AVERAGE
(O3)	Feelings	22	56	HIGH
(O4)	Actions	13	42	LOW
(O5)	Ideas	21	52	AVERAGE
(O6)	Values	14	35	LOW
Agreeableness facets				
(A1)	Trust	22	53	AVERAGE
(A2)	Straightforwardness	18	45	AVERAGE
(A3)	Altruism	24	53	AVERAGE
(A4)	Compliance	18	50	AVERAGE
(A5)	Modesty	16	45	AVERAGE
(A6)	Tender-Mindedness	16	40	LOW
Conscientiousness facets				
(C1)	Competence	24	54	AVERAGE
(C2)	Order	18	48	AVERAGE
(C3)	Dutifulness	24	52	AVERAGE
(C4)	Achievement-Striving	17	44	LOW
(C5)	Self-Discipline	16	36	LOW
(C6)	Deliberation	22	61	HIGH

				TM
Client name	:	**Jake**		**NEO–PI–R**
Test date	:	**00/00/00**		**INTERPRETIVE REPORT**

VALIDITY INDICES

Validity indices are within normal limits and the obtained test data appear to be valid.

BASIS OF INTERPRETATION

This report compares the respondent to other adult men. It is based on self-reports of the respondent.

At the broadest level, personality can be described in terms of five basic dimensions or factors. NEO–PI–R domain scores provide good estimates of these five factors by summing the six facets in each domain. Domain scores can be calculated easily by hand and are therefore used on the (hand-scored) Profile Form. More precise estimates of standing on the five factors, however, are provided by factor scores, which are a weighted combination of scores on all 30 facets (see Table 2 in the NEO–PI–R Professional Manual). Factor scores are best calculated by computer.

Because factor scores have somewhat higher convergent and discriminant validity, they are used as the basis of this report. In general, domain T scores and factor T scores are very similar; occasionally, however, they differ. In these cases, the factor T score, which incorporates information from all 30 facets, is usually a more accurate description of the individual.

Factor scores are used to describe the individual at a global level, based on a composite of facet scale scores. To the extent that there is wide scatter among facet scores within a domain, interpretation of that domain and factor becomes more complex. In these cases, particular attention should be focused on the facet scales and their interpretation.

GLOBAL DESCRIPTION OF PERSONALITY: THE FIVE FACTORS

The most distinctive feature of this individual's personality is his standing on the factor of Extraversion. Such people enjoy the company of others and the stimulation of social interaction. They like parties and may be group leaders. They have a fairly high level of energy and tend to be cheerful and optimistic. Those who know such people would describe them as active and sociable.

This person is average in Openness. Average scorers like him value both the new and the familiar, and have an average degree of sensitivity to inner feelings. They are willing to consider new ideas on occasion, but they do not seek out novelty for its own sake.

Next, consider the individual's level of Neuroticism. Individuals scoring in this range are average in terms of their emotional stability. They experience a normal amount of psychological distress and have a typical balance of satisfactions and dissatisfactions with life. They are neither high nor low in self-esteem. Their ability to deal with stress is as good as the average person's.

This person is average in Agreeableness. People who score in this range are about as good-natured as the average person. They can be sympathetic, but can also be firm. They are trusting but not gullible, and ready to compete as well as to cooperate with others.

Finally, the individual scores in the average range in Conscientiousness. Men who score in this range have a normal level of need for achievement. They are able to set work aside in pursuit of pleasure or recreation. They are moderately well-organized and fairly reliable, and have an average amount of self-discipline.

DETAILED INTERPRETATION: FACETS OF N, E, O, A, AND C

Each of the five factors encompasses a number of more specific traits, or facets. The NEO–PI–R measures six facets in each of the five factors. An examination of the facet scores provides a more detailed picture of the distinctive way that these factors are seen in this person.

Neuroticism

This individual is calm, relaxed, and generally free of worry. He seldom feels frustrated, irritable, and angry at others, and he has only the occasional periods of unhappiness that most people experience. Embarrassment or shyness when dealing with people, especially strangers, is only occasionally a problem for him. He reports being poor at controlling his impulses and desires, but he is able to handle stress as well as most people.

Extraversion

This person is average in his level of warmth toward others, but he usually enjoys large and noisy crowds or parties. He is forceful and dominant, preferring to be a group leader rather than a follower. The individual has a high level of energy and likes to keep active and busy. Excitement, stimulation, and thrills have great appeal to him, and he frequently experiences strong feelings of happiness and joy.

Openness

In experiential style, this individual is somewhat open. He has an average imagination and only occasionally daydreams or fantasizes. He is like most people in his appreciation of beauty in music, art, poetry, and nature, and his feelings and emotional reactions are varied and important to him. He seldom enjoys new and different activities and has a low need for variety in his life. He has only a moderate level of intellectual curiosity, and he is conservative in his social, political, and moral beliefs.

Agreeableness

This person has moderate trust in others but is not gullible, recognizing that people can sometimes be deceptive. He is generally frank and sincere, and he is reasonably considerate of others and responsive to requests for help. This individual holds his own in conflicts with others, but he is also willing to forgive and forget. He views himself as an average person, neither better nor worse than others. Compared to other people, he is hard-headed and tough-minded, and his social and political attitudes reflect his pragmatic realism.

Conscientiousness

This individual is reasonably efficient and generally sensible and rational in making decisions. He is moderately neat, punctual, and well-organized, and he is reasonably dependable and reliable in meeting his obligations. He has limited aspirations and might be considered somewhat lackadaisical or lazy. He sometimes finds it difficult to make himself do what he should, and tends to quit when tasks become too difficult. He is cautious and deliberate and thinks carefully before acting.

PERSONALITY CORRELATES: SOME POSSIBLE IMPLICATIONS

Research has shown that the scales of the NEO–PI–R are related to a wide variety of psychosocial variables. These correlates suggest possible implications of the personality profile, because individuals who score high on a trait are also likely to score high on measures of the trait's correlates.

The following information is intended to give a sense of how this individual might function in a number of areas. It is not however, a substitute for direct measurement. If, for example, there is a primary interest in medical complaints, an inventory of medical complaints should be administered in addition to the NEO–PI–R

Coping and Defenses

In coping with the stresses of everyday life, this individual is not very likely to react with ineffective responses, such as hostile reactions toward others, self-blame, or escapist fantasies. He is likely to use both faith and humor in responding to threats, losses, and challenges. In addition, he is somewhat more likely to use positive thinking and direct action in dealing with problems.

Somatic Complaints

This person likely responds in a normal fashion to physical problems and illness. He is prone neither to exaggerate nor to minimize physical symptoms and is fairly objective in assessing the seriousness of any medical problems that he might have.

Psychological Well-Being

Although his mood and satisfaction with various aspects of his life will vary with the circumstances, in the long run this individual is likely to experience the normal course of positive and negative feelings and generally be happy.

Cognitive Processes

This individual is likely to be about average in the complexity and differentiation of his thoughts, values, and moral judgments as compared to others of his level of intelligence and education. He would also probably score in the average range on measures of ego development.

Interpersonal Characteristics

Many theories propose a circular arrangement of interpersonal traits around the axes of Love and Status. Within such systems, this person would likely be described as dominant, assured, warm, loving, and especially gregarious and sociable. His traits are associated with high standing on the interpersonal dimensions of Love and Status.

Needs and Motives

Research in personality has identified a widely used list of psychological needs. Individuals differ in the degree to which these needs characterize their motivational structure. The respondent is likely to show high levels of the following needs: affiliation, cognitive structure, dominance, play, and sentience (enjoyment of sensuous and aesthetic experiences). The respondent is likely to show low levels of the following needs: achievement, change, and harm avoidance (avoiding danger).

CLINICAL HYPOTHESES: AXIS II DISORDERS AND TREATMENT IMPLICATIONS

The NEO–PI–R is a measure of personality traits, not psychopathology symptoms, but it is useful in clinical practice because personality profiles can suggest hypotheses about the disorders to which patients are prone and their responses to various kinds of therapy. This section of the NEO–PI–R Interpretive Report is intended for use in clinical populations only. The hypotheses it offers should be accepted only when they are supported by other corroborating evidence.

Psychiatric diagnoses occur in men and women with different frequencies, and diagnoses are given according to uniform criteria. For that reason, information in this section of the Interpretive Report is based on Combined Sex norms.

Axis II Disorders

Personality traits are most directly relevant to the assessment of personality disorders coded on Axis II of the DSM-IV. A patient may have a personality disorder in addition to an Axis I disorder, and may meet criteria for more than one personality disorder. Certain diagnoses are more common among individuals with particular personality profiles; this section calls attention to diagnoses that are likely (or unlikely) to apply.

Borderline Personality Disorder

The most common personality disorder in clinical practice is Borderline, and the mean NEO-PI profile of a group of patients diagnosed as having Borderline Personality Disorder provides a basis for evaluating the patient. Profile agreement between the patient and this mean profile is lower than half the subjects in the normative sample, suggesting that the patient is unlikely to have a Borderline Personality Disorder.

Other Personality Disorders

Personality disorders can be conceptually characterized by a prototypic profile of NEO–PI–R facets that are consistent with the definition of the disorder and its associated features. The coefficient of profile agreement can be used to assess the overall similarity of the patient's personality to each of the nine other DSM-IV personality disorder prototypes.

It is unlikely that the patient has Schizoid Personality Disorder, Schizotypal Personality Disorder, Avoidant Personality Disorder, or Dependent Personality Disorder because the patient's coefficients of profile agreement are lower than 50% of the *subjects* in the normative sample.

TREATMENT IMPLICATIONS

This patient scores relatively low in Neuroticism, compared to other psychotherapy patients. His problems are likely to be due to a recent stressor or a difficult situation, and treatment may focus on dealing with those specific issues.

Because he is extraverted, this patient finds it easy to talk about his problems, and enjoys interacting with others. He is likely to respond well to forms of psychotherapy that emphasize verbal and social interactions, such as psychoanalysis and group therapy.

The patient scores low on Agreeableness. He is therefore likely to be skeptical and antagonistic in psychotherapy, and reluctant to establish a treatment alliance until the therapist has demonstrated his or her skill and knowledge. Individuals with extremely low levels of Agreeableness are unlikely to seek treatment voluntarily, and may terminate treatment early.

STABILITY OF PROFILE

Research suggests that the individual's personality profile is likely to be stable throughout adulthood. Barring catastrophic stress, major illness, or therapeutic intervention, this description will probably serve as a fair guide even in old age.

END OF REPORT

Appendix

to Chapter 5

The Lifetime NORC DSM-IV Screen for Gambling Problems

The screen is set up to run first a lifetime screen for all items and then ask about the past year only for those items endorsed for lifetime.

How to score the items:

Lifetime: Add 1 point for every YES to any of the following items:

1 or 2	3	5	7	8 or 9	10
12	13		14 or 15 or 16		17

Past year: Add 1 point for every YES to any of the following items:

18 or 19	20	22	24	25 or 26	27
29	30		31 or 32 or 33		34

If gambler responds YES to more than one item in a response cluster (e.g. "8" or "9"), count them together as a single point.

Under the NODS typology, a gambler who scores zero points is a low-risk gambler, and one who scores a one or two is an at-risk gambler. Scoring three or four would mean one is a problem gambler, which corresponds to what certain studies have called a "possible pathological gambler." A gambler who scores five or more on the NODS is a pathological gambler, by DSM-IV criteria.

1. Have there ever been periods lasting two weeks or longer when you spent a lot of time thinking about your gambling experiences or planning out future gambling ventures or bets?
    YES
    NO

2. Have there ever been periods lasting two weeks or longer when you spent a lot of time thinking about ways of getting money to gamble with?
    YES
    NO

3. Have there ever been periods when you needed to gamble with increasing amounts of money or with larger bets than before in order to get the same feeling of excitement?
    YES
    NO

4. Have you ever tried to stop, cut down, or control your gambling?
    YES
    NO

5. On one or more of the times when you tried to stop, cut down, or control your gambling, were you restless or irritable?
    YES
    NO

6. Have you ever tried *but not succeeded* in stopping, cutting down, or controlling your gambling?
    YES   GO TO 7
    NO   GO TO 8

7. Has this happened three or more times?
    YES
    NO

8. Have you ever gambled as a way to escape from personal problems?
    YES
    NO

9. Have you ever gambled to relieve uncomfortable feelings such as guilt, anxiety, help-lessness, or depression?
    YES
    NO

10. Has there ever been a period when, if you lost money gambling one day, you would return another day to get even?
    YES
    NO

11. Have you ever lied to family members, friends, or others about how much you gamble or how much money you lost on gambling?
    YES
    NO

12. Has this happened three or more times?
    YES
    NO

13. Have you ever written a bad check or taken something that didn't belong to you from family members or anyone else in order to pay for your gambling?
    YES
    NO

14. Has your gambling ever caused serious or repeated problems in your relationships with any of your family members or friends?
> YES
> NO

15. ANSWER ONLY IF YOU ARE IN SCHOOL. Has your gambling caused you any problems in school, such as missing classes or days of school or your grades dropping?
> YES
> NO

16. Has your gambling ever caused you to lose a job, have trouble with your job, or miss out on an important job or career opportunity?
> YES
> NO

17. Have you ever needed to ask family members or anyone else to loan you money or otherwise bail you out of a desperate money situation that was largely caused by your gambling?
> YES
> NO

Past-Year Problems

COMPLETE THIS SECTION ONLY IF YOU HAVE GAMBLED IN THE PAST YEAR

18. [ANSWER ONLY IF 1 = YES]
Since [current month] [last year], have there been any periods lasting two weeks or longer when you spent a lot of time thinking about your gambling experiences or planning future gambling ventures or bets?
> YES
> NO

19. [ANSWER ONLY IF 2 = YES]
Since [current month] [last year], have there been periods lasting two weeks or longer when you spent a lot of time thinking about ways of getting money to gamble with?
> YES
> NO

20. [ANSWER ONLY IF 3 = YES]
Since [current month] [last year], have there been periods when you needed to gamble with increasing amounts of money or with larger bets than before in order to get the same feeling of excitement?
> YES
> NO

21. [ANSWER ONLY IF 4 = YES]
Since [current month] [last year], have you ever tried to stop, cut down, or control your gambling?
>   YES
>   NO

22. [ANSWER ONLY IF 5 = YES]
Since [current month] [last year], on one or more of the times when you tried to stop, cut down, or control your gambling, were you restless or irritable?
>   YES
>   NO

23. [ANSWER ONLY IF 6 = YES]
Since [current month] [last year], have you ever tried *but not succeeded* in stopping, cutting down, or controlling your gambling?
>   YES   GO TO 7
>   NO   GO TO 8

24. [ANSWER ONLY IF 7 = YES]
Since [current month] [last year], has this happened three or more times?
>   YES
>   NO

25. [ANSWER ONLY IF 8 = YES]
Since [current month] [last year], have you gambled as a way to escape from personal problems?
>   YES
>   NO

26. [ANSWER ONLY IF 9 = YES]
Since [current month] [last year], have you gambled to relieve uncomfortable feelings such as guilt, anxiety, helplessness, or depression?
>   YES
>   NO

27. [ANSWER ONLY IF 10 = YES]
Since [current month] [last year], has there been a period when, if you lost money gambling one day, you would return another day to get even?
>   YES
>   NO

28. [ANSWER ONLY IF 11 = YES]

Since [current month] [last year], have you lied to family members, friends, or others about how much you gamble or how much money you lost on gambling?

    YES

    NO

29. [ANSWER ONLY IF 12 = YES]

Since [current month] [last year], has this happened three or more times?

    YES

    NO

30. [ANSWER ONLY IF 13 = YES]

Since [current month] [last year], have you written a bad check or taken money that didn't belong to you from family members or anyone else in order to pay for your gambling?

    YES

    NO

31. [ANSWER ONLY IF 14 = YES]

Since [current month] [last year], has your gambling caused serious or repeated problems in your relationships with any of your family members or friends?

    YES

    NO

32. [ANSWER ONLY IF 15 = YES]

Since [current month] [last year], has your gambling caused you any problems in school, such as missing classes or days of school or your grades dropping?

    YES

    NO

33. [ANSWER ONLY IF 16 = YES]

Since [current month] [last year], has your gambling caused you to lose a job, have trouble with your job, or miss out on an important job or career opportunity?

    YES

    NO

34. [ANSWER ONLY IF 17 = YES]

Since [current month] [last year], have you needed to ask family members or anyone else to loan you money or otherwise bail you out of a desperate money situation that was largely caused by your gambling?

    YES

    NO

The South Oaks Gambling Screen

1. Please indicate which of the following types of gambling you have done in your lifetime. For each type, mark one answer: "not at all," "less than once a week," or "once a week or more."

	not at all	less than once a week	once a week or more	
a.	____	____	____	play cards for money
b.	____	____	____	bet on horses, dogs or other animals (at OTB, the track or with a bookie)
c.	____	____	____	bet on sports (parlay cards, with a bookie, or at Jai Alai)
d.	____	____	____	played dice games (including craps, over and under or other dice games) for money
e.	____	____	____	gambled in a casino (legal or otherwise)
f.	____	____	____	played the numbers or bet on lotteries
g.	____	____	____	played bingo for money
h.	____	____	____	played the stock, options and/or commodities market
i.	____	____	____	played slot machines, poker machines or other gambling machines
j.	____	____	____	bowled, shot pool, played golf or some other game of skill for money
k.	____	____	____	pull table or "paper" games other than lotteries
l.	____	____	____	some form of gambling not listed above (please specify) _____

2. What is the largest amount of money you have ever gambled with on any one day?
   - ____ never have gambled
   - ____ $1 or less
   - ____ more than $10 up to $100
   - ____ more than $100 up to $1,000
   - ____ more than $1,000 up to $10,000
   - ____ more than $10,000

3. Check which of the following people in your life has (or had) a gambling problem.
   - ____ father
   - ____ brother or sister
   - ____ my spouse/partner
   - ____ another relative
   - ____ mother
   - ____ grandparent
   - ____ my child(ren)
   - ____ a friend or someone else important in my life

4. When you gamble, how often do you go back another day to win back money you lost?

   ____ never

   ____ some of the time (less than half the time I lost)

   ____ most of the time I lost

   ____ every time I lost

5. Have you ever claimed to be winning money gambling but weren't really? In fact, you lost?

   ____ never (or never gamble)

   ____ yes, less than half the time I lost

   ____ yes, most of the time

6. Do you feel you have ever had a problem with betting money or gambling?

   ____ no

   ____ yes, in the past but not now

   ____ yes

7. Did you ever gamble more than you intend to?   ____ yes   ____ no

8. Have people criticized your betting or told you that you had a gambling problem, regardless of whether or not you thought it was true?   ____ yes   ____ no

9. Have you ever felt guilty about the way you gamble or what happens when you gamble?   ____ yes   ____ no

10. Have you ever felt like you would like to stop betting money or gambling but didn't think you could?   ____ yes   ____ no

11. Have you ever hidden betting slips, lottery tickets, gambling money, IOUs or other signs of betting or gambling from your spouse, children or other important people in your life?   ____ yes   ____ no

12. Have you ever argued with people you live with over   ____ yes   ____ no
     how you handle money?

13. (If you answered yes to question 12): Have money   ____ yes   ____ no
     arguments ever centered on your gambling?

14. Have you ever borrowed from someone and not paid   ____ yes   ____ no
     them back as a result of your gambling?

15. Have you ever lost time from work (or school) due to   ____ yes   ____ no
     betting money or gambling?

16. If you borrowed money to gamble or to pay gambling
     debts, who or where did you borrow from? (check "yes" or "no" for each)

		no	yes
a.	from household money	____	____
b.	from your spouse	____	____
c.	from other relatives or in-laws	____	____
d.	from banks, loan companies or credit unions	____	____
e.	from credit cards	____	____
f.	from loan sharks	____	____
g.	you cashed in stocks, bonds or other securities	____	____
h.	you sold personal or family property	____	____
i.	you borrowed on your checking account (passed bad checks)	____	____
j.	you have (had) a credit line with a bookie	____	____
k.	you have (had) a credit line with a casino	____	____

South Oaks Gambling Screen Score Sheet

Scores on the SOGS itself are determined by adding up the number of questions which show an "at risk" response:

Questions 1, 2 & 3 not counted.

_____ Question 4 — most of the time I lose
or
every time I lose

_____ Question 5 — yes, less than half the time I lose
or
yes, most of the time

_____ Question 6 — yes, in the past but not now
or
yes

_____ Question 7 — yes
_____ " 8 — yes
_____ " 9 — yes
_____ " 10 — yes
_____ " 11 — yes
Question 12 not counted
_____ Question 13 — yes
_____ " 14 — yes
_____ " 15 — yes
_____ " 16a — yes
_____ " 16b — yes
_____ " 16c — yes
_____ " 16d — yes
_____ " 16e — yes
_____ " 16f — yes
_____ " 16g — yes
_____ " 16h — yes
_____ " 16i — yes
Questions 16j & 16k not counted

Total = _____ (there are 20 questions which are counted)

0 = no problem
1–4 = some problem
5 or more = probable pathological gambler

Introduction to Clinical Interventions: A Plea for Family Involvement

The next eleven chapters are in modular form and provide the clinician with a series of strategies typically required for treating pathological gambling. Each module presents a strategy in a logical rather than chronological sequence, that is, the choice is left to the clinician's judgment as to the exact sequence of interventions. For example, abstinence control involves restricting monetary access as a first step in managing impulsive gambling. However, if the patient represents a considerable suicidal risk, then mood control would become the priority.

EMPIRICAL BASIS

The empirical basis of these strategies requires some discussion. As the literature review made clear, the gambling treatment field lacks controlled treatment-outcome studies. No strategy to date has been found effective in relationship to a credible placebo or other demonstrably effective interventions—the hallmark of efficacy in clinical treatments (Wells, 1999). Nevertheless, in accord with this book's motif, clinicians cannot wait for efficacious outcome studies. The strategies presented here either have empirical support in controlled-substance-abuse research or are components in gambling treatment studies that demonstrated reasonable success rates (e.g., better than 40%).

TREATMENT MODALITIES

Due to the sparse treatment literature, we can conclude little about treatment *modality*. Given that so little is known about the effectiveness of various interventions, *how* the interventions should be delivered is an even greater unknown. Individual, group, and family interventions have all been employed.

My personal bias at this point is that individual clinicians working in a traditional outpatient model can make greater inroads in treatment using a couples modality wherever possible. My reasons for this conclusion are several-fold:

1. Obtaining objective data about the gambler's behavior early on in the therapeutic process is crucial. With no urine-test equivalent to assess gambling behavior, the clinician must rely on collateral sources of information to supplement the minimizing that occurs before full trust is established.

2. In the treatment of any addiction, motivation is critical. Family and significant relationships often represent the ultimate level of

motivation for the client. Given the high salience of the gambling press, it is crucial to combat that attraction by focusing the gambler's attention on alternative motivating forces. Nothing brings these forces front and center into consciousness as the physical presence of significant individuals in the therapist's office.

3. Relationship modalities help overcome one of the thorniest clinical problems in treating pathological gambling—the high dropout rate. In the early stages, families are usually more motivated for recovery than the gambler. Families and significant others often have more leverage to ensure treatment attendance than the clinician working in an individual format.

4. Financial bailouts impede recovery in that they allow the person to continue gambling. Educating the family can halt this practice.

5. Gamblers frequently opt for paying back gambling debts initially to bookies or other persons who are directly related to the gambling enterprise. Not only does this maintain a high-risk relationship, it directs much-limited finances away from the essentials of family maintenance.

6. Relationship counseling reduces the long communication delays that occur between busy family members and therapists. With all persons present, the therapist can point out issues family members need to consider. For example, families simply do not imagine that their loved one could invade the retirement account, take the children's college funds, or forge their spouse's name on a second mortgage.

7. In the case of legal problems, particularly those related to state or federal taxes, having family members present is necessary. Sometimes spouses must obtain independent counsel to protect their own credit or avoid criminal liability. Government agencies will prosecute on the premise that a person who signed a tax return assented to all information provided.

8. As a result of these insights, the most useful approach is a couples/family intervention model, with individual sessions increasing as recovery continues. In my experience, this approach leads to improved attendance, increased compliance with treatment recommendations, and longer abstinence. As the client achieves stable abstinence, reducing the frequency of family sessions and shifting to an individual modality to work on long-term recovery issues is often warranted. After transitioning to an individual modality, periodic family sessions ensure maintenance of treatment gains.

Consequently, throughout the following chapters, couples and family issues are integrated. Although Chapter 14 develops family-relationship issues in more detail, family involvement can be incorporated with little effort into most of the strategies described.

FORMAT

The remaining chapters are presented in the form of modules, with each unit containing worksheets for client handouts. As a group, pathological gamblers are notoriously reluctant to complete written homework assignments outside of session. However, they seem to enjoy structured questionnaires or in-session worksheets (Melville *et al.*, 2000). Each of the modules addresses an important aspect of pathological gambling recovery skills or growth issues. Each has an implicit or explicit connection to self-regulation theory.

The next chapter begins with the foundational issue for all addiction treatment—namely, motivation—an area that has seen remarkable strides in recent theory and research.

Motivational Enhancement, Stages of Change, and Goal-Setting

Addictive behavior inevitably creates conflict within the individual. "Getting rich quick" is generally incompatible with "slow and steady wins the race." The desire to feel euphoric every waking moment is incompatible with the tedium of intimate relationships that typically include worry, separation, and misunderstanding. Addiction obliterates people's awareness of less intense but more satisfying long-term goals. Releasing oneself from impulsive, self-defeating choices becomes the primary task in recovery.

Clinicians and researchers are increasingly paying attention to enhancing motivation to change as a key component in breaking this addictive cycle. In fact, a cold-hearted look at addictive behavior could easily lead one to conclude that motivation is the only *necessary* ingredient in breaking the cycle. When an astute layperson (nonclinician) hears a description of our behavioral change strategies, the general reaction is to see them as little more than common sense. Obviously, if one wishes to give up gambling, it is important not to attend the races. If you want to give up heroin, stay away from the people, places, and things associated with it. Building motivation is the true clinical challenge, whereas the action strategies are relatively straightforward.

THE CONTEXT OF MOTIVATIONAL ENHANCEMENT

Sharon Cheston's (2000) overview of the counseling process (discussed in Chapter 1) provides a useful model to anchor motivational enhancement within the context of therapy. Recall that her model divides the therapeutic endeavor into one of three parts. Although logically distinct, they are united in reality much as the way length and width encompass the area of a rectangle.

The first dimension is the *way of being*, and this represents the relationship factors occurring within the therapeutic enterprise. These factors, called the "non-specific factors," are generic to various schools of therapy and highly related to therapeutic outcome. This dimension refers to the precise interpersonal style the therapist uses. Does the therapist primarily ask questions, respond empathetically, remain silent, challenge the client, give advice, offer interpretations, or provide information?

The second dimension is *way of understanding*. Each therapist has some conceptual understanding of the client's problem. That understanding might be related to some established theory (e.g., Jungian, Adlerian, cognitive-behavioral) or involve the clinician's personal viewpoint.

Finally, counseling involves a *way of intervening*. All therapists actually *do something*. Again, these distinct therapeutic interventions may derive from some established therapeutic school or from the therapist's own experience.

The model seems especially relevant for understanding the distinct processes of motivational enhancement. Motivational enhancement as described here is primarily a way of being with minimal interventions. The second hinge in this chapter—the stages-of-change model—provides both a way of understanding and intervening. Together, then, they represent a comprehensive and holistic approach to the therapeutic process.

ORIGINS OF MOTIVATIONAL ENHANCEMENT

Motivational enhancement for our purposes involves intertwining two approaches to changing intractable behavior. William Miller, a preeminent alcoholism-treatment researcher in the cognitive-behavioral tradition, developed the first strand, called *motivational enhancement* (Miller & Rollnick, 1991).

Miller maintained that many of the commonly used addiction-treatment methods directly contradict research findings from social psychology on gaining compliance in interpersonal situations. After reviewing that data, he concluded that typical addiction interventions might actually be *strengthening* resistance to change. He then proposed a different approach based on that same research.

The second strand developed out of the work of psychologists James Prochaska and Carlo DiClemente (1986), who termed their approach a "transtheoretical approach." They studied people who were successful in overcoming difficult-to-change behaviors. They investigated problems related to alcoholism, drug addiction, tobacco addiction, failure to exercise or maintain health regimens (e.g., diabetic diets), poor dental hygiene, gambling, obesity, and how people kept their New Year's resolutions. From a database of over 20,000, people they postulated a series of stages that people typically go through in changing unwanted behavior.

Miller intertwined his own motivational enhancement approach with the insights from the stages-of-change model to formulate a comprehensive conceptual and clinical approach to addictive disorders. Project MATCH (Project MATCH Research Group, 1997), the largest psychotherapy outcome study ever conducted, randomly assigned over 1200 alcoholics to cognitive-behavioral therapy, 12-step therapy, or motivational enhancement. All treatments were equally effective at 2-year follow up, yet participants in the motivational enhancement modality received only four individual sessions, compared to twelve in the other two groups.

To date, only one study has used motivational enhancement strategies as the major modality for pathological gambling treatment (Hodgins *et al.*, 2000). The study compared motivational enhancement interventions delivered through telephone contact only with a group using a self-help workbook. At 12-month follow-up, persons in the motivational enhancement condition with less severe gambling problems maintained their gains over those receiving the workbook alone. Although limited, the study is remarkable in that such minimal contact could affect change.

STAGES-OF-CHANGE MODEL

The stages-of-change model rests on three premises (for details, see Prochaska *et al.*, 1992, 1994). For most people, change is not a discrete, all-or-none event, but a gradual process that has an identifiable sequence. People make use of different strategies at various stages on the road to long-lasting change. The research approach was to study people who were successful at changing their lives rather than those who were chronic failures. The stages-of-change model challenges assumptions many practitioners bring to addiction treatment. The standard approach provides clients with action strategies for coping with their addiction. These change strategies might involve environmental interventions such as attending 12-step meetings, initiating family counseling, and so on. Yet research indicates that fewer than 20% of those entering treatment are ready to take action.

As Prochaska and DiClemente (1986) pointed out, we tend to believe that change is dramatic and discrete. Many people, therapists included, view recovery from addictions similarly to a religious conversion experience. Perhaps the prototypical religious conversion in history is that of St. Paul, who went from being an avid persecutor of early Christians to their chief spokesman following getting knocked off his horse by heavenly intervention. This conversion metaphor filtered into the 12-step tradition via William James, a preeminent psychologist, and one of the earliest to study religious phenomena. James (1985) primarily focused on intense or unusual religious experiences. His fascination with conversion is notable in that he devoted more space to the phenomenon of religious conversion in his book than to any other.

Many conversion experiences described in his *Varieties of Religious Experience* involve alcoholism and drug addiction. This should not be surprising, given the absence of effective treatment for these conditions in the nineteenth century. What may surprise the contemporary reader is how central religion was for many people's recovery in that era. What is important for our discussion, however, is the *sudden dramatic nature* of these conversion experiences. The core of these experiences is the moment of enlightenment, the sudden discovery, the powerful impact of healing grace. From the history of Alcoholics Anonymous (Kurtz, 1999), we know that James's book had a profound influence on shaping AA's early philosophy, particularly the centrality of surrender in recovery. It is not surprising that metaphors of sudden, discrete change remained forceful in addiction lore. Had James taken an interest in everyday religious experience, the stages-of-change model might be less alien in the addiction field. Clinicians encounter many clients with addiction problems who seem to be waiting for the proverbial thunderbolt to galvanize them into recovery. Prochaska and DiClemente have done the field an enormous service by pointing out how people need not become victims of their own metaphors.

Precontemplation means that the person is not considering change. The advantage of this stage is that it is failure-proof. I cannot fail at recovery if I do not have a problem to begin with. People in this stage are maximally defensive, projecting blame onto others: "I have to gamble just to satisfy her need for money." The following case represents pathological gambling in the precontemplation stages despite years of treatment.

> Alex was 42 years old when he entered outpatient treatment. Five years previously he had been in inpatient treatment for his gambling problem. His 15-year history of pathological gambling included a $13,000 judgment against him for illegal commodities trading. His wealthy parents subsidized him, his wife, and his children. Alex's attitude toward this subsidy was one of entitlement. "I paid my dues" meant that he worked for his father's company for 2 or 3 years and received in return his mortgage payment, children's private school tuition, family vehicles, and a guaranteed monthly income. He would not attend mutual-help groups because "I am a celebrity." The clinician wrote at the time of intake, "The patient is excessively concerned with impressing interviewer with his family background and his own amazing skills." At the intake session, Alex greeted the therapist saying, "What are you going to do for me?" His speech was characterized by an earnest, engaging, manipulative, and highly entertaining style. Alex became quite angry when the therapist pointed out the discrepancy between Alex's belief in his "investment skills" and being deeply in the hole financially after 20 years of investing in silver futures. The patient estimated he lost over 2 million dollars in the market, yet interpreted the losses as a failure to hold otherwise good positions. Alex's gambling behavior was to sit in front of his quote machine six hours daily. At the time of admission, he owed $25,000 to his broker, a sum that he wished to keep secret from his wife, whom he feared would leave him. He refused to accept his father's solution to his financial problems that required Alex to accept a salaried position as the father's personal secretary for $65,000 annually in return for a promise to pay off his son's debts.
>
> Alex left treatment after about 6 months and returned 8 years later approximately $250,000 in debt. He had gone through $150,000 in the prior three months, including $50,000 in lottery winnings [possibly fictitious], and was now quite concerned that his wife would leave him. He was also skimming money from jointly held funds. This phase of therapy involved an 18-month cycle of family meetings, structured bailout plans that the patient

foiled by revealing further debts and continued gambling. He refused to get a job, resulting in conflict with his wife, but agreed to a 30-day residential program that ended outpatient therapy. None of these interventions led to Alex giving up gambling or seeing himself as a professional investor. When the therapist asked Alex how he could see himself as a "market professional" despite more than 20 years of financial ruin, Alex put forth his thesis. "Well, you see, if you are going to invest in commodities or options, you need to have a system. And if you are going to maintain your system, you have to have the courage to hold to it even when the market starts to make certain moves against you. However, in order to hold your position against certain moves, it means that you have to have a substantial account to begin with. If you start with a smaller amount of money than is required, when the market starts to make certain moves, this forces you into taking premature action. That's what happened in my case. Every time I've been forced to move out of a position for lack of funds, my original position would've made me a hell of a lot of money." In summary, Alex maintained, after 20 years of treatment including two inpatient residential programs and years of outpatient therapy, that his only problem was that his family had undercapitalized him.

Contemplation represents a stage of ambivalence wherein the person can see the need to change but at the same time is aware that change requires effort or loss. Miller uses the analogy of a seesaw in a children's playground to visualize the person balanced evenly in midair between the forces for change and the counterforce against it. The following case illustrates a multiple-problem gambler who was stuck in ambivalence for many years.

Sarah was a 62-year-old divorced woman who had a long history of substance abuse and pathological gambling. She currently lived with an older widowed man whom she was romantically involved with. Due to her history of pathological gambling, she had few financial assets but contributed to the household costs through her full-time job in real estate. Sarah's longest period of abstinence was approximately 5 years when she had transitioned out of real estate work into mental health counseling as an addiction counselor. During that period, however, her relationship with her children unraveled due to the huge debts she had run up during her gambling period. Her ex-husband had to assume enormous financial burdens following Sarah's departure from the family as well as the burdens of raising the remaining younger children at home. None of the family members remained in contact with Sarah, and, due to crushing amounts of guilt, she was unable to attempt any reconciliation.

Sarah's drinking and gambling pattern over the last 8 years was periodic abstinence followed by playing video poker machines, which led inevitably to chronic drinking. Despite this pattern, Sarah's fiance remained loyal to her for many years. Following her most recent episode, he informed her that, despite the fact that he loved her intensely, he could no longer cope with living with her. Sarah agreed to reform and therefore sought outpatient treatment. She described how her recent binge left her at the top of a high bridge with the intention of jumping. A chance encounter with a security guard led to her going to the emergency room, where doctors discovered a severe coronary condition that required immediate surgery. While she was in the critical care unit, hospital authorities found the name of her companion and called him. After visiting, he agreed to take her back.

Sarah was clearly aware of all of the positives and negatives of her gambling and alcoholic lifestyle. From her work as an addiction counselor, she could recite recovery lingo and turn it on herself in a self-deprecating manner. She had significant insight into the factors maintaining her continued drinking and gambling. She knew her gambling was an escape and that once she began gambling chronic drinking rapidly followed. She also knew that guilt over her family situation was the major reason for desiring to escape. She could blot out this pain only so long until she turned to gambling for relief. For the first six to eight sessions, Sarah continued to talk about the pain of facing her children but then failed to keep a series of appointments and eventually relapsed.

Preparation implies that the person is close to taking action and is taking steps necessary to prepare the way for change. A dieter might make an appointment for a physical exam; a gambler might investigate a treatment program or contact the employee assistance program.

Action means that people have taken some steps toward changing the behavior: attending a mutual-help group, cutting up the credit cards, or coming clean with their family.

Maintenance means the change has continued for a considerable period, usually 6 months or more.

Termination suggests that returning to the undesirable behavior is highly unlikely. Whether this is an expected stage for persons with pathological gambling or substance dependence is a controversial question that need not concern us in early treatment. Some in the field do not believe addiction recovery is ever a permanent state.

Recycling, however, is a consensus experience in the addiction field. Slips, lapses, or relapses are normative in pathological gambling and other addictions. When action or maintenance fails people are prone to recycle through the stages of change. The model proposes that, when people have a slip or lapse, *there is no necessary fall to an earlier stage*, for example, precontemplation. People may recycle immediately to contemplation or action as well. Educating clients about this fact is one aspect of managing slips and relapses described in the next chapter.

In the stages-of-change model, progress often means spiraling around and through the various phases with success not uniformly linear.

STRATEGIES USED TO CHANGE

The stages-of-change model describes nine strategies people typically use to change undesirable behavior.

1. *Consciousness-raising* is the most common early strategy and involves bringing into awareness the depth and level of the problem.

2. *Social liberation* is a process that changes social environments (e.g., laws banning gambling in the state).

3. *Emotional arousal* uses intense feelings to counteract a person's indifference to the negative consequences of his behavior.

4. *Self-revelation* challenges the person through examining the personal values her behavior conflicts with.

5. *Commitment* is telling others in a public manner that one is attempting to change.

6. *Countering* substitutes adaptive for maladaptive behavior.

7. *Environmental control* makes lapses less possible by changing the environment, for example, giving one's excess cash to a spouse.

8. *Rewards* are often used in the aftermath of achieving some goal related to the new behavior.

9. *Helping relationships* provide support in keeping people on track.

A main finding (Prochaska *et al.*, 1992) was that people used certain strategies more in one stage than another. We discuss the early-stage strategies in the next section under motivational enhancement and sprinkle the later-stage strategies throughout the remaining treatment intervention chapters.

MOTIVATIONAL ENHANCEMENT APPROACH

Motivational enhancement focuses specifically on the earliest phases of treatment. In essence, it provides a microanalysis of the actual conversion experience itself—that slow movement from resistance to taking responsibility for changing one's behavior. Motivational enhancement combines social psychological research regarding interpersonal influence with the stages-of-change model to create a dynamic blend of motivators presented in a caring, collaborative relationship.

The climate the therapist creates with motivational enhancement is as important as any strategy. I summarize that climate as "Rogerian with an agenda." Research indicates that the Rogerian triad of accurate empathy, genuineness, and nonpossessive warmth carries 25–66% of the variance with outcome in psychotherapy (Miller & Rollnick, 1991). The addiction field developed a style of harsh confrontation that is related to treatment failure and psychological casualties (Lieberman *et al.*, 1973). The first step, therefore, requires accurate empathy, warmth, and positive regard because many pathological gambling patients view themselves as losers or moral degenerates

Addictive disorders, however, require more than warm environments to ensure change. Motivation to change requires that *the person develop a discrepancy between who they currently are and who they wish to be*. Facilitating this discrepancy represents the key skill in the therapeutic toolbox. First, a therapist must create an accepting climate wherein clients speak honestly without minimizing their problems. Second, through caring feedback, the therapist holds up a mirror that clients can tolerate looking into.

In line with social psychological research, developing intrinsic motivation means the person resists outside influences. Therapists accordingly must avoid arguing or persuading no matter how rational their goals. An exercise routinely used in motivational enhancement training workshops illustrates this point. A person from the audience who is in the process of making some decision volunteers to examine his choices with the workshop leader. The topics typically discussed include buying a house, sending a child to private school, taking a job in another town, and so on. In the demonstration, I first spend a few minutes making sure I have understood the volunteer's dilemma by using accurate empathy. At some point in the discussion, when I have a reasonably good feel for the problem, I mentally "flip a coin" and go with one choice over another. The following dialogue demonstrates one such exchange:

> **Leader**: It certainly sounds as if you have excellent reasons for either decision about what to do with your antique pickup truck. On the one hand, you've had it since you were young, and it represents a real love affair with your past. You enjoy taking it to shows or just riding around and watching heads turn as you go down Main Street. You enjoy the camaraderie of the group that restores old vehicles. Yet you realize that it is not practical for your lifestyle now. It limits the range you can travel, you worry about taking it on certain roads, and you stated how expensive its upkeep is. Furthermore, because you only have enough income to support one vehicle, you are wondering if it does not make sense to sell it. [*Then I arbitrarily take a position.*] Well, after listening to both positions, it seems clear that the only sensible thing to do is sell it. It probably makes sense to put behind you the things of your youth now. From an economic perspective, it's only reasonable. You will get decent money from the sale, have a vehicle that will meet more of your needs, and have a range of freedom you don't have now.

Without fail the participant replies in a manner similar to this volunteer:

> **Volunteer**: You know, you are probably right about the practicalities. It does make more sense. But I have always been my own person in a lot of ways by not doing the sensible thing, and I am really attached to my truck. Do you know how many coats of paint I've put on it?

The point of the demonstration becomes clear to the audience, and we process what happened. People's need for autonomy leads them *to develop counter-arguments* when external choices are thrust on them. Developing motivational enhancement skill is often difficult for addiction counselors whose approach with clients is "Look, your way hasn't worked. Where has it gotten you? Now you need to listen to someone else" (meaning, of course, the counselor). Guidelines for motivational enhancement treatment include the following:

Principle 1: Be a Rogerian

Initial interactions with a client must have huge doses of acceptance, empathy, and positive regard. Too often this is alien in addictions treatment. A young African-American counselor, who was on maternity leave from her job in an inner-city drug program for heroin addicts, expressed gratitude to the workshop leader for the perspective motivational enhancement training gave her. She stated that while on leave she looked for work outside the mental health field because staff told her, "You have to get angrier with the addicts. You're entirely too nice to them." She said she didn't *want* to get angry with them, that the abusive things she heard said to them violated her religious principles, and she wasn't even sure it worked. Now, she believed, she could return to work, be effective, and maintain her values.

Principle 2: Be a Rogerian with an Agenda

Having empathy does not mean being blind to the ravages of addiction. *Selective empathy* means having the persistence and tenacity of a bulldog in zeroing in on the downside of gambling or any destructive behavior in the person's life. The skill most needed to carry out this agenda is *double-sided reflective statements*. The following scenario represents the first group therapy session at an inpatient program for impaired clergy.

The group therapist, as was customary, invited Father John to tell a bit of his story to the group, particularly how he ended up in treatment. In many ways, it was typical of the downhill slide from gambling and using prescription drugs. This bright, young researcher-educator gradually became more and more impaired and could no longer effectively teach or carry out his other responsibilities. John's mother was terminally ill, and his religious superiors ordered John to take a leave from teaching to be with his mother in her final months.

John complied, but the leave led to an ever-increasing descent into addiction. Desperate for money and pills, he stretched out his cancerous mother's pain medication to have an ample pill supply to sell for gambling money and use himself. His mother's confused mental state meant family and friends did not notice John's tactics, and even praised him for his caretaking of the mother. As John told the story, however, his focus was mostly on his own internal pain. With a novelist's gift of narrative, he captured the group's attention. Tears streamed down his face, and several group members cried with him as he described all the wrongs his gambling and drug use engender. The group leader, using a motivational enhancement framework, framed the situation differently. On one hand, John was feeling a considerable degree of emotional pain coming to grips with what gambling and drugs had cost him. At the same time, he minimized its impact through a self-centered framework. The leader could have focused with empathy on John's pain or opened the wounds further with harsh confrontation. Instead, he opted for double-sided reflection that included both empathy and holding up a mirror to John's behavior with the data John provided the group.

"First of all, I want to thank John for being so open and honest, especially here at his first meeting. We know how difficult that can be, particularly in a group of total strangers. But most here will probably affirm that it's the only way to grow. Also, judging the group members' reactions, it seems that many of you feel for John in his pain and can identify with what he has experienced through his addiction. I'm sure that support will help him throughout treatment and you could all grow by reaching out to him. It always stuns me to see just how much hurt addiction causes a person and we can see John's pain today is visible. What I especially appreciated was how John was able to be so honest and direct about the effects of his addiction, not just what it cost him, but also what it did to others. He was able to share with us that his need for money and drugs was so strong that it led him to steal pain medication from his dying mother."

The last sentence had the effect of a thunderbolt on the group. It brought home how John's addiction was not just a private matter, but that it violated basic social bonds. Yet it was said simply, in a caring tone, without harshness or personal attack. Weeks later, John shared how that one remark started him looking honestly at his addiction. It is doubtful that John could have looked into that mirror if the therapist had called him a derogatory name or engaged in moralizing and finger wagging.

Principle 3: Elicit Self-Motivational Statements

This principle implies two separate skills. First, do not provoke counter arguments, as was demonstrated in the workshop example, by taking sides. Second, the therapist elicits self-motivational statements, so that *the client is the one who argues for recovery and recovery-linked behaviors.*

Eliciting Self-Motivational Statements

Worksheet 7.1* assists the client in examining the consequences of gambling in a dispassionate manner. The client fills out the worksheet once the therapist believes she has established trust and then uses it as data for constructing reasons for changing in the next exercise (decisional balance). The therapist also explores the client's responses on the checklist to *elicit client self-motivational statements for change.* For example, if the client checks off "family members criticized you" and was quite bothered by this, the therapist seeks examples. She asks the client to describe what that experience felt like and what it made him feel like doing when it happened. She also asks how this fits in with his values and his view of himself.

Developing the ability to elicit self-motivational statements means learning the proper way to ask questions. In asking questions, the hope is that clients will see what is in their own best interest. The first good habit to get into is *rephrasing declarative statements of advice into interrogative ones* that will lead clients to self-exploration and ownership of the insights. The following dialogue illustrates this approach, with the interviewer's internal dialogue in italics. The case concerns a pathological gambling patient who strongly wishes to stop gambling but feels trapped in a vicious cycle of needing to hold off creditors by writing bad checks, then feeling a need to gamble to cover the checks, and so on:

Counselor: Can you tell me about this pattern of writing so many bad checks?

Client: Well, it's not like I want to, but I can't seem to figure any way out. I got into so much debt from my gambling that my credit is shot. I write checks at retail places to pay off the creditors who are screaming the loudest.

Counselor: You said earlier that you don't even *like* gambling anymore, yet you sometimes play the video poker machines.

Client: Yeah, at the end of a bad day, when I haven't made money fixing anything, I'll stop at a bar and throw a few bucks in the machine. But that's not because it's fun anymore, I'm just hoping to get lucky.

Counselor: So you're gambling more or less as a way of solving your financial problems not because it makes you feel good?

Client: Right.

Counselor: [*John is not into gambling for the effect anymore but simply as a life solution. The task now would be for him to see that his current "solutions"*

---

*All worksheets may be reproduced for use with individual clients.

have created a vicious cycle. If he can come to understand that, perhaps he will be open to other problem-solving approaches.] Could you tell me how you spend a typical day?

Client: Well, I get up at about 6:30 or 7:00 a.m. and go down to my work area in the basement. I look at my ledger with all the bills I owe. There are 35 people I have borrowed from or wrote bad checks to. I speak to about half of them every day and tell them I'll see them at such and such a time later that day or the next. Then I figure out just how much I have to make to give them something.

Counselor: And how many of the ones you promise to pay to do you follow through on?

Client: It depends on how much I make that day. If business is good, I can get to all of them; other days just a few—but I never give all of them what I promise.

Counselor: So how do they react when that happens?

Client: They're really mad, but I put them off by telling them I'll bring something by tomorrow. The ones who yell the loudest or threaten legal stuff I give more to or see them every day.

Counselor: And you give these people cash?

Client: Yes. Well, that's the thing. Most of the time I do. But when work is tight I'll write a check to keep them quiet.

Counselor: How can you do that?

Client: I don't have any legit checking accounts, but I have a bunch of checkbooks from an account that closed years ago. So I write checks on that because it takes a week or two for them to find out they're no good.

Counselor: Okay, I'm getting the picture. Could you continue, then, with your day?

Client: So starting at about 8:30 or 9:00 a.m., the calls start coming in from people demanding their money. I stay on the phone for about 3 to 4 hours giving everybody a song and dance about paying and telling them I'll be in to see them. About noon or so, I hit the streets soliciting repair business from all the retail outlets I know and work like a dog. I only take cash; I tell them I'm a small operation, and I pass on the savings in overhead directly to them in reduced costs. Some of them don't like the cash thing. It messes up their books. But they're small businesses too, so they do lots of stuff on the sly as well. And they know they're not going to get better rates or a better job. So about 6:00 p.m. or 7, I've collected enough cash for my own expenses and then I make the rounds of the establishments I owe money to. I tell them we're in a business downturn and work is slow, etc., which they know themselves, and I give them only a portion of what I've promised. They're mad as hell, but they know I come around every day with something, so in a way it keeps them from doing something drastic. Then I get home around 8:30 p.m., and maybe my wife has left me something to eat, and we watch TV for an hour or two and go to bed.

Counselor: [*Several major issues here to address. First, his debt-reduction method is a vicious cycle. That means he will continue to turn to gambling as a solution. Second, this has got to be exhausting given that this is a 7-day-a-week existence, not to mention totally unsatisfying. Third, what impact is all of this having on his marital relationship? My instinct would be to tell him these things directly as observations. However, it will have more impact if he reaches these conclusions on his own.*] Could you describe for me what it must feel like for you at the end of a typical day? [*This is an interrogatory alternative to, "You must be exhausted!"*]

Client: To be honest, I try not to think about it because if I do then I get real depressed. I'm depressed all the time anyway. But it gets real bad when I focus on it.

Counselor: And if you chose to focus on it, what would you notice? [*Here emotional arousal could highlight and punctuate motivation for recovery.*]

Client: When I focus on it, I see I'm going nowhere fast, that people are going to stay on my case, and I'm digging myself deeper into a hole.

Counselor: There's no end in sight.

Client: Right.

Counselor: And when you feel that there's no end in sight ... ? [*This is being "Rogerian with an agenda," not content to simply empathize that there's no end in sight. If John explores his pain, perhaps it will provide motivation toward corrective action.*]

Client: I begin to think I'm going to have no choice but to run. I'm not ever going to jail again. So I'll run.

Counselor: And what would that mean?

Client: It means I won't be able to contact my wife and family. I'll have to go underground. I know how to do that. It's no big thing, but I really don't want to.

Counselor: Why not?

Client: I've got nothing without my family. I'm already broke with a miserable existence. At least they know by being in treatment I'm trying to do something with my life. I think I could improve things with the kids, but not if I go underground.

Counselor: So although you feel you might have to go underground to end this vicious cycle, you really don't want to do it.

Client: Right.

Counselor: [*Time to summarize.*] So when you look at the pattern you've developed with the bills, you see it's a dead-end. It sets you up to gamble every now and then even though you've seen what gambling has done to your family. And it makes you feel so terrible that you can't see any other way out but to run.

Client: Yeah.

Counselor: Is this what you want for yourself? [*Rather than, "What a miserable existence, surely you want to change this!"*]

Client: No. I want to be normal.

Counselor: [*Now he's given me a metaphor. "Normal." Something to use as a goal to work toward. Could never have guessed that being normal was important to him.*] What would normal look like?

Client: Normal means I've paid off my bills. I can work six days a week instead of seven. That I can spend Sundays with my wife, kids, and their families. I get home at night and have supper with my wife, and we can go to the store sometimes or watch TV. It means I don't have to gamble ever again. Not just because I don't want to anymore but because I don't need to.

Counselor: [*One more chance to develop discrepancy between the real and the ideal and perhaps interest him in some other solutions.*] And when you look at this picture of normal and where you'd like to be, how does it compare to where you are now? [*Again, rather than telling him about the huge discrepancy, the interviewer attempts to get the client to describe, experience, and reflect on it.*]

Client: It's a mess. I can't see any way out of it.

Counselor: [*At this point, it might be useful to explore some action strategies to get out of this vicious cycle. I'm not sure what he'll buy into right now, but he'll need to commit himself to some change to make this work.*] What would a program have to achieve before you could agree to it? [*Rather than make suggestions at this point, I need to assess the parameters of an acceptable solution.*]

Client: I will not go to jail; so anything we try that means somebody's going to get mad and try to prosecute me for fraud or something, I won't do.

Counselor: So the most important piece in any plan is staying out of jail. And that gets done by keeping the creditors from getting mad and retaliating by bringing legal action.

Client: Right, but I don't see any way to do that.

Counselor: [*Well, I have some thoughts about how to bring this off (see debt reduction strategies in Chapter 13), but, however I present it to him, he has to see that we will have the same goals. Better present it tentatively because, after all, I can't be absolutely sure what the creditors will do. He's put them off so long, there's no telling what their actual intentions are, and some of them are shady characters.*] What would you feel about a strategy that allowed you to work from 8 or 9 a.m. daily instead of being on the phone for those 4 or 5 hours? [*Versus, "You need to develop a strategy that allows you to work from 8 or 9 a.m. daily because you could double your income".*]

Client: That would be great. It would mean that I would double my income.

Counselor: If you doubled your income, what would that mean?

Client: Well, I would be able to pay off the creditors quicker and have extra money to give to my wife for the household bills.

Counselor: And if you did those things, how would that make you feel?

Client: Terrific. The pressure would be off.

Counselor: Would that feel normal?

Client: Absolutely.

Counselor: [*Time to link all of this back to his gambling addictions.*] If the pressure were off and you were feeling normal, what effect would this have on your urges to gamble?

Client: Honestly, I don't even know why I would have an urge to gamble anymore. This relapse only started because the money situation got so bad from the last binge, I *had* to gamble or *felt* I did.

Counselor: [*Summarize.*] So, an acceptable payment plan would take off the daily pressure, cause you to feel less depressed, mean you wouldn't have to go underground, make you feel respectable in the eyes of your family, reduce or even eliminate the urge to gamble, increase your earning potential, and give you more time to spend relaxing and being with your family.

Client: Yes.

Counselor: Well, maybe this would be a good time to look at your finances in detail.

This scenario illustrates the translation challenge in motivational enhancement. When the interviewer sees a road the client needs to travel, the required skill is asking questions so that the client determines the path. That takes place several times in the above dialogue. Notice that the questions the interviewer asked *did not imply that he or she knew the answer in advance.* If this point is missed, the interview will sound as if it's a cross-examination or a midterm exam instead of self-discovery.

MOTIVATIONAL ENHANCEMENT AND GOAL-SETTING

As stated throughout, goal-setting is crucial to adaptive functioning and rests at the core of self-regulation theory. In self-regulation theory, goals play a dual role representing two sides of the same coin. They set the content of our aspirations and become the incentives driving us toward them. Together they organize our behavior into coherent patterns, or, in the words of the great Yankee baseball player Yogi Berra, "If you don't know where you're going, you're liable to end up somewhere else."

Goals receive much of their self-regulatory capacity from their connection to attentional mechanisms. Within self-regulation theory and control theory attention is central (Carver & Scheier, 1998). We can only change that which we pay attention to. As noted in Chapter 4, casinos are set up to provide both a timeless ambiance with no clocks and one that increases the likelihood of self-escape via an absence of mirrors and the fostering of alcohol consumption. It would be a mistake to presume that addicts in general or pathological gamblers in particular lack goals. Rather, they are pursuing implicit, self-defeating goals that operate outside of awareness. Motivational enhancement attempts to make these implicit goals explicit, or, in the poetic language of psychoanalysis, to make the unconscious conscious. Then the therapist and client collaboratively must determine which new goals are in order.

Preparation for Planning Goals

Between consciousness-raising and setting new goals lies the intermediate step of making a commitment to change. A major tool in developing a commitment to change is the Decisional Balance Exercise (Worksheet 7.2). In keeping with self-regulation theory, the Decisional Balance Exercise is yet another way to focus one's attention. This strategy is quite ancient. Many years ago, I introduced the decisional balance to a nun whom I was seeing in therapy. Having recently read it in a counseling manual (Miller & Jackson, 1985), I eagerly described it to her as a tool developed by a creative behavior therapist. Sister studied the form for a minute or so, looked up, and said, "Oh, yes, this comes out of the *Spiritual Exercises* of St. Ignatius Loyola" (ca. 1491–1556). Naturally, it affirmed my cleverness to have a client point out that my advice was at least four centuries old.

Clients usually adapt well to this tool and offer little resistance. It strikes them as evenhanded and devoid of lecturing, and they engage the task actively. The therapist can suggest advantages or disadvantages left unmentioned, but only when the client is stuck or misses obvious elements. With minimal guidance, a commitment to change should follow this exercise. Goal-setting, then, is the next logical step.

Goal-Setting

Goal-setting can be as simple as a one-page exercise or as complex as the commercially available planners and organizers that command a high price in mall and airport shops catering to business executives. This chapter opts for an intermediate approach that attempts to touch on the goals relevant to recovery from pathological gambling. Pathological gamblers as a group tend to comply less with homework assignments than other patient groups. Therapy sessions provide a forum for doing the exercises, and the task itself elicits significant clinical material. Even though consciousness-raising precedes the goal-setting, motivational enhancement should never stop. As the client discovers new goals or reformulates old ones, the therapist connects the positive future vision with abandoning the pathological gambling experience: "Yes, that leisurely retirement is possible, but not if gambling wipes out your pension." Periodic commercials for recovery are powerful reinforcers as long as they are not overdone.

Overview

The approach outlined here proceeds in three steps accompanying the worksheets. First, clients with therapeutic assistance determine their goals across the major areas of social and psychological life. Second, clients review all of their goals as a whole. Unless they look at the totality, they may miss potential conflict areas or set impossible standards for themselves. Third, clients develop specific implementation plans for each content area. These worksheets were developed to reflect empirical research on the relationship between goal-setting and subjective well-being. For our purposes, the research demonstrates three important aspects of personal goals (Cantor & Sanderson, 1999). First, people choose goals at various levels of specificity. Contributing to the good of the human race versus giving directions to a person lost in the city describe higher- and lower-order goal pursuits, respectively. Second, people differ in their preferences for higher- or lower-order personal goals. Some people respond to goals described by grand visions; others connect with sweeping the sidewalk. Yet the same task (e.g., sweeping the sidewalk) could achieve either person's goal. Third, trade-offs exist in the pursuit of higher- versus lower-order goals. Higher-level ones provide people with a greater sense of meaning but are associated with greater levels of negative affect. Lower-level ones result in less negative affect but are also associated with more physical illness. This has been termed the meaningful-manageability trade-off. "The most adaptive form of self-regulatory behavior may be to select concrete, manageable goals that are linked to personally meaningful, higher-order representations" (Emmons, 1999, p. 54).

Therapists can use the following format to develop precisely that balance of concrete-manageable goals with ones that are linked to higher-order representations. In this way, the recovery process will not frustrate pathological gamblers with "magnificent obsessions," an excess of higher-order goals, nor mire them in "trivial pursuits," that is, lower-level goals (Emmons, 1999, p. 54, quoting Little, 1989).

Goal-Setting Exercise

Worksheets 7.3–7.10 divide life's goals into eight major content areas: recovery-abstinence, financial, relationship, family, spiritual/religious/character, health, occupation, and recreation/leisure. They subdivide goals chronologically according to those over the next 10 years, 5 years, and 1 year. Pathological gambling leads to tunnel vision regarding the future. The person's emphasis is on the here-and-now—"eat, drink, and be merry"—with little forethought. Focusing on the long term enables the patient to choose a positive vision that looks beyond the immediate turmoil of remaining abstinent. Envisioning a long-term future is in itself a motivational enhancement technique (Miller & Rollnick, 1991). This is especially recommended with younger clients, for whom "long-term" translates into what they're doing next summer.

Task A-4 ("Goals if I died in six months") on Worksheets 7.3–7.10 requires explanation. This idea comes from a popular time-management source (Lakein, 1973), and therapists could adapt it as they find suitable. Imagine you have an incurable disease, one that will cause you no great physical pain or disability but that will ensure you die precisely within the next 6 to 12 months. Under those circumstances, what goals would you choose for each content area? This question helps people establish priorities that otherwise might seem unclear.

Following the development of goals for each content area, the client achieves an overview by filling in all the goals on the Goals-Summary Worksheet (Worksheet 7.11). Viewing all the goals as a totality provides motivation for seeing the big picture and permits troubleshooting around having too many goals or conflictual ones. Item D on the Goals-Summary Worksheet involves ranking each goal according to level of importance. This establishes priorities as well as alerts the clinician regarding motivational level for each content area.

Worksheet 7.12 represents the Goal-Planning Worksheet onto which the client transfers each goal and generates an action plan. Therapists can easily incorporate goals into standard treatment plan documentation. These worksheets not only establish goals but also develop the steps for attaining them. Naturally, the therapist provides assistance as required for creating action plans.

Completing all eight worksheets early in the therapeutic process could intimidate the patient. We provide all eight here for an overview of the process. Clients normally will focus on a few in the early stages, for example, abstinence/recovery and financial goals. Therapist and client can revisit others in detail when relevant. Therefore, before addressing strategies for financial (Chapter 13), relationship (Chapter 14), or spiritual (Chapter 15) recovery, the client would complete goal planning for the designated area.

Resolving Goal Conflicts

Sometimes people pursue conflicting goals, for example, become vice-president for sales, working 70–80 hours a week, while at the same time desiring to maximize time spent with small children. Worksheet 7.13 is designed to aid in resolving goal conflicts. Using the decisional balance strategy, the person notes the advantages and disadvantages of each goal. The client then sets priorities using the well-established Premack principle from operant conditioning using high-frequency behaviors to reinforce low-frequency ones. The worksheet simplifies this to "grandma's rule," pointing out that people can arrange their lives to do the less probable behavior *prior* to the more probable one ("If you eat your spinach, you get the ice cream."). A third strategy is a variation of the Gestalt therapy two-chair technique. Seated in one chair, the client argues the case for one goal, switches chairs, and then argues the case for the other goal. This exercise clarifies priorities.

Finally, people can resolve goal conflicts through visualization (Miller & Rollnick, 1991). In this technique, the person transforms the conflict from words to an image, for example, being handcuffed, caught between two enticing doors, or coming to a fork in the road. The person visualizes selecting one goal with all its consequences. These consequences would include feelings, behavior, beliefs about oneself, what others will think, and so on. The person then visualizes the second goal in the same way. Again, this exercise will typically set priorities. Therapists can use these last two strategies to supplement the decisional balance exercise to develop a commitment to change. When the advantages/disadvantages quadrant does not generate enough powerful motivators, the two-chair visualization technique may tap into feelings and increase the therapeutic power.

This section has emphasized getting clients started on thinking about goals and using them as a motivating force. Goals ought not to die in the early stages of change as if they have served their purpose. Self-regulation theory states that goals remain primary motivators so that continued focus on them is essential for maintaining change. Many popular books in the self-help sections of bookstores do little more than encourage people to focus continually on goals related to abstinence. The titles advocate regular self-examination—for example, *Twenty-Four Hours a Day*—within the structure of daily reflection. Although Chapter 15 discusses daily reflection under spirituality and character formation, its foundation begins with the goal assessment described throughout this chapter. These goals represent for the patient a work in progress that requires continual awareness, reevaluation, and implementation. With an overall plan for life change, the person can approach with an integrative perspective the specific challenges discussed in the following chapters.

Worksheet 7.1

Consequences of Gambling Checklist

Name: _____

Date: _____

Place a checkmark next to any item that occurred as a result of gambling.

For each item checked please rate how bothered you were by that consequence

0	1	2	3	4
not at all		somewhat		very much

	Occurred (checkmark)	Bothered (0–4)
Occupied too much time	＿＿	＿＿
Conflict at work	＿＿	＿＿
Felt out of control	＿＿	＿＿
Couldn't keep mind on job	＿＿	＿＿
Arguments with spouse/partner	＿＿	＿＿
Arguments with children	＿＿	＿＿
Arguments with other family members	＿＿	＿＿
Lost self-respect	＿＿	＿＿
Felt guilty	＿＿	＿＿
Spent less time at work	＿＿	＿＿
Time away from family activities	＿＿	＿＿
Spent less time with nongambling friends	＿＿	＿＿
Told lies	＿＿	＿＿
Didn't give others attention	＿＿	＿＿
Unpaid debts to friends	＿＿	＿＿
Unpaid debts on credit cards	＿＿	＿＿
Unpaid debts to banks/lending institutions	＿＿	＿＿
Late paying household bills	＿＿	＿＿
Late paying loans	＿＿	＿＿
Late paying credit cards	＿＿	＿＿
Illegal acts (other than gambling itself)	＿＿	＿＿
Unable to take vacations	＿＿	＿＿
Spouse/partner criticized you	＿＿	＿＿
Friends criticized you	＿＿	＿＿
Family members criticized you	＿＿	＿＿
Employer/co-workers criticized you	＿＿	＿＿
Violated your personal values	＿＿	＿＿
Unable to reach your career goals	＿＿	＿＿
Unable to reach your family goals	＿＿	＿＿
Unable to reach your financial goals	＿＿	＿＿
Unable to reach your spiritual goals	＿＿	＿＿
Kept secrets from people you're close to	＿＿	＿＿
Became violent	＿＿	＿＿
Thought about dying	＿＿	＿＿
Thought about hurting yourself	＿＿	＿＿
Tried to hurt yourself	＿＿	＿＿
Lost a job	＿＿	＿＿
Had things you purchased repossessed	＿＿	＿＿
Late paying rent	＿＿	＿＿

Decisional Balance

Continuing to gamble	Stopping gambling
Benefits	Benefits
Costs	Costs

Goal-Setting Worksheet

A. Developing *Abstinence/Recovery* Goals

    1. Goals for the next 10 years.

    2. Goals for the next 5 years.

    3. Goals for the next year.

    4. Goals if I died in six months.

B. Values Clarification

As I inspect these goals, do they appear to take into consideration my highest values? If not, add or adjust individual goals accordingly.

C. Finalized goal to work on immediately

Worksheet 7.4
Goal-Setting Worksheet

A. Developing *Occupational* Goals

    1. Goals for the next 10 years.

    2. Goals for the next 5 years.

    3. Goals for the next year.

    4. Goals if I died in six months.

B. Values Clarification

As I inspect these goals, do they appear to take into consideration my highest values? If not, add or adjust individual goals accordingly.

C. Finalized goal to work on immediately

Worksheet 7.5
Goal-Setting Worksheet

A. Developing *Family* Goals

   1. Goals for the next 10 years.

   2. Goals for the next 5 years.

   3. Goals for the next year.

   4. Goals if I died in six months.

B. Values Clarification

As I inspect these goals, do they appear to take into consideration my highest values? If not, add or adjust individual goals accordingly.

C. Finalized goal to work on immediately

Goal-Setting Worksheet

A. Developing *Relationship* Goals

1. Goals for the next 10 years.

2. Goals for the next 5 years.

3. Goals for the next year.

4. Goals if I died in six months.

B. Values Clarification

As I inspect these goals, do they appear to take into consideration my highest values? If not, add or adjust individual goals accordingly.

C. Finalized goal to work on immediately

Goal-Setting Worksheet

A. Developing *Health* Goals

    1. Goals for the next 10 years.

    2. Goals for the next 5 years.

    3. Goals for the next year.

    4. Goals if I died in six months.

B. Values Clarification

As I inspect these goals, do they appear to take into consideration my highest values? If not, add or adjust individual goals accordingly.

C. Finalized goal to work on immediately

Goal-Setting Worksheet

A. Developing *Financial* Goals

   1. Goals for the next 10 years.

   2. Goals for the next 5 years.

   3. Goals for the next year.

   4. Goals if I died in six months.

B. Values Clarification

As I inspect these goals, do they appear to take into consideration my highest values? If not, add or adjust individual goals accordingly.

C. Finalized goal to work on immediately

Goal-Setting Worksheet

A. Developing *Recreational/Entertainment* Goals

    1. Goals for the next 10 years.

    2. Goals for the next 5 years.

    3. Goals for the next year.

    4. Goals if I died in six months.

B. Values Clarification

As I inspect these goals, do they appear to take into consideration my highest values? If not, add or adjust individual goals accordingly.

C. Finalized goal to work on immediately

Goal-Setting Worksheet

A. Developing *Spiritual/Religious/Personal Character* Goals

1. Goals for the next 10 years.

2. Goals for the next 5 years.

3. Goals for the next year.

4. Goals if I died in six months.

B. Values Clarification

As I inspect these goals, do they appear to take into consideration my highest values? If not, add or adjust individual goals accordingly.

C. Finalized goal to work on immediately

Fill in from *item C* on the previous worksheets for *each of the content* areas.

Abstinence-Recovery:

Occupational:

Family:

Relationships:

Health:

Financial:

Recreational/Entertainment:

Spiritual/Religious/Personal Character

D. *To become aware of the potential conflicts among your goals, rate each one as to how important it is to you.* On a scale from 1 to 10, with 1 having little importance, and 10 having great importance. Put the number right next to the goal.

E. If any goals present a major conflict; problem-solve around them, and adjust accordingly.

F. **Now transfer your goals onto the Goal-Planning Worksheet, and add specific steps for accomplishing each one.**

Worksheet 7.12
Goal-Planning Worksheet

I.   Using your Goals-Summary Worksheet, develop a plan for each content area.

II. Circle the content area for this plan.

   Abstinence   Family   Relationship   Health

   Financial   Recreational   Spiritual/Character   Occupation

III. Overall Goal:

IV. Steps necessary to attain goal

   1.   Date completed

   2.   Date completed

   3.   Date completed

V.   Possible obstacle(s)

   Specific steps to overcome obstacle(s)

   1.

   2.

   3.

140

Resolving Goal Conflicts Worksheet

Strategy I. Decisional Balance

Benefits of achieving Goals A and B

Disadvantages of achieving Goals A and B

Benefits of *not* achieving Goals A and B

Disadvantages of *not* achieving Goals A and B

Strategy II. Setting Priorities, or Grandma's Rule

Some goals that appear to be in conflict can be resolved simply by setting priorities. For example, keeping a clean house vs. going fishing. Grandma's rule says, *Do the least appealing project **before** doing the more appealing one.* Grandma put it differently, "If you eat your spinach, you'll get your ice cream."

How could setting priorities resolve my goal conflicts?

Strategy III. Two-Chair Technique

1. Set up two chairs.
2. Identify one chair for Goal A, another for Goal B.
3. Argue the case aloud for Goal A in first chair.
4. Switch chairs. Argue the case for Goal B in second chair.
5. Do this until you notice a clear sense of direction toward one or the other.

Strategy IV. Visualization

1. Visualize conflict by changing it to a picture or metaphor, being handcuffed, being caught between two attractive entertainments, etc.
2. Visualize selecting Goal A.
3. Visualize all the consequences of this choice, feelings, behavior, what you think of yourself, what others will think, etc.
4. Visualize all consequences of Goal B in similar fashion.
5. Now which seems to be of more benefit?

Abstinence Control and Relapse Prevention

BUILDING A FENCE AROUND TEMPTATION

If there is a way to obtain money, some pathological gambling patient somewhere has tried it.

Doreen and Sam were in their mid-sixties. Children of poor immigrants, both worked their way through school, married, retired, and now enjoyed traveling and seeing their grandchildren. Sam had a thriving and hectic insurance business in this northwestern rural U.S. county. He purposely worked 50 to 60 hours a week so that he could retire at age 60 and enjoy the good life with his family while he had good health. Doreen had stayed home to raise their three children but now worked as a hospital volunteer several days a week.

One Saturday afternoon, Doreen came in with the mail and mentioned to Sam that there appeared to be a computer glitch with their old mortgage company. Five years ago they had paid off their house mortgage, and the lines of credit they had used over the years to pay their children's college tuition. The letter Doreen opened included a payment coupon book for a new $250,000 mortgage on their home, very close to the 80% full value of the dwelling. Sam didn't react too strongly, reminding Doreen how a couple times the mortgage company messed up on their escrow accounts. "George told me last week when we were golfing that the bank was having trouble with the new computer system now that some big bank out of LA took them over. But I'll give it to Bill [their attorney] to check out."

The following Wednesday, Bill paid a visit to Doreen and Sam. He apologized for taking so long to deal with this issue but he had to do some checking. He showed them a document from the county clerk's office indicating they had deeded joint ownership of their home to their oldest son, Alan. Bill then produced a loan application for $250,000 containing Alan's signature as well as Doreen and Sam's. Bill knew the couple well enough to see from the look on their faces that Alan had forged both documents. In a small town, people often complete business deals on a handshake and have total trust in a person they've known all their life. To make that even more credible was the fact that Alan was the town's representative to the state legislature. Dumfounded, the couple asked Bill about their options. "Well, of course, you can press charges," Bill mentioned. "Insurance companies need to see charges brought before they will reimburse the bank for fraud. Once the insurance company pays back the bank, that wipes out your responsibility for the loan. I'm sure Alan could get jail time for this." The couple blanched even further when they considered the impact of such a family scandal, the end of Alan's career, and the loss of the only income his four children and homemaker wife had to live on. Ironically, if they prosecuted Alan, they would end up supporting his children.

As Doreen and Sam later discovered, Alan took out the loan to cover gambling debts, so the money was not recoverable. Furthermore, he had still more sizable outstanding debts. Doreen and Sam entered counseling to come to grips with needing to change all their expectations about the retirement they had spent more than 35 years preparing for.

The next case represents a different scenario.

Jennifer sat huddled under the kitchen table hugging tightly her 2-year-old boy. Four large, nonchalant men were carrying out the family's living room, dining room, recreation room, and master bedroom furniture. The family was not moving; rather, the loan company was repossessing all the furniture that her husband had put up as collateral to obtain money to gamble. The only piece he missed—a wedding gift—was the kitchen table and chairs. Jennifer gravitated beneath them as the one safe spot for her and her son while the environment rapidly dissolved around her. She later recalled her surreal thinking during that unnerving episode. In her pocket were two dollars, her only available money. Touching the money for reassurance, she could not make up her mind how to spend it. Her choice was difficult. Should she use it to buy peanut butter to feed her child or toilet paper?

Sad stories are all too familiar in the wake of pathological gambling. Their purpose is not so much to highlight the impact of pathological gambling on families (the subject of Chapter 14), but to illustrate the ingenuity and loss of restraint in obtaining money to gamble. The present chapter focuses on how patients, therapists, and families need to mobilize resources to neutralize this powerful drive for money and prevent it from destroying the lives of pathological gambling patients and their families. The chapter begins by defining abstinence control and its components, then links these components to self-regulation theory, and then describes the strategies themselves in some detail. In conjunction with abstinence control strategies, the chapter examines relapse prevention techniques to contain slips before they snowball.

DEFINING ABSTINENCE CONTROL

Unless controlled gambling is the therapeutic goal, abstinence control is the primary focus in gambling treatment. Developing initial abstinence usually is a threefold process:

1. Discovering the triggers or links in the chain leading to gambling.
2. Containing the impulse by managing the environmental triggers, or as this chapter describes it, "building a fence around the impulse."
3. Controlling the impulse by managing the urges, negative emotions, and cognitive expectations that lead to gambling.

The first two parts of the process are discussed in this chapter; the next two chapters examine the final part.

Managing the environment as a change strategy is well known in the history of behavior therapy or behavior modification (Bandura, 1969). With recourse to the concept of "stimulus control," therapists used applied behavioral analytic techniques to reduce the likelihood that maladaptive behaviors will occur and to increase the likelihood of adaptive behavior. Following a functional analysis of an identified behavior, a therapist might suggest altering the links in the chain that lead to the problem. For example, if a dieter keeps breaking a healthy eating regimen with a nightly bag of potato chips in front of the television, stimulus control procedures might suggest: (a) keep the potato chips out of the house and/or (b) have a firm rule never to eat while watching TV. Stimulus control involves managing gambling behavior first by learning the *sequence* of events leading up to the gambling and with that information devise strategies to *interrupt* the sequence.

Stimulus Control and Self-Regulation Theory

Managing the environment via stimulus control has direct links to self-regulation theory. Self-regulation theory emphasizes the importance of attention, and the first step in stimulus control is a functional analysis of one's gambling. Functional analysis is a form of self-monitoring that heightens awareness of the multiple factors involved in the decision to gamble. It alters perceptions of gambling from a runaway impulse to an event with consistent patterns. A functional analysis suggests any number of entrance points for a person to implement self-regulation theory strategies, thereby interrupting the sequence.

Gambling is linked to *choices* people make at various decision points in the chain. This permits them to see how they start the snowball going down the hill ("acquiescence" in self-regulation theory). Although this awareness of personal choice increases gambler's responsibility for their behavior with the potential for increasing guilt, the trade-off is decreasing the need to see themselves only as victims and developing an increased potential for autonomy.

STIMULUS CONTROL ASSESSMENT

Identifying the Links in the Chain

Social learning theory suggests that a variety of environmental links exist for human behavior. Behavior is seldom related to a single causal entity. Many environmental cues signal the context for action (Bandura, 1986). We stop at red lights, cut steak with a knife at a dinner party instead of tearing it with our hands, and have sex in private.

Social learning theory goes further and suggests that any behavior is like the last link in a chain of multiple behaviors that together form a whole sequence. Social learning theory differs from psychoanalytic theories on the one hand and chaos theory on the other in its units of analysis. Psychoanalytic theories tend to emphasize antecedents in childhood and chaos theory emphasizes nonlinearity and unpredictability (McCown & Chamberlain, 2000). In social learning theory, the task is to identify the various immediate links, those approximating a waking day, with the hope of shifting them to alter the outcome. If one wants to stop an adulterous affair, not being alone together increases the odds of reaching that goal. Stimulus control procedures are at the heart of many clinical interventions discussed in the treatment outcome review (see Chapter 3). So essential are they for attaining abstinence that studies primarily interested in other treatments' components usually have included some stimulus control strategies.

The Gambling Triggers Worksheet (Worksheet 8.1) is a tool for assisting a functional analysis of the gambling behavior. It has two parts that work together: one verbal, one visual. In the textual component, the person recalls the major events of the day prior to gambling. Another verbal approach is for the therapist to ask a series of questions similar to a newspaper reporter's. The therapist asks, "*Who, what, when, where, how, why, how often*, and *how much*," to understand the gambling episode. A leisurely discussion of each question will uncover much of the same data as the worksheet. This worksheet introduces self-monitoring as a self-management tool, whereas answering questions is a passive experience typical of the role of "patient." Through the aid of the worksheet's visual component, the person tracks feelings, activities, and urges sequentially prior to and following gambling. Using the worksheet within sessions communicates a nonjudgmental and scientific approach to analyzing gambling. The therapist might introduce the worksheet as follows: "It will be great if you never gamble from here on, but we need information about everything leading up to gambling. So let's review everything that happened prior to your last episode. From now on, if you gamble, fill out the worksheet afterward as soon as you can. If you don't get it done before our session, we will complete it here." The therapist treats every gambling episode as interesting data that she wants to explore in detail. Gambling is never an occasion for scolding or disappointment but an opportunity to learn more about the dynamics of gambling for the patient. If patients can absorb this mentality from the therapist, they can look at their slips as a learning experience—a topic discussed under relapse prevention.

Over time, keeping a record of the antecedents and consequences of gambling results in identifying patterns. Those patterns will indicate external environmental situations and internal feeling states that correlate with gambling. Similarly, noting what happens to the person *after* gambling can indicate the *function* gambling plays for the person as a solution to emotional or cognitive needs. When clients are unable or fail to keep track between sessions, therapists invite them to complete it in session. Doing it together often reveals new information as well as helps gain understanding into the client's lack of motivation. All motivational deficits, including failure to complete homework assignments, should be treated in the manner discussed in the chapter on motivational enhancement. Using the principle of "successive approximations" or "shaping," the therapist can describe "success" as having the client think about the task between sessions, while gradually increasing the level of task difficulty in keeping the record.

Bill, a triply addicted person (gambling, cocaine, and alcohol) described a typical sequence leading to gambling. Until this analysis, Bill saw his gambling behavior only as a reaction to "feeling bad." He broke down the gambling antecedents into smaller units that encompassed his thoughts as well. The sequence started with financial concerns, which led to believing he could not adequately support his pregnant fiancee and their child. These concerns led to thoughts about suicide, which in turn led to gambling. For Bill the racetrack served as a distraction to drown out suicidal ideation.

Francesca's gambling triggers were more straightforward. She succumbed whenever the state lottery reached a critical mass around a million dollars. She became aware of this from the billboard in her inner-city neighborhood and at night when they selected the lottery winning numbers during intermission of her television game shows. Inevitably, this led her to the nearest convenience store to buy tickets. Therapists need to be aware that a functional analysis uncovers the idiosyncratic and specific triggers to gambling that lead *this* person to gamble under *these* circumstances.

Worksheet 8.2 moves the analysis of slips from the level of motor acts toward understanding intention and choice. Here the therapist guides the patient from seeing the slip as an irresistible impulse to an act composed of mini-decision points (Marlatt & Gordon, 1985). This worksheet, in conjunction with the triggers exercise, should provide patient and therapist with a multilevel look at each gambling episode. If the therapist remains consistent with this process, patients become much more attentive to their triggers for no other reason than dealing with the mandatory therapeutic debriefing.

STIMULUS CONTROL AND ENVIRONMENTAL MANAGEMENT

Consistent with the theme throughout this book, we recommend relationship or family counseling as an effective modality for achieving the second prong in a stimulus control approach—namely, managing the environment. I will use the generic term "support person" to represent a spouse, partner, family member, employer, professional financial manager, or other friend who chooses to participate in the gambler's recovery program. Support persons play many roles in the recovery process, but here the focus is assisting gamblers in building a fence around obtaining money for the purpose of gambling. The support person needs to be present for as many sessions as possible until the patient maintains suitable control. If no support person is available, a professional financial manager or accountant can help. Legally, a professional financial manager is required to follow the client's wishes, which allows the patient to override an established plan on impulse. Recourse to legal roadblocks such as a trust fund may derail impulsive actions. An agreement is also useful, with the client's permission, to have the financial professional report periodically to the therapist about withdrawals. When no support person of any type is available, the therapist functions as the client's support in managing the environment. For ethical reasons, the therapist may not get directly involved in handling client funds or accounts, even though clients request that service.

Follow the Money

The following list represents the wide variety of legal ways gamblers can have access to financial resources and therapists need to evaluate the gambler's potential to access them:

Savings accounts, checking accounts, credit card borrowing, stocks and bonds, trust funds, pension funds, personal loans, borrowing from acquaintances, home equity loans, second mortgages, borrowing from lending institutions, using financial accounts or personal possessions as collateral.

Only the pathological gambler's resourcefulness and lack of scruples limit illegal means of obtaining money. The following represent only some of the illegal ways pathological gambling patients have obtained money:

Embezzling client accounts (bank, stock, trust funds, pensions), embezzling funds one oversees (religious institutions, boys' and girls' clubs, research grant money to university departments, homeowner's association funds), writing checks "on the float," insurance fraud, and even armed robbery.

The financial desperation sometimes results in bizarre and tragic schemes. A real estate agent who catered to the wealthy lost enormous sums gambling and owed many people huge amounts. The only solution in her mind was to prevail on a friend to assist in making her death look like murder instead of suicide. She could thereby bequeath her insurance benefits directly to her creditors and die with her debts resolved. Unfortunately for her creditors, good detective work uncovered the plan but not, sadly, before she had killed herself.

Illegal acts to obtain money raise the issue of determining a differential diagnosis for antisocial personality disorder. Although it is helpful to maintain some index of suspicion about this early in the assessment process, the majority of pathological gamblers committing antisocial acts who seek treatment do not meet criteria for antisocial personality disorder. First, the antisocial acts are not usually present in early adolescence. Second, much of the antisocial behavior is clearly linked to gambling behavior rather than being one aspect of an antisocial lifestyle. Often the very ineptness of the crime assists in the diagnosis.

> A police officer, whose wife was a homemaker with three small children, was about to lose his house due to gambling debts. He held up a bank teller at a drive-through window. When he handed the teller a note asking for a sum equal to his mortgage debt he alerted her to the gun sitting next to him on the passenger seat. He was apprehended in less than 3 hours because his badge and police number sat on the same seat easily in range of the security camera and the teller's alert vision.

In the presence of the support person, the therapist queries the patient about the many potential legal and illegal sources of income as is reasonable. A few individual meetings beforehand should give the therapist a sense of how honest the client is likely to be.

Relationship Principles

The goal of the support person's presence in therapy is to assist the client in developing stimulus control skills. In order to achieve that goal, a collaborative relationship is essential between the support person and the patient, particularly when the support person is a spouse or intimate partner.

The therapist might explain the following guidelines as tools for building a fence around the temptation to gamble. Persons in intimate relationships who use these tools have the added bonus of increasing communication that no doubt was dormant or nonexistent

1. **Flood the partner with information**. The presenting dynamic in the relationship is usually one in which the pathological gambler's primary goal is to keep the partner in the dark. As a result, communication is not only minimal, it is often purposely deceptive. Breaking that pattern is no small task, so the operative strategy is

"do the opposite," namely, go to the other extreme in telling the partner more than he or she may want to know. The rule of thumb at the beginning of therapy is *no information is too trivial to communicate*. This particularly relates to the gambler's movements when outside the house. No visit to the grocery store, no side trip to look at scenery, and no change in lunch plans is too minor to relate.

2. **Make no assumptions about what your partner already knows**. This flows from the preceding rule. If there is any assumption, it should be that he or she knows nothing. Just 2 or 3 weeks of using this strategy can produce major climate changes through reducing needless worry for the family.

Disarmament

This strategy for improving the relationship is an adaptation of Integrative Behavioral Couple's Therapy (Christensen & Jacobson, 2000), a method explored more fully in Chapter 14. That strategy involves enriching intimacy by having the partners engage in "disarmament." In distressed relationships, partners know how to push the hot buttons of the other person and use the strategy when desiring revenge or to get what they want. Disarmament calls for pathological gamblers coming clean with all their "tricks of the trade," including:

1. What their psychological state looks like when they are gambling.
2. Their behavioral patterns when they are beginning to gamble.
3. Ways they try to deceive family members and others into thinking no gambling is going on.
4. Ways they are likely to go about looking for money to gamble.
5. The when, where, why, and how of gambling for them.

Worksheet 8.3 is a tool the couple can use for this process, and the therapist can mediate the discussion around the data. The rationale behind disarmament is that, if the pathological gambler were truly committed to abstinence, he or she would want others to know all the likely patterns or schemes to assist in building a fence around the impulse to gamble. If they don't want others knowing their secrets, then the issue should be raised as to whether they are truly motivated to change. If they are not, then the therapist should engage in the motivational enhancement strategies discussed in the previous chapter.

In the early stages, the couple reviews, monitors, and adjusts the environmental management goals with the aid of the therapist. Although the therapist facilitates this process initially, the goal is to have the couple or family conduct this independently.

Financial Control Strategies

Reducing access to money is the first major component in abstinence control. That component goes hand in glove with budgeting and developing an overall financial plan (see Chapter 13). But financial control cannot wait until every aspect of budgeting is complete.

Phase one evolves out of the overall clinical assessment of the patient's method of operating as well as the behavioral chain assessment described above. Once high-risk situations are identified, the next step is to limit access to financial resources to gamble with. To illustrate the challenge involved in this step, consider the nature of substance abuse. People do not need to have alcohol or heroin in their possession to manage the activities of daily life. Money, on the other hand, is essential, but money is intricately linked to the gambling compulsion.

The first phase involves planning which financial resources the patient will control on a daily basis and what system for accountability will be used. Some require severe restrictions; perhaps enough money for lunch or transportation. Strict accountability may also be essential, for example, keeping receipts for all expenditures.

Controlling access to funds is also critical, that is, writing checks, making loans, using credit cards for cash advances, and so on. Families may need to prevent access to certain accounts, write letters to the bank stopping all loan applications, change automatic teller machine passwords, and set up a post office box number to ensure that bills, credit card applications, and the like go directly to the support person. Chapter 13 offers further suggestions for support persons to protect themselves financially and legally from the gambler's illegal or irresponsible use of money.

Individualized assessment is essential in taking any of these steps. In the most severe cases, patients should carry a limited amount of money and have strict accountability, with no access to other income. Other patients may require minimal monitoring. A good rule of thumb is to start with minimal access and minimal amounts but to gradually increase both as recovery progresses and trust develops. Naturally, monitoring and renegotiating these guidelines are a continual process.

Typically, the support person is wary at the outset and favors severe monetary restrictions. Usually, the patient attempts to renegotiate this after a few weeks of success, with the support person resisting change. The support person often describes feeling either scared about what kind of financial damage the gambler will do or guilty for acting like a parent who is infantalizing the patient. Open discussion usually resolves these issues by reassuring everyone that this is a temporary phase in the recovery process that helps both parties achieve their goals.

Managing Other High-Risk Situations

The functional analysis conducted earlier should alert all involved as to what the gambler's high-risk situations are other than simple possession of money. As a result of that assessment, all strategize together as to how best to cope with these events. In the case of John in Chapter 7, we saw that creditors threatening to take legal action constituted a high-risk incentive to gamble. Developing an overall payment plan eventually reduced the pressure of that experience.

The therapist uses the idea of a behavioral chain or starting the snowball to discuss how to eliminate behavior that starts the gambler down that path. Video poker machines, for example, are illegal in many states but are often easy to find in bars and restaurants that serve alcohol. The recovering video poker machine player needs to arrange her life so as not to go in a bar unless accompanied by a support person. These changes may require altering aspects of social life, expanding the circle of friends, not participating in certain forms of recreation (e.g., the semiannual trip to Atlantic City), or similar attention to activities that are linked to eventual gambling. Any of these plans could be incorporated into the goals development strategies discussed in Chapter 7.

Containing a Slip

The strategies discussed so far aim to prevent the patient rolling the snowball down the hill in the first place. Now we turn our attention to another under-regulation failure—letting the snowball continue rolling down the hill or, in this case, failing to contain a slip before it spirals out of control. Cognitive-behavioral work in addictions refers to this process as relapse prevention (Marlatt & Gordon, 1985). Relapse prevention has gained great popularity in addiction circles—one type as a commercial therapeutic program (Gorski & Miller, 1982) that has no controlled research, and the cognitive-behavioral version, which is weaker than many focused alcoholism interventions (Miller *et al.*, 1998). Nevertheless, we offer a cognitive processing analysis to patients as one more tool to shift their attention away from helplessness beliefs to ones emphasizing self-efficacy.

Worksheet 8.4 instructs patients to analyze slips in such a way as to prevent two common negative beliefs. The first relates to thinking a slip justifies giving up altogether and counters the loss of self-esteem that routinely results. The stages-of-change model (Chapter 7) demonstrated that people could return immediately to their highest stage following a slip without needing to cycle back to precontemplation. The worksheet also directs the patient toward an objective analysis of what he could have done differently. This shifts attention away from self-deprecation to problem-solving. Finally, the exercise directs the patient to list personal and environmental resources that can enhance her ability to feel more in control.

SUMMARY

This chapter has reviewed two major aspects of stimulus control or ways for gamblers to manage their environments to reduce risk of gambling. These strategies included:

1. A functional analysis of thinking, feeling, and behaving that leads to gambling.
2. Assessing the methods the gambler used to obtain money to gamble or cover it up.
3. Developing methods to restrict access to money through the help of support persons and thus prevent impulsive gambling.
4. Developing strategies to cope with the physical situations that increase the probability of gambling.

The next chapter describes how patients in their attempt to cope with gambling urges inadvertently increase their intensity, duration, and frequency through the process of misregulation. To cope effectively with these urges the chapter extends the therapeutic strategy of acceptance into the realm of gambling treatment.

Gambling Triggers Worksheet

1. **Describe a situation when I gambled recently**.
   What did I do earlier in the day?
   What did I do an hour before gambling?
   What did I do 30 minutes before gambling?
   What did I do 5 minutes before gambling?
   Feelings? Mood?

2. **Triggers Chart**.   Rate the intensity of urge to gamble at each stage.

   Urge Intensity Scale
   0–2   minimal
   3–4   moderate
   5–6   intense
   7–8   overwhelming

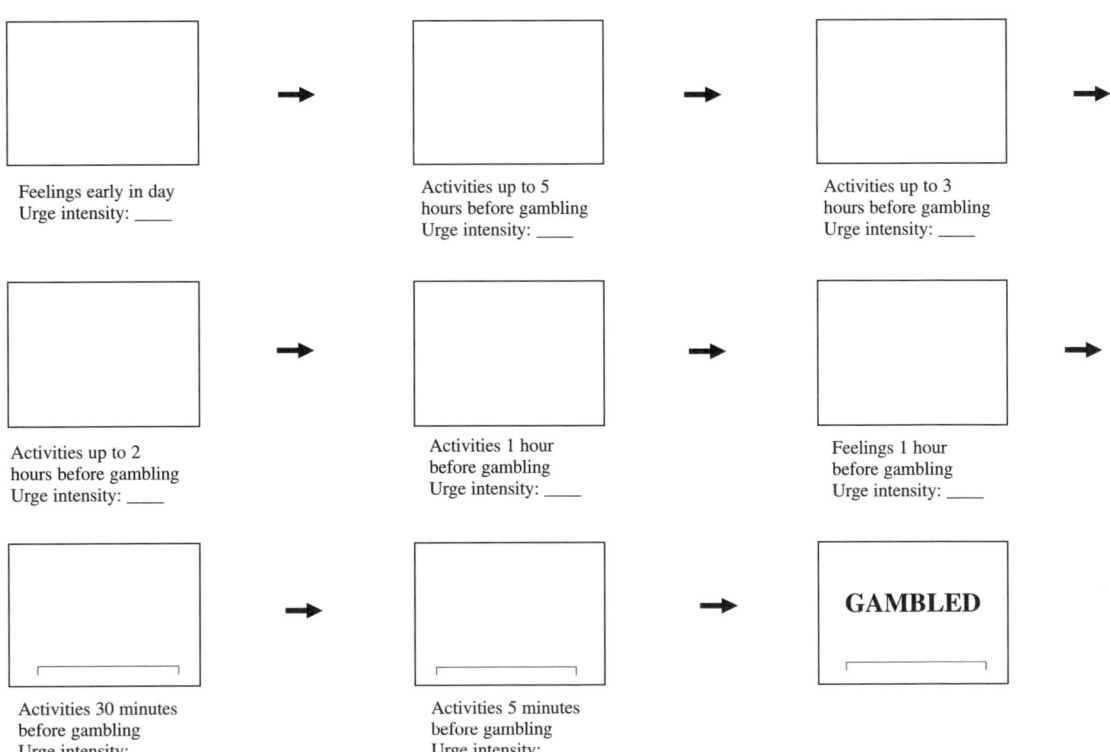

Feelings early in day
Urge intensity: ____

Activities up to 5
hours before gambling
Urge intensity: ____

Activities up to 3
hours before gambling
Urge intensity: ____

Activities up to 2
hours before gambling
Urge intensity: ____

Activities 1 hour
before gambling
Urge intensity: ____

Feelings 1 hour
before gambling
Urge intensity: ____

Activities 30 minutes
before gambling
Urge intensity: ____

Activities 5 minutes
before gambling
Urge intensity: ____

GAMBLED

Coping with Relapse
Lapse/Slip Analysis Worksheet

1. When a slip/lapse occurs, people often feel blindsided by the event. Yet they fail to see how they may have put the blinders on themselves. Slips usually occur when people take a step early in the slip process that makes resistance extremely difficult. Problem gamblers who were admitted to the addiction treatment hospital where I worked would sometimes decide to drive through Atlantic City. It was actually 200 miles out of the way, but they wanted to take "the scenic route." Did they consciously intend to gamble? Some didn't. Was it sensible? What do you think?

2. The purpose of this worksheet is to dissect a recent slip/lapse to see whether you did things early in the process that made the slip more difficult to resist.

3. Use your Triggers Worksheet to analyze a recent slip/lapse.

4. Break down the event roughly into these stages:

    Preparatory:

    Middle:

    Ending:

5. What choice(s) did you make in the preparatory stage that you can now see set the stage for the slip/lapse?

    a. How did this/these choice(s) contribute to the slip/lapse?

    b. How aware were you *at the time* that this choice could be closely linked to a slip?

    c. How aware now?

    d. What do you need to do differently to keep the blinders off?

Gambling Behavior Warning Signs

Warning signs that I may be gambling or feeling urges to gamble

   1.

   2.

   3.

   4.

   5.

   6.

   7.

   8.

   9.

10.

11.

12.

Coping with Relapse
Containing a Slip by Stopping Snowballing

1. Describe your slip/lapse.

2. Negative Thoughts about the Slip/lapse.

    A. Thoughts related to: *I messed up, might as well go all the way and do it right.*

    B. Thoughts related to: *It's no use, what's the point, I'm not strong enough anyway.*

3. Consequences of Negative Thoughts

    A. Negative Feelings.

    B. Effect on My Self-Esteem

    C. What I feel like doing right now.

4. Challenging the Negative Thoughts.

    A. Yes, I messed up—*but*, how worse will a binge make my situation?

    What resources do I have to get back on my feet?

    Who will support me even now if I sincerely try?

    Even though I made a mistake what personal qualities do I still have that are worthwhile?

    What evidence do I have that I still have some personal control?

    B. How can I use the slip as a learning experience?

    What would I do differently?

5. New Way of Thinking and Feeling

6. Plan for my Next Step.

Who do I contact and share?

What do I do next to get back in recovery?

Managing Urges
Through Acceptance

Problem gamblers and other people whose behavior appears out of control often feel overwhelmed by their urges and cravings to engage in self-defeating acts. Whether it is gambling, alcohol, drugs, overeating, inappropriate sex, or other powerful drives, people have the notion that strong cravings *demand* acting on them.

CRAVINGS AND SELF-REGULATION THEORY

Self-regulation failure has multiple avenues, but this chapter focuses primarily on managing what are popularly termed the immediate urges or cravings to gamble. Self-regulation theory points out (Baumeister *et al.*, 1994) that, technically speaking, no one exercises impulse control. By definition, impulses simply arise and therefore are uncontrollable. People only control the *actions* that impulses instigate. This fact leads many people mistakenly to use the wrong strategy in self-regulation. As we shall describe below, these attempts exacerbate their desires or thoughts rather than regulating them.

Self-regulation theory's analysis of impulses (Baumeister *et al.*, 1994, pp. 132–138) provides the framework for the strategies suggested in this chapter. "An impulse often consists of a transformation of a long-term motivation" (Baumeister *et al.*, 1994, p. 135). Thus, there are three aspects to impulses.

1. **Latent motivations**. Refers to the entire range of wants and needs people have, everything from hunger to wanting to become president. At any given moment, these motivations are on or off the radar screen in people's current activities.

2. **Activating stimulus**. Describes the immediate situation that triggers the impulse. Therapists need to be aware in their assessment of gamblers' triggers that activating stimuli are of two types. One type derives from the external environment in the form of people, places, or things associated with gambling. People see lotteries advertised on a billboard, television broadcasts a sporting event to bet on, or a person drives by a casino. Often, however, impulses arise internally from either the physiological or emotional state of the individual. A person may associate conflict in an intimate relationship with the urge to gamble or have a similar reaction to a setback in one's career.

3. The **impulse** itself is experienced as the resultant interaction of the latent motivation with the activating stimulus.

This analysis also establishes the structure of the various clinical interventions used in this section of the book. We focus here on the *immediate* aspects of self-regulation that requires dealing with urges and impulses. Ordinarily, this is the earliest focus in maintaining abstinence control. The previous chapter looked at avoiding certain external activating stimuli—particularly around having access to money. But such an approach is incomplete. People with compulsive behaviors encounter a wide range of activating events. Sooner or later, the gambler will see the racing results in the sports pages, feel the lure to play the lottery from a TV commercial, or hear golfing friends suggest betting on shots "to make it interesting." Gamblers cannot avoid all external activating stimuli forever, so learning to cope with the impulses that arise from them is essential.

From a complete therapeutic approach, however, dealing with immediate impulses is incomplete. If we agree that impulses arise out of latent motivations, self-regulation requires addressing those motivations in some fashion. Chapter 15 identifies character and spirituality themes that ask people to examine their latent motivations as well. The 12-step tradition has a long history of working on what it terms "character defects" for aiding long-term recovery. We also saw in Chapter 5 how gamblers score significantly lower on measures of conscientiousness, the latent motivation around key aspects of self-regulation (Piedmont, 1998). From the standpoint of self-regulation theory, therefore, the clinical sections of this book address strategies that support dealing with immediate impulses and longer-term personality issues that together increase the probability of self-regulation failure.

ACCEPTANCE RATIONALE

Modern clinical psychology in its openness to a broad range of human behavior, including religious behavior, has recently explored the usefulness of standard spiritual practices as tools for behavioral self-regulation. The source of the openness has many strands but has coalesced around emotion-regulation strategies termed acceptance or mindfulness. Clinical researchers have applied acceptance to a wide range of clinical populations, including borderline personality disorder (Linehan, 1993), substance dependence (Marlatt, 1994), severe chronic pain (Kabat-Zinn, 1990), inappropriate sexual behavior (LoPiccolo, 1994), distressed couples (Jacobson & Christensen, 1996), anxiety disorders (Hayes, 1994), and depression (Teasdale, 1999). What may seem counterintuitive is that researchers in the behavior-therapy tradition conducted the bulk of clinical studies using this method. The clinical approach that emerged from the laboratories of Skinner, Pavlov, and Watson now finds commonalities with the traditions of ancient Christianity and Buddhism (Goleman, 1997).

From a strategic standpoint, acceptance/mindfulness has two major psychological characteristics—one derived from empirical psychology and one derived from meditation practices. One justification emerges from the empirical literature on the downside of trying to suppress thoughts (Wegner, 1989; Wegner & Erber, 1993). Thought suppression leads to a "rebound" of the suppressed thought when the individual's defenses are down. Wegner named this the "white-bear effect" from Leo Tolstoy's childhood experience when his older brother devilishly told him they could play together once Leo finished thinking about white bears. It points to the futility of direct assaults on controlling one's thoughts. From a technical standpoint it means that the brain's software (i.e., the program that is directed to scan for thoughts about gambling) *has to be thinking about gambling* in order to carry out its mission. Paradoxically, efforts to suppress thinking about gambling cause one to have gambling thoughts! Self-regulation theory contends that self-control failure can arise from this futile strategy. Here scientific psychology and 12-step traditions have similar analyses. The 12-step program derides "white-knuckle" sobriety, an image describing someone holding onto recovery for dear life by sheer effort of the will *not* to drink or think about drinking. The tradition also alerts its members to the conditions likely to trigger a "rebound" of urges or cravings through the mnemonic HALT: hungry, angry, lonely, and tired. This coincides with viewing self-regulation as a muscle that will fail in its ability to suppress thinking when overtaxed (Baumeister & Exline, 1999).

Thus far in the discussion, psychology tells us what will not work in regulating urges or cravings but does not suggest methods for countering strong urges. Research clinicians working with extreme emotional disorders and addicted populations (Linehan, 1993; Marlatt, 1994) adapted applied meditation practices and older Gestalt sensory awareness methods (Perls *et al.*, 1951) to the task of emotion regulation. These methods advocate calm awareness of the urges rather than forceful resistance. The hoped-for outcomes are similar whether using the Zen image of viewing the mind as a lake with thoughts rippling past, or Christianity's metaphor of letting thoughts grow together like weeds and wheat. Although these strategies arose in traditions that were interested in character training, they bear some resemblance to emotional processing theories developed in the learning theory tradition (Foa & Kozak, 1986). These theories form the conceptual basis for exposure therapy of anxiety disorders and suggest that strong emotions dissipate when people process rather than avoid them. The clinical challenge has always been to motivate people to process the emotion by staying with it rather than escaping. The same is the case for managing urges. People who wish to stop gambling try to regulate their urges to gamble by not thinking about it. In this way, they are like snake phobics who avoid watching nature shows on television. Acceptance strategies, like exposure therapy, suggest that processing the feared event is the way to manage it. In effect, acceptance, meditation, and mindfulness allow the person to process the urges without trying to run away. By processing urges through acceptance, they lose power and the person gains self-efficacy around managing them.

This chapter suggests a two-stage approach to emotion regulation: preventive rehearsal and real-life implementation. Mindfulness is a skill requiring practice, and it would be foolish optimism to simply describe it and expect clients to implement it when challenged by their cravings.

REHEARSAL

This section elaborates on the instructions for the urge-surfing rehearsal worksheet (Worksheet 9.1). First, it provides a rationale for the practice stating that many gamblers (and others with compulsive behaviors) wrongly believe loss of control is an irresistible impulse. Pathological gambling patients may believe gambling is out of control, but in reality they do not give in to *every* impulse to gamble. It is assumed that the first rehearsal takes place during therapy, and the therapist may want to provide a more expanded rationale than is on the worksheet. Below is one way to introduce the practice:

> What we want to do is discuss ways you might find helpful in controlling your urges or cravings to gamble. [*Here the therapist might mention some recent client experience of intense cravings/urges.*] Many people believe the best way to deal with gambling thoughts is to try to get rid of them. This is a good idea if you use positive distractions, for example, talk to a friend, exercise, or read a book. We are not talking about a fleeting thought or one that goes away when you get involved in some other activity. We are talking about urges to gamble that stay no matter how hard you try to distract yourself.
>
> Many people, and perhaps you've done this, try to put the thoughts out of their minds. Research shows that this is pretty ineffective and, in fact, even backfires. When the great novelist Leo Tolstoy was a young boy, he had an older brother and, like many younger brothers, Leo always wanted to play with the "big boys." Leo's brother, like many older brothers, thought it was a drag to have his younger brother hanging around, so he devised a scheme to keep Leo out of his hair. He told Leo, "Go stand in a corner and as soon as you can stop thinking about white bears you can come play with us." Leo's brother instinctively knew what modern psychological research confirms: when you *try* to stop thinking about something, you only think about it *more*. [*For some clients, I describe the laboratory experiments, but this may be omitted.*] For example, psychologists brought people into a room and asked them to think about anything they wanted but to keep track of how many times they happened to think about a white bear. Naturally, people did have

some white-bear thoughts. Then they asked the participants to *not* think about white bears and found people could reduce their white-bear thoughts somewhat. But later, when asked to just let their minds wander, people thought about white bears *much more*. In other words, after people try to suppress their ideas, there is a later *rebound*, with the idea coming back more forcefully.

The same process works with compulsive behaviors. When people try really hard *not* to think about gambling, drinking, alcohol, or doing drugs, the thoughts come back in greater force, especially when they are hungry, angry, lonely, tired, or stressed in some other way as the 12-steps say. So, in a strange way, the strategy to control unwanted thoughts backfires and *increases* the thoughts. So what we're going to work on is a strategy that aims to "stop stopping." We want to find a way to let the thoughts be, but in a way that also does not lead to losing control. What I hope you will learn ultimately is that having certain thoughts in and of itself is not harmful; thoughts come and go and can be managed but not controlled.

Next follows the actual acceptance/mindfulness rehearsal. The task outcome is for the client to have a controlled experience of thoughts about gambling that yield several insights:

1. Thoughts are difficult to control and have a life of their own.
2. Given enough time, all thoughts eventually decay.
3. Any thought is likely to come *and* go.
4. Waiting out a thought rather than fighting it is the better strategy.
5. The intensity of feelings related to a thought also varies greatly from minute to minute.
6. When put all together, this should (a) decrease anxiety about having the thought and (b) increase self-efficacy paradoxically by not trying to control the thought.

The process, as outlined in Worksheet 9.1 is an imaginal exercise wherein the client visualizes having a typical gambling thought. Using the sensory awareness technique of observe, describe, and don't judge (Linehan, 1993), the client simply attends to his or her thoughts and feelings. Clients rate the intensity of their feelings during the exercise at regular intervals, with the entire process lasting 5 to 10 minutes.

In the debriefing (analysis) section, clients report their observations. The two observations for therapeutic comment are how thoughts come and go when people stop trying to control them, and how much the feeling level fluctuates even over this brief period. Clients who experience a high intensity level without a decline might require a second, longer imaginal exercise to achieve the effect.

Following the worksheet outline (section B), therapist and client discuss the implications of this experience. This includes a range of topics such as what is the nature of "control" and how it works, especially when related to thinking. An important discussion would be how this experience might be helpful to the client when confronted in the future with cravings. Could remembering this exercise help in some way to reduce the sense of anxiety or panic about having thoughts to gamble?

The final section (conclusions) gives the client a concept and term, "urge surfing" (Marlatt, 1994), that consolidates all aspects of the discussion. Urge surfing is an image associated with a highly skilled sport, but one that works through creative harmony, not effortful struggle. The point is we can "control" enormous forces of nature only by flowing with them.

IMPLEMENTING ACCEPTANCE AND URGE SURFING

Worksheet 9.2 guides the client toward acceptance of urges to gamble that arise in real-life situations. This exercise begins, as do all self-monitoring tasks, with a description of the situation. Next the client notes its intensity level, that is, how impelled to gamble the person feels. Item #3 reminds the client about the downside of thought suppression via the white-bear phenomenon, with the next item suggesting a different approach.

The heart of this worksheet (item #5) is an abbreviation of acceptance/mindfulness that the client learned from previous rehearsals. This process includes: observe, describe, but do not evaluate the goodness or badness of the urge/craving. Be aware that it simply *is*. Note, perhaps, that the urge/craving decreases at times, increases at other times, and may altogether disappear. Repeated emphasis of this point drives home the self-regulation idea that when it comes to self-control we almost always operate within that "zone of indifference" (Baumeister *et al.*, 1994), meaning we are rarely compelled to act on any impulse. Only the legally insane person cannot control impulses, and even then an isolated impulse—not every waking activity. Give an impulse enough time and it fades.

This worksheet suggests various images such as surfing the urge in the same way a swimmer rides a wave or observing the movement of sea life. The client records the urge intensity periodically to increase awareness of its shifting nature.

The client continues this process until feeling more in control—not of the impulse, for we do not control them: impulses simply come and go on their own (item #6). Rather, the client continues until reaching a comfort zone that permits a peaceful coexistence with a less intense gambling thought. Finally, the client conducts a postmortem on the experience (item #7) that functions as a debriefing. When these worksheets are brought to therapy, they provide important data as to how well the client is managing these urges.

To this point, we have outlined strategies for building an environmental fence around impulsive gambling and acceptance strategies to manage the impulses themselves. In the next chapter, we examine a host of negative feelings that often provide an impetus to gambling as a means of escape.

Worksheet 9.1

Emotion Regulation
Introduction to Urge Surfing: Rehearsal Worksheet

1. **Rationale**. People often feel overwhelmed by their urges and cravings to engage in self-defeating behavior such as gambling, drinking alcohol, using drugs, overeating, and inappropriate sex. They more or less have the idea that strong urges/cravings *require* acting on them.

   In reality, we control the majority of our urges most of the time. Scientific proof of this statement comes from the fact that a great percentage of infants prone to screaming in the middle of the night reach their first birthday despite the homicidal urges of sleepy parents in the middle of the night.

2. In the following exercise, you are asked to *imagine* some aspect of your problem behavior, particularly situations that typically tend to trigger that urge in you. For a gambler, it might be reading about the point spread for football games in the newspaper or hearing a hot tip on a horse. For other problem behavior, it might be passing a bar or street corner where you did drugs.

3. Close your eyes and calmly visualize yourself in that setting. Imagine as clearly as you can its sights, sounds, colors, emotional feelings, energy, excitement, allure, and your own reactions. Play the scene out slowly as if you were watching it on video.
   A. As you begin, note the intensity of any urges to engage in your problem behavior that may perhaps arise. Describe its intensity on a scale of 0–9, with 0 being no intensity at all, and 9 being as intense as you could ever imagine.
   B. Continue to play the scene out in your head for 4–5 minutes, periodically jotting down the intensity level that you are experiencing.

4. Analysis
   A. What did you notice about your urge levels throughout the exercise?
      a. You may have noticed that it was not nearly as intense for you as the real situation, because it was only imaginary.
      b. If you are like most people, you may have also noticed *both* (a) your attention wandered a lot, making it difficult to keep thinking about the situation, and (b) your urge intensity fluctuated considerably over time.
   B. Assuming this was the case for you, what are the implications of how easy it is for our minds to wander, and how rapidly urges change their intensity over time?
      a. What does this suggest about your ability to maintain control over your urges?
      b. What would be a sensible emotional response to having these urges, instead of a sense of panic about being overwhelmed?

5. **Conclusions**. Thousands of years ago, spiritual masters discovered how to draw on the mind's power to control strong urges, and today psychologists are studying these methods scientifically. Spiritual masters call this practice "acceptance."
   A. Some psychologists who have applied these tools to recovery call this skill "urge surfing." The idea is not to fight the thoughts about gambling, drinking, using, etc., but to let the thoughts "surf" your mind in the same way that surfers handle strong waves—not by fighting or resisting, but by moving in harmony with them.
      a. Rather than being overwhelmed by this powerful force, people can learn how to let its energy work for them, and, most importantly, not to flee from them.
   B. If you would like to try out urge surfing, use the Acceptance–Urge Surfing Worksheet to see how it might work the next time you experience a notable urge or craving.

W o r k s h e e t   9 . 2

Emotion Regulation
Acceptance—Urge Surfing Worksheet

1. Describe the situation in which you currently are experiencing an urge to gamble.

2. Rate its intensity level (0 very low; 9 extreme).

3. Resisting the idea creates "The White Bear Effect." The novelist Leo Tolstoy's older brother told Leo when he was a child that they could play together as soon as Leo would go in a corner and truthfully say he was not thinking about white bears. Naturally, his brother's suggestion meant Leo could never get the idea out of his mind, so his brother was never bothered by Leo.

4. Instead of fighting the thought/urge, consider urge surfing it or accepting it.

5. Process:

   A. Observe, describe, but do not evaluate the goodness or badness of the urge/craving. Be aware that it simply *is*.

   B. You will note, perhaps, that the urge/craving fades somewhat at times, increases at other times, and may altogether disappear.

   C. Can you think of yourself surfing the urge the way a swimmer surfs a wave?

   D. Or, perhaps, observing the urge is like watching a fish in a large aquarium. It moves around, sometimes stopping in the middle to stare back at the spectator, sometimes moving left to right, sometimes disappearing altogether behind the sea plants.

   E. Every so often write down the intensity of the urge.

Observation	Intensity Level

6. Continue the process until you notice you are feeling much more in control—not of the urge (after all, the urge *is* not-you) but in control of yourself existing side by side with the urge or craving.

7. Conclusions you have drawn from this experience?

Depression, Anxiety, and Guilt: Cognitive Strategies

Thisis chapter describes standard cognitive-behavioral processing strategies for negative emotions. As such, they represent a fairly direct self-regulation strategy that attempts to alter the belief systems presumed to drive these emotions. The reader may already be familiar with and/or experienced in their application. Although numerous clinical manuals devoted to these negative emotions exist (Beck *et al.*, 1979, 1985; Burns, 1989; Ciarrocchi, 1995b; Craske *et al.*, 1992; Wells, 1997), there are advantages to having gambling-specific applications in one place.

ANXIETY MANAGEMENT

In this section, we refer mainly to anxiety in the generic sense of negative rumination or worry about possible negative future outcomes. We want to distinguish this generic anxiety from anxiety associated with specific disorders such as posttraumatic stress disorder, obsessive-compulsive disorder, social phobia, specific phobias, or panic disorder. Each of those disorders has its own presumed etiology and treatment approach (Barlow, 1988). To keep this section manageable, two basic approaches to managing anxiety are emphasized. The first derives from cognitive processing approaches (Craske *et al.*, 1992) and the second from emotional processing ones (Foa & Kozak, 1986).

Cognitive Processing Strategies

Cognitive processing approaches originate from a model that sees two major information-processing influences on anxiety development (Barlow, 1988). In this model, susceptible individuals (whether from biological, genetic, or socialization factors) process stressful events in ways that incline them to seeing the events not as challenges but as threats. First, anxiety often involves the tendency to overestimate the probability of negative consequences. When people are prone to believe on an emotional level that the sky is falling, they have the expected emotional, cognitive, and behavioral reactions. The second characteristic is the tendency for the person to believe that, if the actual negative outcome occurred, the results would be catastrophic. In other words, people have the assumption that they could not cope with the untoward event were it to happen. Again, this belief results in a range of emotional and behavioral consequences.

For our purposes here, the downside of these beliefs is the resultant *ruminative* response. Rumination refers to an intellectual "spinning of the wheels" that the person feels compelled to engage in to ward off the anticipated disaster, but that actually is far removed from true problem-solving (see Chapter 12). Rumination, since it focuses on danger, leads to negative emotional arousal. Negative emotional arousal is problematic in that it increases the probability of self-defeating risk-taking in many people, not just those with addictions (Leith & Baumeister, 1996).

Cognitive processing of anxiety, then, is a straightforward process (Worksheet 10.1). First, the person identifies the worry. Second, the person identifies the negative beliefs (over-predicting the likelihood of bad outcomes or thinking one can't cope if difficulties occur). Third, the person looks at the emotional consequences of this belief (intensity of worry). Fourth, and this is the therapeutic task, the person challenges these negative beliefs with alternative ideas or perspectives.

Succeeding at step 4 involves responding to a series of questions that can help the person see the negative beliefs in a different light. Such questions include:

1. Is there any evidence supporting this belief?
2. Is there evidence contradicting this belief?
3. Am I jumping to conclusions or over-predicting the negative outcomes?
4. Am I engaging in emotional reasoning, that is, assuming that my feelings about the situation are actual facts?
5. What evidence do I have that I would totally fall apart if this were to happen?
6. What evidence do I have that I *could* manage this situation if it turned out the negative way I predicted?

Phil, following this outline, analyzes his anxiety about telling his grown children and their families about his gambling problem. His negative thoughts include the following:

1. This will be a severe burden for them.
2. They will think much less of me as a person, father, and role model.
3. They will ignore me and keep the grandchildren away from me.

The negative emotional consequences of these beliefs were:

1. Intense anxiety and worry.
2. Feeling badly about himself.
3. Fear of separation from his family.
4. Desire to go to the track to forget his troubles.

With his therapist, Phil first addressed the issue of how probable these outcomes were. He concluded:

1. My children are highly resilient; rather than a burden, they would be more hurt if I *tried to keep them in the dark*.
2. They indeed may think less of me, be angry or disappointed in me, but this does not negate all the positives in our life together.
3. There is no evidence from past experience that they are punitive and would keep the grandchildren from me. In fact, they have often talked about how important that relationship is for their children.
4. Gambling, although a temporary escape, only postpones the inevitable and destroys whatever confidence in my recovery I've built up.

Next Phil listed his resources for coping with any negative effects of his telling the children. They included:

1. My wife's support for my recovery.
2. I can talk about it at GA.
3. We have a bond of love; I can trust that in time positive feelings will return—*if I work my program*.
4. Their pain could help me be aware of how serious my gambling problem is, and motivate me to not let it happen again.

In alleviating anxiety, assessing the degree to which either problem-solving or overcoming procrastination is a viable remedy takes precedence over cognitive processing. Many issues that cause anxiety in recovery relate to avoidance behaviors. In those instances, the long-lasting therapeutic approach is to solve the problem rather than simply feel better about its nonsolution. For example, in Chapter 12 we discuss Regina's anxiety about her credit problems. Accepting the situation through cognitive processing would not have improved her credit rating and would leave her at increased risk to gamble as a solution.

Emotional Processing Strategies

One final strategy for anxiety management comes from behavior therapy strategies that emphasize the importance of emotional processing for habituation—the process of getting used to negative emotions. This strategy calls for staring down the anxiety-provoking thoughts rather than processing them away.

Mary cannot get to sleep worrying about finances. Rumination is not problem-solving, so if Mary cannot distract herself, the next best thing is to become bored by thoughts. Behavior therapy advocates "worry time," that is, setting aside 30–40 minutes during which Mary repeatedly goes over her list of worries. This can be done on the spot in the case of insomniac worry or postponed to a later time. Clients are usually amused when you suggest to them that they put off worries until a specifically scheduled time. Their amusement stems partially from wondering whether this is possible, and also from appreciating how its very outrageousness might work. Clients discover that when the appointed worry time arrives they cannot *make* themselves worry. This demonstrates convincingly the fleeting nature of intrusive thoughts.

MANAGING DEPRESSION

This section applies cognitive processing (therapy), a well-researched and effective clinical treatment for depression (APA, 1994), to regulating depression. The intention is to focus on specific applications for managing negative beliefs associated with depression.

Overview

Cognitive therapy and its cousin, rational-emotive therapy (Ellis & Harper, 1975), postulate that people's negative beliefs drive their emotional distress. Cognitive processing, as noted above, involves the following steps (Worksheet 10.1):

1. Identifying the negative assumptions.
2. Understanding the link between these assumptions and the person's current distress.
3. Challenging the assumptions.
4. Reevaluating one's emotional state following the reframing of one's beliefs.

A further level of cognitive processing involves identifying the broader information-processing style of the person—the so-called "schemas" (Beck *et al.*, 1985)—or, more recently, "metacognitions" (Wells, 2000). Schemas involve generalized assumptions about the universe as opposed to how the person views the current situation. For example, I may be upset today because my boss didn't say hello when passing me in the corridor, but not because I believe she must always think well of me (schema). It may be that this is the annual period for salary adjustments and I am especially tuned in to her reactions and concluded (perhaps falsely) that I am out of favor (negative automatic belief). Schema processing takes place after the person becomes adept at identifying the here-and-now negative beliefs that trigger upset. We are not concerned with all potential depression-inducing schemas, but we will focus on themes that frequently characterize recovering gamblers. Therapists interested in other depression-related schema issues may want to consult relevant sources (e.g., Beck *et al.*, 1985).

One caveat about cognitive processing is in order. Although cognitive therapy is a powerful tool for managing negative emotions, it is also a therapy that is easy to do poorly. Taking a list of either typical negative beliefs or schemas and shoehorning them onto clients will surely backfire. Cognitive therapy requires skill in the process of *guided discovery*, a Socratic dialogue involving dispassionate examination of the upsetting events and the beliefs behind them. Working with gamblers requires empathic questioning, so that assumptions or themes serve only as illustrations. No list can replace a careful, individualized assessment of the client's own worldview. With this concern in mind, we examine typical negative assumptions pathological gambling patients have in relationship to Beck's triad.

Negative View of Self

Gamblers routinely believe that they are failures, inept, have nothing to show for, are out of control, and have nothing to offer anyone. As with all addictions, these conclusions are not necessarily unrealistic given the sorry state the process causes. Cognitive therapy does not deny reality but tries to moderate the extreme beliefs that lead people to feel helpless and hopeless. Cognitive therapy is not a Pollyannish attempt to whitewash the harsh effects of gambling but a collaborative search for hope.

Negative View of the World

Depressed pathological gamblers often have pessimistic worldviews. They believe, for example, that life is stacked against them, that they are unlucky, that nothing goes right, or that the world is unfair. That these pessimistic views can coexist side by side with optimistic cognitive distortions about winning at gambling is a tribute to people's ability to maintain apparently inconsistent beliefs. How do we understand Alex in Chapter 7, who had lost more than three-quarters of a million dollars in the stock market and maintained that his "system" can still theoretically work given the right amount of capital? At the same time, Alex often asserted that he was unlucky. In a similar fashion, gamblers may maintain a series of inconsistent beliefs about other people. Some of these beliefs are: people fail to support me, I can't count on others, people think I'm a loser, I'll never get respect, people should love me no matter what I've done, and so on. Notice that there are two types of negative beliefs in these statements about others. One set relates to assumptions that the gambler has personally failed in some way (e.g., people think I'm a loser, I'll never get any respect). For other beliefs, the assumption is *others fail to give what I am entitled to*. Both sets of beliefs lead the person to feeling hopeless or discouraged, but they have dissimilar origins and clinical meaning. Challenging the first set of assumptions proceeds by looking at whether the situation is as grim as the client portrays. The second set of assumptions requires looking at the client's expectations of others, particularly the notion that they are so special that people treat them unfairly by withholding affirmation or holding them accountable. Cognitive therapy, or any therapy for that matter, that reinforces a sense of entitlement is sacrificing long-term character change for short-term mood enhancement. Maintaining a victim status via entitlement expectations encourages the unrealistic, grandiose expectations that reinforce patients' beliefs they are capable of overturning even the laws of probability.

Intervention

Since all change requires focusing attention, the first step is to identify the feelings and the negative automatic thoughts behind the feelings. Beginning with a recent episode provides the client with a model for analysis. In reviewing this event, the therapist, by Socratic questioning, elicits the thought, idea, or expectation behind the negative feeling. In those instances, when the relationship between the belief and feeling is unclear or the belief itself seems vague or nonexistent, recourse to the so-called *downward arrow* (or vertical arrow; Beck *et al.*, 1985) is helpful. Peter feels depressed because he can't trade in his car for a brand new one. When first asked what the negative thought behind that feeling is, he simply replies that he wants a new car. Since wanting a new car is not necessarily negative, it is essential to understand the *meaning* of his not getting one. The therapist elicits this information through questions such as, "What would be so bad about [not getting a new car]?" "Why would [not getting a new car] be such a problem?" or, "What would it mean if [you did not get a new car]?" The therapist continues questioning the event's meaning until the client repeats the same belief. In this case, Peter believed he would never impress his customers with his 5-year-old luxury car, and this would lead to loss of business.

Once the client identifies these negative assumptions, the therapist invites Peter to challenge these beliefs using the same techniques for challenging anxious negative beliefs. First, the client determines whether he or she is looking at the situation through the filter of extreme negativity such as all-or-none thinking, catastrophizing, minimizing positives, blowing negatives out of proportion, or emotional reasoning (turning feelings into facts). Second, the client examines the belief dispassionately by weighing the evidence both for and against the idea to see whether the statement is exaggerated. Third, if this discussion still leaves the person clinging to the belief, client and therapist together can develop experiments to test out the belief as if it were a scientific hypothesis. Sometimes the experiment can be retroactive. Is Peter right now losing business? If so, is that loss clearly attributable to the client's beliefs about his car? What is the evidence for this? Sometimes the experiment is set as a homework assignment: do a financial analysis of your income, plotting profits from 1 year prior to buying your car through the last 5 years. Do the data clearly show that business improves significantly *from the moment you bought the new car* and declined gradually as the car aged?

Fourth, as a result of this analysis, the client writes down alternative ways of looking at the situation—ways that provide a more balanced, optimistic view of the situation. Finally, should the belief be fairly close to reality, the focus could shift to dealing realistically with the circumstances that led to the displeasing situation. Is it amenable to problem-solving (Chapter 12), seeking forgiveness, committing oneself to a program of character reform (Chapter 15), or setting new goals (Chapter 7)? There is no point in using cognitive processing strategies to accept your spouse's anger over not taking out the trash when the solution is to take out the trash.

Before leaving cognitive processing strategies, it is useful to remember the "behavior" in cognitive behavior therapy. Although Beck calls his method cognitive therapy, he makes significant use of behavioral strategies (Beck *et al.*, 1985) to help depressed individuals feel better. A large body of research shows that when depressed people become more physically active through engaging in pleasant events and exercise they experience significant mood improvement (Lewinsohn & Gotlib, 1995). Often gamblers are depressed in early recovery because their former life of excitement and activity ended. They are used to intense forms of entertainment and can no longer "smell the roses." They have the belief that fun involves three days at a casino or spending elaborate sums. Realistically, many have few financial resources left for recreation. They need to pursue pleasant activities that are inexpensive yet mood enhancing. They may not yet have such activities in their repertoire or have long ceased doing them. Initiating such activities may require problem-solving.

MANAGING GUILT FEELINGS

Depression and guilt often go together for recovering people, making it difficult to disentangle them. Intense guilt often means the person is simultaneously depressed as a result of their negative self-view. We separate it here because it is important to distinguish appropriate from inappropriate guilt. One of the drawbacks of a disease model is that it may lead some to see themselves as passive victims of their disorder. This extreme view not only can eliminate a sense of personal responsibility for past actions but can also reduce one's self-efficacy for changing the future. The 12-step tradition has coped with this dilemma by suggesting that people are not responsible for their status as alcoholic or drug addict, but are clearly responsible for taking the first drink today. It is an approach that combines a large dose of acceptance with a firm expectation about accepting responsibility. Pathological gambling creates even more of a problem with the disease model. Although some arguments can be made for suggesting that alcoholics have biological, genetic, or physiological predispositions (Zuckerman, 1999), similar evidence for pathological gambling is sparse.

On the one side, pathological gambling patients face inappropriate guilt. Extreme forms of information processing characterize these beliefs as all-or-none thinking, emotional reasoning, and absolute pessimism. Little needs to be added here to the strategies discussed above for processing negative beliefs and schemas. Therapist and client together can identify the beliefs, examine the evidence for the belief, and develop alternative viewpoints. Appropriate guilt, on the other hand, represents a genuine therapeutic challenge. Therapists are trained to be value-free, so the whole notion of helping clients acknowledge guilt may seem alien if not outright unethical. Others may wonder if dealing with appropriate guilt constitutes "beating a man when he's down." Many therapists are also predisposed to view guilt as *absolutely* negative. A number of years ago, a philosopher addressed the American Psychological Association's annual convention and received an enthusiastic reception with his thesis about the uselessness of guilt as an emotion (Kaufmann, 1973). Twelve-step programs know that guilt is a core aspect of recovery and do not hesitate confronting their members. Through the process of "working the steps," particularly the fourth and fifth steps, members honestly identify past misdeeds and discuss them with another person. Further action comes at the ninth step, when members make amends for their behavior to the offended parties. Gamblers Anonymous has built into its 12 steps the obligation to repay one's debts whether to individuals or to institutions, thereby holding recovering gamblers directly responsible for the negative consequences of their gambling. GA understands, as many religious traditions have, that when people correct their misdeeds in the social sphere it can also represent the occasion for a change of heart.

Strategies for Challenging Negative Automatic Thoughts Associated With Guilt

The following model is one way to help clients navigate guilt feelings to avoid the extremes of emotional paralysis or moral disregard. One influential theory of depression, called learned helplessness, maintains that depression sets in after failure experiences, when people make certain kinds of explanations for the events (Seligman, 1991). Imagine that recovering gamblers Veronica and Rachel fail their real estate license examination. Attributional theory (explanations for the causes of events) states that the explanations a person makes render them invulnerable to or immune from depression. Three types of explanations or attributions are relevant for depression.

1. **Personal explanations**. The failure was due to some external cause or me. Rachel believes that she failed the test because she was stupid; Veronica holds that the test was unfair.

2. **Permanent explanation**. The failure represents a weakness that cannot change or is temporary. Rachel believes that no matter how hard she would study for the next exam it will be just as difficult and she will do just as poorly. Veronica maintains that once she understands the "bias" of the examiners, she will be able to beat the test.

3. **Pervasive explanations**. The failure extends to just about everything I do or was limited to the situation. Rachel believes her failing the licensing exam is just typical of how stupid she is, whereas Veronica believes that she has many intelligent capabilities but that finance is one of her weak areas.

Attribution theory goes on to say that, when people make personal, permanent, pervasive explanations after setbacks (Rachel), they are likely to experience depression; but when they make external, temporary, and specific explanations of failure (Veronica), they are less likely to experience depression. This theory fits neatly into cognitive therapy because it predicts that the way people process information about events influences emotions. Not only is this a useful theory for depression, it is a helpful template for assessing and working with clients' guilt feelings. It is particularly useful for the dilemma involving appropriate versus inappropriate guilt. Most of us would agree that complete absolution from personal responsibility for wrongdoing would create a lawless society. On the other hand, as clinicians we are highly attuned to the negative effects of excessive guilt. Attribution theory presents a way out of the dilemma. Appropriate guilt involves *not* externalizing the reasons for the situation. The person needs to acknowledge that he or she stole the money and that no one put a gun to their heads to make them do it. Even if therapists help people put their thievery in context (e.g., the immense pressure to pay the mortgage, feed the kids), personal responsibility remains.

Inappropriate guilt, however, means exaggerating the negative self-view through *permanent* and *pervasive* attributions. In other words, "Yes, I stole the money, and that was wrong (personal attribution). I will never be able to recover from this evil action (permanent attribution). I am an immoral person and degenerate in every way imaginable (pervasive attributions)." When people make all three assumptions about their misdeeds, inappropriate guilt is the result. When they limit their explanations to "I did this act and it was a wrong thing to do," they may have a temporary negative feeling but one that can allow an appropriate moral and psychological rebound.

In cognitive processing (Worksheet 10.1), the client proceeds very differently when evaluating appropriate (personal) causal statements from exaggerated ones (permanent and pervasive).

Processing guilt involves dialogue similar to the following with Linda, who is distraught over the pain her gambling caused her daughter.

Client:	I really let people down.
Counselor:	What evidence do you have for that?
Client:	I gambled the money for Melissa's summer camp and now she can't go with the other kids in June.
Counselor:	How do you feel?
Client:	Terrible. I don't deserve to live.
Counselor:	Let's start with feeling terrible. How is it you feel so bad?
Client:	We had promised her all winter she could go; she's really been a trooper, not making many demands on us because money has been tight, but I know it meant the world to her to go with her friends. You know what middle-schoolers are like, and it's going to be hard for her to save face.
Counselor:	So it sounds like feeling bad is a reasonable way to react to the situation.
Client:	It is, but I don't deserve to live.
Counselor:	You feel you've done the worst thing imaginable. Could you tell me what thoughts you've had about improving the situation for your daughter?
Client:	Well, it's too late to do anything about summer camp. My husband and I talked last night about something else Melissa really loves—going to the beach. Last year her older sister took a friend and had a great time, and I know Melissa would enjoy that too.
Counselor:	How would you make that happen?
Client:	Well, I missed the deadline on the deposit for her summer camp because we didn't have the money at the time, but we could get a place down the beach for August.
Counselor:	What would that involve?
Client:	If I work Saturdays for the next four or five weeks, I'm pretty sure we could swing it; in fact, if I don't gamble, I *know* we could swing it.
Counselor:	How would it feel if you could tell your daughter that even though there wasn't money in time for camp, she can take a friend to the beach?
Client:	It would feel great. Even though I can't change her disappointment about camp, at least she's going to have a good time at the beach with a friend.

> **Counselor:** [*This led to a discussion about how the client would monitor the impulse to gamble as her typical "solution" to needing money for the vacation.*] But I want to get back to something you said earlier about deserving to die. Do you still feel that way?
>
> **Client:** Well, in a way I do; but I feel much better knowing I can do something to make things better. I've already apologized, but she's heard me do that so many times it doesn't mean anything anymore. I think it will definitely mean something if I do it this way.

In this vignette, the therapist chose to address the realistic aspects of the situation rather than focusing on the initial, extreme guilt statements. In realistic guilt, people generally feel better when they take some corrective action. Cognitive processing at that point does not rectify the social disruption caused by the gambling. When intense guilt remains despite corrective action, then cognitive processing is useful.

Challenging inappropriate guilt involves identifying the permanent and pervasive nature of the negative automatic thoughts. When clients say they deserve to die, they are usually exaggerating the pervasiveness of their character defects, making themselves into moral monsters. Some therapists pull in the ready example of Hitler to use as a benchmark. This usually leads people to nuance their own degree of guilt. Other approaches involve having the client construct a moral data log—a record of events that identifies the good things they do in the course of an average month.

SUMMARY

As we emphasize throughout, there are multiple avenues to pathological gambling and relapse. This chapter described strategies for coping with the major negative emotions that lead to gambling relapse (Marlatt & Gordon, 1985). Self-regulation theory *specifically* maintains that the actual strategies people use to cope with these issues often backfire and result in relapse. People may relapse when they fail to regulate negative emotions and rely on gambling as their default mode for coping with emotional pain. In line with this model, the chapter described clinical strategies for coping with emotions triggered by negative beliefs. We now turn our attention to the positive beliefs and cognitive distortions that maintain problem gambling.

Challenging Beliefs Leading to Negative Feelings

Situation: Describe the situation around the time you were feeling anxious, depressed, guilty, or angry.

Beliefs: What negative *beliefs* or *expectations* automatically went through you mind when you were in that situation?

Feelings: What painful feelings did these beliefs or expectations lead to?

Challenging the Beliefs or Expectations: Is there any evidence that those beliefs or expectations are not totally accurate? Describe the contrary evidence.

Coping with the Situation: Even if the situation can't change, what evidence do you have that you could manage it? Based on your talents? Your past experience? Support persons? Resources?

New Perspective: What is a different way to now look at the situation?

Changed Feeling: How did your feelings change after you looked at the situation differently?

Changing Beliefs About Gambling: The Downside of Hope

INTRODUCTION

Chapter 3 provided the conceptual underpinnings for a cognitive treatment approach with pathological gamblers. In that chapter, we saw at least three strands of research that implicated information-processing influences in gambling persistence. This has led several research groups in the pathological treatment field to develop strategies based on these findings.

To date, no consensus exists within the field as to the best strategy for applying cognitive therapy to pathological gambling. The published and unpublished treatment research reports involve an amalgam of cognitive, behavioral, and problem-solving techniques, so it is unclear which treatment component is the effective one or if all together are required. As we have maintained throughout, however, the practicing clinician cannot wait for the ultimate empirical conclusion. For that reason, this chapter highlights the general nature of a cognitive approach to pathological gambling along with a few intervention examples. This is a rapidly developing area with much interesting work occurring internationally. However, despite a theoretical leaning toward cognitive explanations, each group is pursuing slightly different applications. This is to be expected in the initial development of an applied treatment, but we will have to wait until a consensus emerges from research and practice.

APPLICATION

To briefly summarize the three strands of social cognitive psychology, we can recall from Chapter 3 the various information-processing strategies related to gambling persistence. Recourse to cognitive explanations evolved in a way analogous to cognitive explanations for other disorders, for example, anxiety. Learning theory maintains that nonreinforced behavior tends to extinguish. But why does a person who is socially anxious, for example, continue to anticipate all sorts of dreadful consequences in her social life when in fact this seldom happens? Researchers claim that only social cognitive theories can explain this anomaly. People remain anxious because of what they tell themselves about the situation rather than from some automatic reaction to the laws of conditioning.

In similar fashion, why do people in obvious violation of the laws of learning persist in a punishing event (losing money) despite ample data that the situation will not improve? Recourse to the law of variable ratio responding will not do in the case of pathological gambling given the extreme punishment of the outcome. Therefore, to make sense of this phenomenon, social cognitive psychology states we have to look at how people process information to understand the *meanings* they give to their gambling experiences.

The first of these information-processing explanations relates to the *illusions of control* that gamblers maintain. People believe their odds of winning a chance event improves under any of the following conditions: personal choice (picked the ticket), practice, early wins, familiarity with the event, and feeling superior to a competitor. The second relates to distortions around the so-called *gambler's fallacy*, meaning that people misinterpret the concept of randomness. Randomness is the idea that the occurrence of an event is independent of any preceding event. Many people develop beliefs that fail to take randomness into account (e.g., "number six *has* to come up soon") and gamble accordingly.

Third, even though people may have many negative gambling experiences, they persist because of *the explanations* they make about these experiences. Specifically, they may conclude that their wins are the result of special qualities or skills that they personally have, but their losses are the result of various external or situational influences. Social cognitive theory when applied to gambling treatment, therefore, suggests that pathological gamblers need to be aware of the information-processing strategies they use if they are to counter their influence.

EVALUATING CLIENT BELIEFS

The first step in cognitive processing requires assessing the client's gambling beliefs. Scales for this purpose are in development (Breen & Zuckerman, 1999), but full psychometric standards are not established. Worksheet 11.1 lists typical beliefs about gambling and reasons for gambling for individualized assessment. The list encompasses many illusions of control, randomness errors, self-serving explanations, as well as a few functional reasons for gambling. The list can serve as a starting point for the idiosyncratic meaning each client brings to gambling.

The dialogue below between Morgan and his therapist attests to the uniqueness of gambling beliefs for clients. Morgan recently relapsed after 8 months of abstinence, was $4,000 further in debt on top of a recent bankruptcy, and had jeopardized his relationship with his fiancee as a result. Divorced once due to his gambling, he desperately wanted to maintain his current long-term relationship with his supportive and sensitive partner.

Therapist: Can you think back to when you went to the track the first time with this latest round? Can you recall what you were thinking?

Client: I can remember it as clear as a bell. I told myself, "This is a wonderful woman. You're so fortunate. She deserves so much. She's put up with all my debt, has managed my finances, and sacrificed a lot. I want to take

> this relationship to the next level and that means becoming engaged. To get engaged I need $5,000 for an engagement ring." So I manipulated her into giving me control of the finances so I could get my hands on enough cash to get to the races.

Therapist: So the thing that was primary in your mind was a strong desire to formalize your relationship with Denise, to let her know how much she meant to you, and tell her you wanted to be committed to her. And you saw an engagement ring as saying all those things.

Client: Right.

Counselor: I'm interested in how you came to link gambling to that desire for an engagement ring. Given the last 7 years of the destructiveness of gambling, personally and financially, how did that pop up as a solution for you?

Client: I know it's crazy, but I still haven't stopped believing that I can hit it big—that the way for me to get my hands on that much money is to win at the track.

In this case, the belief relates to *gambling as an enterprise*, that is, as an overall coping strategy. For other clients, the beliefs that relate to *gambling process* are more relevant. These involve beliefs related to controlling the outcome: lucky numbers, talismanic objects, favorite machines, lucky dealers, and so on. These beliefs may be best accessed via a think-allowed assessment during imaginal betting (Ladouceur *et al.*, 1998). In that procedure, the therapist audiotapes the clients' verbalizations around their beliefs and expectations as they imagine themselves betting in their preferred manner. Therapist and client then review the tape to challenge the various maladaptive beliefs.

[margin note: ENTERPRISE ↓ MEANS TO AN END]

CHALLENGING GAMBLING BELIEFS

[margin note: PROCESS ↓ NATURE OF OUTCOMES]

Challenging client beliefs about gambling occurs at two levels. In the case history above, it is necessary to challenge the client's belief about gambling as an enterprise. In other words, this client, and many others, view gambling as a solution to their problems. In the second instance, and this is the area receiving most research attention currently, therapy challenges the client's beliefs about gambling as a process. This distinction is important because, although both sets of beliefs relate to faulty information-processing, the former's faulty view involves seeing gambling as a means to an end, while the latter's involves faulty perceptions around the intrinsic nature of gambling outcomes. Even though we will propose a similar structure in combatting these perceptions, each has distinct dynamics. Combatting the first involves closely examining individual motivation, whereas combatting the second challenges the perceptions directly.

Challenging Illusions of Control and Attributional Biases

Worksheet 11.2 provides a format for challenging motivations to gamble that relate to maladaptive beliefs. In Chapter 10, we used a similar format to manage negative feelings. The model presented there assumed that negative emotions derived from negative beliefs about preceding events. It assumed that shifting to more positive perspectives would also positively affect moods or feelings.

In this chapter, the model suggests that examining one's beliefs can interrupt the automatic behavioral tendency to gamble when stress arises. Instead of managing stress in the given moment, this strategy attempts to change the unexamined assumptions that drive deeply ingrained gambling responses. In addition to the negative consequences of gambling questionnaire, the Gambling Timeline (Worksheet 11.3) can help examine gambler's assumptions. A 3- to 6-month period is usually an adequate data set in the life of a pathological gambler to test the hypothesis that "Gambling is an effective way to make money." The gambling research study group at the University of Memphis (personal communication, 2000) has a creative intervention based on this concept. They ask the client how much money they hoped to win in the course of the time period and also how much money they actually spent. Showing the contrast by writing out the hoped-for payoff against the actual losses, the therapist then calculates how much money the patient would have if he or she had worked for minimum wage at a fast-food restaurant. This illustrates that not only did gambling put them in the hole financially but also how much wealthier they would have been flipping hamburgers.

Worksheet 11.2 directs clients to examine in the harsh light of reason any and all assumptions inherent in their gambling behavior. Using a cognitive processing approach, they state the evidence for and against these ideas. This approach harmonizes with the advice given throughout this book: *never argue with a client*. Even though the gambler's beliefs appear irrational to the therapist, seldom does anyone give up pathological gambling through sheer force of logic. The therapeutic premise here is that cognitive processing can take hold only in an accepting environment where people examine, perhaps for the first time, *the negative consequences for their life if they continue to maintain their beliefs*. The idea is not for the therapist to persuade clients that it is "irrational" to gamble. Hundreds of millions of people gamble daily. Rather, this client, in this situation, with these beliefs, needs to see whether those assumptions actually work.

Gambling and Positive Automatic Thoughts

Cognitive behavior therapy uses different terms to describe the belief systems that lead to dysfunctional behavior and feelings. Albert Ellis called these beliefs "irrational" (Ellis & Harper, 1975). The field has moved away from this term, partly because of its pejorative tone and partly because research points out that an unrealistic optimism, which could count as "irrational," actually buffers people against depression (Alloy & Abramson, 1979). We have accepted Beck's notion of negative automatic thoughts (Beck *et al.*, 1979) because the research consensus links negative automatic thoughts to emotional disorders such as depression and anxiety (Wells, 2000).

In my opinion, addiction treatment requires further adapting the terminology of cognitive therapy. The antecedents for compulsive behavior are often *positive automatic thoughts*. The previous chapter reviewed treatment approaches for changing painful emotions that might precipitate gambling as an escape. An equally important treatment target is the positive automatic thoughts that create beneficial expectations in patients' minds. My thesis is that *positive expectations and automatic thoughts frequently drive addiction, including pathological gambling*. Cognitive therapy must address positive beliefs as vigorously as it addresses negative ones. The dieter may eat the chocolate cake to escape stress, but she also expects that the cake will enhance her mood. The pathological gambling patient gambles when feeling down because of her financial situation, but she does so in the belief she has a good chance of winning.

The dialogue below illustrates one approach to changing positive automatic thoughts. Morgan wrote down his five beliefs about gambling. They included his belief that he is more likely to win when he "has that special feeling" (illusion of control), as well as believing he is "more knowledgeable than others." Evidence for these ideas included the few times he has actually won significant amounts. Evidence against these ideas included "Why am I $65,000 in debt?" Completing the positive and negative consequences of gambling and not gambling was revealing. On his first attempt he wrote, "none" under positive consequences of gambling. This led to the following discussion:

Therapist: You wrote "none" under positive consequences if you gamble. And, "the consequences are only negative." I'm wondering why anyone would do anything that was *only* negative?

Client: Oh, I see what you mean. The positive part was the short-term feeling, but that's all.

Therapist: Could you describe that?

Client: Well, it's the most intense feeling I ever have. When I'm at the track, I can actually feel a sensation starting at the base of my spine that has me in its grip when I'm watching a race, especially when my horse has a chance of winning. It's a slightly tense but deeply pleasurable feeling. I'm totally focused on that race and feeling it is like nothing else in the world.

Therapist: It's more exciting than anything else you can imagine.

Client: Exactly. I can't tell anyone that because they don't understand. When I told my first wife that, she would say, "How come you don't get that feeling with me." And even Denise [*his fiancee*] wouldn't understand.

	She would be crushed if she felt that being at the track felt better for me than being with her.
Therapist:	And how does your memory of that feeling make it difficult to sustain your recovery?
Client:	Because I know that there's nothing like it in the world, but I know at the same time that I have to give it up.
Therapist:	And what makes it so difficult to give up?
Client:	Actually, I have given it up for fairly long stretches, but the idea of never feeling it again is very tough. And I feel guilty that I feel this way, especially seeing what it's done to my relationship.
Therapist:	So what you are telling yourself is that you can't imagine *never* experiencing that intense feeling again.
Client:	Yes.
Therapist:	What makes that so difficult?
Client:	It's something I have to give up forever.
Therapist:	And giving it up forever would mean ... ? [*Here the therapist is engaging in a downward arrow strategy to get at the core assumption in the client's belief, as described in Chapter 10.*]
Client:	It means I would be deprived of that feeling.
Therapist:	And that would be bad because ...?
Client:	I guess I just feel I need it.
Therapist:	So underneath this memory of intense feeling is the assumption that it would be very difficult to have a full life if you didn't experience this particular, intense feeling that comes with gambling [*core assumption*].
Client:	Ridiculous, isn't it?
Therapist:	Well, it may seem ridiculous when looked at logically, but these beliefs can be pretty convincing. What do you conclude by looking at your worksheet?
Client:	I conclude that I have to tell Denise every crazy idea I get because that puts it out in the open and she can help me look at it objectively.
Therapist:	Including the idea that not even the relationship is as intense as gambling?
Client:	I wouldn't know how to tell her about that. What do you think I could say?
Therapist:	Maybe she's making the same mistake you are. Maybe she's equated pleasure with happiness.
Client:	What do you mean?
Therapist:	Let's accept the fact that in terms of sheer intensity gambling is the most pleasurable experience in the world for you. Does that make it the most satisfying?
Client:	Absolutely not.

Therapist:	Why not?
Client:	Because feeling close to Denise is the most satisfying thing to me.
Therapist:	Exactly. It's not the most pleasurable all the time, but it's what brings you the most happiness. And you've often made the mistake of thinking pleasure equals happiness, so that's what's made it easy for you to gamble. If she gets upset hearing how great gambling makes you feel, she's making the same mistake thinking pleasure is the only experience that represents happiness to *you*. But you're saying now you can't limit your idea of happiness to a fleeting moment of pleasure.

This dialogue illustrates two aspects of cognitive processing for this client. First, the client identified his beliefs that maintain his gambling persistence. Those ideas related to being knowledgeable and having a special feeling that "assured" him he would win. Filling out the worksheet led to seeing that the available data overwhelmingly contradicted these beliefs. This approach is especially necessary in the case of *skill* gamblers, that is, gamblers who participate in betting that favors more knowledgeable persons. Indeed, the client noted on his worksheet that many people simply pick a number at the track rather than study the horses' background as he did. The beliefs of skill gamblers often resist cognitive restructuring around the gambler's fallacy. In challenging the gambler's fallacy, therapists educate clients around the concept of randomness, that is, that an outcome is independent of what happened previously. The number 15 doesn't *have* to hit in Las Vegas Keno (and had not as of this writing). Skill gamblers, however, believe they have "an edge" over other players because of their experience, a belief that is often difficult to challenge directly. They often *have* more extensive gambling experience than recreational gamblers. It is better to roll with resistance (Miller & Rollnick, 1991) than hit it head-on. That often means admitting the client's vast experience but also requesting they look at the complete picture, that is, the evidence that their "expertise" has not fulfilled its promise. In this case, Morgan was able to do just that. He noted, in effect, "If I'm so smart, how come I'm not rich?" The Gambling Timeline is a tool for examining beliefs about one's expertise. For example, a physicist won $30,000 at blackjack during one of his first casino visits. He described winning amounts ranging from $30,000 to $50,000 several times over the next two years. But when he used the Timeline to view his gambling *as a whole*, he could see how rapidly he accumulated $250,000 in debt. His more frequent losses far outstripped his remarkable wins, necessitating declaring bankruptcy.

The second belief that emerged for Morgan is a common one in addiction: one cannot lead a fulfilled existence without the rush associated with the behavior. The therapist happened on this when directing the patient to examine the positive consequences of gambling. As indicated in the chapter on motivational enhancement, understanding the positives of gambling is essential for addressing future goals. Without that understanding, it is impossible to consider alternative experiences that will provide some substitute for the gambling. Using the downward arrow technique, the therapist unearthed the core assumption. Core assumptions are usually in the form of conditional statements ("If, then"; see Wells, 2000). In this case it was "If I don't experience this intense pleasure, I will be deprived of some essential ingredient for living a fulfilled existence." Addressing this assumption had the added bonus of raising an important issue in the client's intimate relationship. He wanted to communicate at a deeper level with his fiancee but often felt that certain revelations might drive her over the edge. Therefore, the notion that something other than the relationship could feel that intense seemed destined to upset her. Eventually, he was able to process how both he and his fiancee were equating pleasure with happiness—a common assumption in modern life.

The draw of positive illusions increases when people believe gambling is the only way out of painful life predicaments. The next chapter discusses ways to decrease people's vulnerability to these illusions by developing problem-solving skills.

List of Beliefs about Gambling and Reasons for Gambling

Check all that apply.

- ❐ I have a system that works.
- ❐ I'm a lucky person.
- ❐ I'm a positive thinker.
- ❐ Fate is on my side.
- ❐ I'm a more knowledgeable gambler than most.
- ❐ My system can beat the odds.
- ❐ I've won before.
- ❐ I'm at my lucky place.
- ❐ I deserve to win.
- ❐ Others can't keep up with me.
- ❐ The time is right.
- ❐ I have this special feeling.
- ❐ I can influence the outcome.
- ❐ I am confident in myself.
- ❐ I have prayed.
- ❐ I have my lucky object.
- ❐ After so many losses, it's the time to win.
- ❐ I am very experienced.
- ❐ My luck has changed.
- ❐ Today is lucky.
- ❐ Gambling will solve my problems.
- ❐ Gambling will make me feel better.

Other: _____

_____

_____

_____

Worksheet 11.2
Gambling Beliefs and Reasons Worksheet

I gambled, desire to gamble, or will gamble because
(select most important reasons from checklist)

1. _____
2. _____
3. _____
4. _____
5. _____

Evidence for these ideas: _____
_____
_____

Evidence against these ideas: _____
_____
_____

Positive consequences if I gamble   **Negative consequences if I gamble**

Negative consequences if I don't gamble   **Positive consequences if I don't gamble**

Decision: _____

Why: _____

Strategies for not gambling: _____

Worksheet 11.3
Gambling Timeline

Name: _____

Date: _____

Part A: Select the most recent week in which you gambled.

Days gambled	Amount gambled	Net loss	Net win
_____	_____	_____	_____

Part B: Think about the three months prior to this most recent week.

First month

	Days gambled	Amount gambled	Net loss/net win
Week 1	_____	_____	_____
Week 2	_____	_____	_____
Week 3	_____	_____	_____
Week 4	_____	_____	_____
Total:	_____	_____	_____

Second Month

	Days gambled	Amount gambled	Net loss/net win
Week 1	_____	_____	_____
Week 2	_____	_____	_____
Week 3	_____	_____	_____
Week 4	_____	_____	_____
Total:	_____	_____	_____

Third Month

	Days gambled	Amount gambled	Net loss/net win
Week 1	_____	_____	_____
Week 2	_____	_____	_____
Week 3	_____	_____	_____
Week 4	_____	_____	_____
Total:	_____	_____	_____

Problem-Solving and Overcoming Procrastination

INTRODUCTION

A pathological gambling career teaches at least two major lessons. One lesson is the advantage of an impulsive lifestyle and the second is the benefit of escaping problems at every opportunity. Chapter 3 revealed the research consensus on the centrality of impulsivity in pathological gambling and escape is a major force in addictive behavior (Baumeister, 1991a). This chapter builds on the abstinence control strategies (Chapter 8) that structure the environment in ways to reduce impulsive behavior. Here we discuss rational decision-making processes that assist people in attaining their goals. Problem-solving is incomplete, however, if escape and avoidance remain strong pulls. The chapter thus details a second set of strategies specifically linked to overcoming avoidance or procrastination.

Self-regulation theory connects directly to both these strategies. Problem-solving corrects attention underregulation, and overcoming procrastination interrupts a misregulation strategy. People attempt to regulate negative moods through avoiding unpleasant or unrewarding tasks. The premise of this chapter, therefore, is that these tools overcome attention underregulation and avoidance misregulation.

PROBLEM-SOLVING

Problem-solving as a clinical tool has a long history (Goldfried & Davison, 1996) and even plays a major role in the conceptualization of marital distress (e.g., Beach *et al.*, 1990). In those models, marital disruption is viewed primarily as a failure to problem-solve, and corrective therapy involves communication training and problem-solving. Proponents of cognitive-behavioral therapy as well incorporate problem-solving within the clinical repertoire. In keeping with self-regulation theory, problem-solving functions by diverting the gambler's attention away from immediate, impulsive goals to longer-term, adaptive ones. Whatever the ultimate explanation for how problem-solving works, it contributes to developing greater attentiveness to higher-order goals, and the steps that lead to them.

The rationale for problem-solving derived from cognitive science. The strategies represent the human mind operating at its most rational and scientific or, in the words of social cognitive psychology, as those of a "naive scientist." When people do their best thinking, they operate like scientists reviewing and eliminating competing hypotheses. Life, however, in its hectic pace leads to taking "mental shortcuts" (heuristics) to solve our problems (see Chapter 3). In general, these shortcuts work, and we buy cereal from the grocery store that at least doesn't kill our family. When the stakes are high, these shortcuts could lead us astray, and that is where problem-solving comes in. Many people instinctively shift into problem-solving mode when making major decisions such as buying a house or choosing a career. Pathological gambling patients newly emerging from the addiction cycle have reinforced impulsivity for so long, they fail to utilize problem-solving even when the stakes are high. They are more likely to engage in automatic, stereotyped behavior rather than in flexible, creative solutions.

FORMAT

With the therapist's assistance, clients fill out Worksheet 12.1 in session.

DESCRIPTION OF THE CURRENT PROBLEM

The first step is *defining the problem*.

Regina was a 39-year-old African-American woman and a single parent. She grew up in a poor neighborhood with dismal schools and little family support. Nevertheless, she was determined to improve her situation and after high school took an entry-level position with a communications conglomerate. Although she could not pursue a degree program, she took advantage of the company's incentive program for college-level technical courses relating to her work. After receiving outstanding job ratings, her company promoted her to mid-level manager. Following her divorce 5 years ago, she found that playing bingo at local churches provided a pleasant distraction. Eventually, she developed a pathological gambling disorder related to bingo and lottery games that resulted in losing her apartment and moving in with her grandmother and sister. Although no longer gambling, her credit rating was sinking due to lack of responsiveness to creditors. She intended to pay everyone, but sent money in a haphazard manner. The situation became serious when her company's travel policy changed. Regina made numerous business trips as a trainer for the company's satellite offices, but a new accounting system meant the company would issue credit cards for travel to department heads. Up until now, travelers received cash advances. The policy change meant that each employee given a credit card had to undergo a credit check, and Regina knew this would be a disaster and possibly end her function as a company trainer. The first order of business was to settle with her creditors in a responsible way. Despite knowing this was a sensible thing to do, Regina avoided making contact with them. Discussion with her thera-pist brought out several different reasons. First, she felt that, even though she was a successful African-American businesswoman, she somehow would be viewed in a stereotypically negative way and this would cause both anger and shame. Second, she was embarrassed to discuss this with a live account agent and felt less guilt by simply mailing in her payments, even if they were regularly late. Third, she worried that if she got serious about resolving her financial crisis she would not have access to any credit cards even in case of an emergency.

Regina defined her problem thus: "Develop a payment plan with the creditors."

In Worksheet 12.1, I have incorporated strategies related to motivational enhancement. Even though problem-solving represents the most rational side of human thinking, people are not computers and require a motivational component in their decisions. For that reason, Question I.2 asks, "How does the problem interfere with important goals in your life?" Regina's response was, "I cannot advance in my career, keep doing the work I love, or accomplish my future financial goals with the situation as it now stands."

Before proceeding to problem solutions, Question I.3 requests an examination of the relationship between the problem and life goals. It asks specifically how the problem relates to lack of goals, rigidity of goals, having incompatible goals, or being overextended in goals. Regina's response fell in the category of aimlessness: "By focusing only on my immediate embarrassment, I am neglect-ing to work toward the kind of life I promised my son and me."

To further motivate the person toward solving the problem, Section II provides a decisional balance exercise similar to the one used in motivational enhancement. Regina responded as follows:

Benefits of following it: "Once I have settled my differences with the credi-tors, I know I can come clean with my supervisor. She has always been supportive; she knows how I am getting help for the gambling, so she'll help me work around this new travel policy."

Benefits of not solving it: "I can continue to pretend there is no problem and not feel the depression that comes with having to think about it."

Negatives of solving it: "I will feel embarrassed when I personally speak to the creditors. I won't like having to tell my supervisor."

Negatives of not solving it: "My credit history remains a mess; I'll never be able to pass a credit check to get my own place; I'll have to make some lame excuse about not wanting to travel anymore—which could hurt my chances for advancement or threaten my job itself."

Taken together, this information leads to a final problem definition, which, in Regina's case was, "Resolve credit problems through developing a payment plan that allows me to deal honestly with my company."

GENERATING SOLUTIONS

The next step assures a good solution through a process that generates as large a number of solutions as is possible.

The first step requires the client, with the therapist's assistance, to generate as many solutions as she can imagine. Before solution generation begins, the therapist describes the basic rules of brainstorming which is familiar to most clients. The two most important rules are: (a) quantity, not quality, and (b) no censorship.

Quantity, Not Quality

It is more important that people generate a large list of potential solutions rather than a perfect list. Brainstorming implies that solutions are fluid and that one idea can easily link to another for a better solution. The therapist coaches the client to consider multiple possibilities and not stay with the conventional.

No Censorship

This rule means every idea, no matter how silly or stupid sounding, is written down. The point is not to choose ridiculous solutions but that the germ of an excellent solution can result from a flawed one. This can't happen, however, unless the therapist creates a climate where flights of fancy are tolerated. When the therapist senses a hesitation to go beyond the conventional, he or she may want to generate quirky solutions. In Regina's case, the therapist suggested, "Run away to Canada."

The following represented Regina's list:

1. run away to Canada
2. borrow money from Uncle Clarence
3. change companies
4. declare bankruptcy
5. take an extra job
6. give up traveling and training
7. contact each creditor individually
8. go to a consumer counseling center

9. do nothing and just stay with her family for a few years until she gets on her feet

10. trade in 2-year old car for used car with no monthly payment

11. drop out of Florida time-share

12. obtain part-time employment

The next step is for the client to evaluate each of the solutions. Solutions that are essentially positive receive a plus sign. Those that are essentially negative receive a minus sign. Ones that are positive with slight drawbacks get a plus sign followed by a minus sign; ones that are negative with some benefits get a minus sign followed by a plus sign. Nuancing solutions in this manner pays off in several ways. Sometimes no solution is totally positive and people have to settle for those that have a degree of merit but might have been overlooked. Often there is more than one solution required and including other choices creates a full problem-solving package. Regina's evaluated list was as follows:

1. run away to Canada –

2. borrow money from Uncle Clarence –

3. change companies –

4. declare bankruptcy –

5. take an extra job – +

6. give up traveling and training –

7. contact each creditor individually + –

8. go to a consumer counseling center +

9. do nothing and just stay with the family for a few years until I get on my feet –

10. trade in 2-year-old car for a used car with no monthly payment – +

11. drop out of Florida time-share + –

12. obtain part-time employment +

Following the evaluation of each solution, the discussion proceeds to the central focus of the exercise—actually making choices. Regina realized that no one solution would entirely solve her financial problems and that it required a multifaceted program. Her priorities were to contact each creditor and also go to a consumer credit counseling service (Chapter 13). But there were other ways to improve her situation. Although she didn't want to change companies, she had the option of doing some consulting one weekend a month to supplement her income. Giving up the Florida time-share made sense, but her son had lost so much due to their moving and the change in lifestyle that she could not bring herself to take away their cherished annual week at Disney World. On the other hand, trading in the car that symbolized independence and status was sensible given that she was responsible for the problem. Although she did not want to borrow money from Uncle Clarence, she knew he had an older car with low mileage available now that Aunt Lois could no longer drive.

IMPLEMENTING THE SOLUTION

An essential ingredient in problem-solving is to faithfully carry out the solution. A common phenomenon in problem-solving, particularly when doing it in a group, is to feel accomplishment and relief when completing the previous steps. This leads to a letdown and a desire to regroup emotionally after expending so much energy. This is the point where the process fails for many because *they assume implementation rather than plan it*. To prevent this, I have listed a series of specific questions to help guarantee solution implementation. For each solution, the client answers the questions of "who, what, when, where, and how." These questions lead automatically into precise planning for implementation. The answers help the therapist determine whether the decisions are reasonable in light of the client's skills, resources, and life situation. They also incorporate measurable goals to monitor overall progress. In Regina's case, her main avoidance was speaking to each creditor personally. She broke down her contacts into groups: credit cards, lending institutions, and personal loans. She then set aside an hour each workday evening to call and explain what would be happening. She even needed to specify where she would make the calls. Without a personal telephone in her current residence, she lacked privacy but found the extension in the basement provided solitude. Both therapist and client have a document to help monitor the actual implementation.

EVALUATE THE SOLUTION

Organizational consultants agree that the bane of all problem-solving attempts is the failure to evaluate solutions. Government is the best (or worst) example. Legislators rarely appropriate money to evaluate the effectiveness of their solutions. The overwhelming majority of bills passed simply hang out there, and it is left to journalists or interested citizens to determine their success. Individuals encounter the same difficulty. The constant flux of existence requires ongoing evaluation of solution implementation with regular adjustments. Worksheet 12.1 provides a means for this last task. Therapist and client discuss together how the solutions are working out and adjust accordingly. If no therapist is present, clients need to carry this task out on their own. In Regina's case, Uncle Clarence had promised Aunt Lois's car to the church, but he put her in touch with a car dealer who gave her top dollar on her car.

Recovering gamblers usually respond favorably to the problem-solving process. They find it engaging, and enjoy the solution-oriented approach. They express sensing improvement as they implement each solution. A major mistake I have made over the years was to expect clients to do any analysis at home. Therefore, I never consider it a waste of time to work through any of the written tools suggested in this text during the actual therapy session. A true waste of time is to postpone interventions because clients fail to do the required analysis on their own.

Ideally, this chapter could end here with clients rapidly implementing all the great ideas generated during the problem-solving process. Self-regulation theory and personal experience alert us to the common issues of avoidance and procrastination to which we now turn.

OVERCOMING PROCRASTINATION

Theoretical Premise

Although overcoming procrastination strategies follows problem-solving, these strategies apply across the board to avoidance of all types. Self-regulation theory views procrastination as linked to goal-setting problems. People either set unrealistically high goals and then avoid them for fear of failure or they neglect to set reasonable short-term goals. Further, because doing unpleasant tasks usually puts people in a bad mood, procrastination becomes a form of misregulation to control negative feelings. Self-regulation theory states that procrastination results from two motivational sources (Baumeister *et al.*, 1994, pp. 73–74). People either worry that doing a specific task will result in some type of negative evaluation or that the task itself is boring. One important avenue to overcoming procrastination, therefore, is realistic goal-setting. We have discussed this remedy at length in Chapter 7. Merely establishing goals in the manner described in that chapter often eliminates considerable procrastination. Sometimes, however, the emotional blocks are too powerful for even goal-setting to overcome. For those situations, a more emotion-focused strategy may prove useful. The strategies described below derive from social cognitive models (Taylor *et al.*, 1998) but can also be conceptualized as exposure procedures common to behavior therapy (Barlow, 1988). The core idea is that avoidance represents an emotional escape. Often, however, the feared negative consequences either (a) don't happen or (b) are manageable. When people interrupt the process via avoidance, they miss the chance to discover those outcomes.

People avoid threatening experiences because at some level it works even though the long-term cost far outweighs the short-term benefit.

Procedure Overview

Worksheets 12.2 and 12.3 portray two integrated avenues to overcoming procrastination. Worksheet 12.2 attempts to challenge the faulty beliefs behind avoidance. Through the use of cognitive strategies, the person identifies the negative thinking associated with the task, examines its consequences, and finally develops alternative ways of viewing the situation. This is fairly standard cognitive therapy protocol. Worksheet 12.3 uses strategies derived from social cognitive psychology to face the task itself through imagery and then plan its behavioral accomplishment through the strategy of shaping or successive approximations.

Cognitive Approach

Worksheet 12.2 begins with a brief explanation of the two major avenues to procrastination: fear of being evaluated and the negative aspects of the task itself. This information helps clients name the roadblock. The client then identifies what they are avoiding (item #2). Regina had put off calling her creditors as described above. She would feel embarrassed and ashamed rather than find it was boring or uninteresting.

Item #3 addresses the negative automatic thinking that is associated with avoidance. In Regina's case, it had to do with two ideas. The first idea was that the people she spoke with would think of her as a deadbeat, when all her life she had tried to act responsibly and raise her child accordingly. The second idea was that calling the creditors meant she was a failure. Tied into this was the notion that, as an African-American woman, she had somehow "let my people down" by getting herself into this jam. Regina did not have any thoughts related to the issue of the task being boring or irrelevant.

Item #4 helps the client examine both the emotional and behavioral consequences of procrastination. Regina had no trouble cataloguing a long list of negatives from her procrastination. On the emotional side, she noted guilt, shame, fear, depression, self-directed anger, and low self-esteem. On the behavioral side, she stopped writing because the list seemed endless: ruined finances, loss of independence, inability to provide adequately for her son, possible bankruptcy, and giving up dreams of buying a home, travel, or retirement.

Item #5 uses a cognitive therapy approach to challenge negative thinking associated with anxiety. That framework states that people become anxious from two standard belief systems (Craske *et al.*, 1992). On the one hand, they over-predict future negative events, that is, expecting that the sky will fall. On the other, if the negative event were to take place they believe they couldn't cope. When Regina examined her fear that her creditors would think she was a deadbeat, her therapist helped her sort out two different scenarios. Some might *treat* her in a condescending manner, while others might *think* of her in a negative way. In looking at these possibilities, she admitted that the few times she had any dealings with the creditors on the phone, it was unpleasant, but no one was abusive. She said, "I could tell most of the time it was some underpaid billing person who was probably feeling as awkward as I was." Regina realized she could not control whether people thought well of her or not. However, since these people were not emotionally important to her, she should not worry about trying to influence their opinions of her.

Far more painful were the guilt, shame, and embarrassment. Here she used a number of different ideas to see the situation differently:

1. "OK, I messed up. Mistakes are human. The important thing is to get back on your feet. That's the message I want to give to my son right now. Calling these people says, 'I'm going to act maturely.'"
2. "No matter what people think of me, I have to do the right thing. I can only take responsibility for myself right now."
3. Finally, "People tell me all the time how much they admire what I've accomplished—those are the people whom I care about—my family, my friends, my people at church. They will support my taking the step because they've been there, they've had real hard times, and they're not going to let me down."

When clients are able to see the situation differently as Regina did, they are less blocked emotionally to take up the challenge of implementation.

Behavioral Implementation

Worksheet 12.3 also begins with a *task description*. However, in this case the client breaks the task down into small, manageable chunks (Item #2). Regina broke her task down into its three parts as follows:

1. Beginning—preparation
    a. Locate all the unopened mail from my creditors.
    b. Gather together all my credit card, loan documents, and account numbers.
    c. Make separate folders for each account and put each account into its own folder.

2. Middle
   a. Call the two consumer credit organizations: the credit union organization at work and the community organization I've seen advertised.
   b. After speaking to each one, make an appointment to visit the one I'm most comfortable with.
3. Ending
   a. Actually show up for the appointment with all my documentation, listen to their plan, and follow their recommendations.

The next phase challenges procrastination through *visual imagery* carrying out each of the steps involved. This is an example of process imagery rather than simply imagining a purely optimistic outcome. The person visualizes each sequence slowly as if watching herself doing the task on video. She visualizes even the smallest step in the process. Regina visualized herself pulling down the large cardboard box on top of her closet, where she tossed unopened bills and payment notices. She visualized going to the basement and finding the small, two-drawer file cabinet she brought from her place but had not looked at since moving in with her family. Finally, she visualized herself stopping at the office supply store on her way home from work to purchase manila folders and labels. Some other examples included visualizing going through the yellow pages to locate the consumer credit organization's phone number.

Item #3 instructs the client to rate feelings as they go through the visualization process. This often provides useful information regarding the areas of greatest resistance. For Regina, most of the anxiety occurred around simply getting started. She found that once she got going her mood improved considerably. This was relevant for her therapy, because it suggested that inertia at the beginning was going to be the major obstacle.

Once the client visualizes the entire sequence, he or she should repeat it to reduce the anxiety further. About 10–15 minutes total visualizing will ordinarily be adequate if the client does the task in session. Visualizing at home may increase motivation as well. Although the task may sound cerebral, it can shock participants by triggering intense feelings. Many interesting new thoughts and feelings emerge as people visualize. These new negative thoughts can then be challenged with the cognitive process used in the prior worksheet. Therapists may also find it useful to try the procedure first on some self-identified procrastination task relevant to their own life. This can give a feel for the procedure and suggest ways to modify it in working with clients.

Action steps are essential in any strategy hoping to overcome procrastination. This procedure uses shaping techniques from behavior therapy to facilitate action. The basic premise is to take the task, break it down into minute, absolutely achievable component parts, and do the first item. This process has a subtle but powerful influence on people. First, breaking it down into its smallest component parts makes the task appear manageable. "There is no way I could develop a payment plan for my bills," Regina told herself. However, buying manila folders *was* something she could imagine accomplishing. Second, this process uses momentum, or as self-regulation theory refers to it, psychological inertia (Baumeister *et al.*, 1994). Regina learned from her experience that she could not resist buying a lottery ticket when she went to the convenience store to buy gum. Inertia works in a positive way also. She found it is easier to go to the consumer credit group once she gained momentum from organizing her bills.

Item #5 initiates this process by identifying and freeing up a time period. Next, the person breaks down the initial task into its smaller component parts. As described in Worksheet 12.3, this might include deciding where the items are to go, what type of containers to put them in, and so on. The person then completes all parts in the first chunk. Clients gain momentum if they rate their positive feelings of accomplishment after each task. This worksheet suggests that they are getting closer to their goal and may want to continue working on the task. They also keep track of what they accomplished and this provides feedback and reinforcement. Regina's reaction was typical: "I can't believe I put this off so long; it was no big deal doing it." If people get stuck, subsection G reapplies the strategy of breaking the step down into its smallest component parts.

SUMMARY

This chapter has outlined strategies for dealing with two major issues that affect the quality of life for recovering gamblers. The first issue was the tendency to neglect rational problem-solving approaches to difficulties in favor of impulsive, reflexive, and short-term ones. It is not that pathological gamblers are unintelligent; rather, they fail to access the naive scientist modes of thinking that characterize the best of rational problem-solving. Problem-solving ensures that they slow down and challenge these instinctive patterns with more deliberate ones. The second issue related to procrastinating on recovery goals. Working on recovery goals generates unpleasant feelings when the tasks are painful reminders of past failures or when they are not interesting. An integrated approach should prevent people from needing to gamble either to solve or avoid their problems.

Worksheet 12.1
Problem-Solving Worksheet

I. Description of current problem

1. Define the problem.

2. How does it interfere with important goals in your life?

3. Is the problem related to any of the following:

    a. aimlessness, i.e., lack of a goal?
    b. too rigid of a goal?
    c. incompatible goals?
    d. overextending; biting off more than I can chew?

4. If yes to any of these, first identify what is the most important goal—the primary goal and purpose in wanting to solve this problem.

II. Motivation for solving the problem

| Benefits of solving it | Benefits of not solving it |

| Negatives of solving it | Negatives of not solving it |

III. Final problem definition

IV. List as many solutions as possible. Quantity, not quality of solutions is important. Do not censor or evaluate solutions, yet.

V. **Place a + or – next to solutions as to their effectiveness**

VI. **Select solution(s)**

VIII. **Identify specifics of implementing the solution**

Who?

What?

When?

Where?

How?

Date completed:

VIII. **Evaluate the solution**

Adjustments?

Worksheet 12.2
Changing Behavior
Procrastination Analysis Worksheet

1. People usually procrastinate for one of two reasons.

    A. *Fear or worry about being criticized* about the task, or not doing it as well as it should be done. The criticism can be from others, or from within me.

    B. The task itself is *boring, uninteresting, or unimportant* to them.

2. Describe the task(s) you are currently procrastinating on.

    A. What part, if any, relates to concern about doing it well?

    B. What part, if any, relates to being boring, uninteresting, or unimportant to you?

3. Describe the negative automatic thoughts behind each part.

    A. Worry concern, e.g., I might not do it well enough

    B. Not important, e.g., I'm wasting my time, it's not important, I should only do things that are interesting and engaging.

4. Consequences of these negative beliefs.

    A. *Emotional* Consequences: As a result of procrastinating what do I end up feeling?

    B. *Behavioral* Consequences: What are the *effects* of procrastinating on my occupation, relationships, health, finances, self-worth, recovery, spiritual/personal development? (Reply to all that are relevant.)

5. Challenging these negative automatic thoughts.

    A. What are alternatives to my *anxiety-related* concerns? What is the evidence I *can* do this adequately?

    B. How might I be over-predicting a bad outcome, thinking in all-or-none terms, fortune-telling what others think or feel, etc.?

    C. Even if I didn't do it perfectly well, or had to admit that I messed up, how could I cope with that?

6. New way of viewing the situation

Worksheet 12.3
Procrastination Change Worksheet

1. Describe the task that you are procrastinating on.

2. Break it down into three parts.

   Beginning/Preparation

   Middle

   Ending

3. *Visualize each sequence slowly*, as if watching yourself doing the task on video.

   Make sure you see yourself doing even the smallest part of each step, e.g., filing individual pages into a folder; opening the paint can with a screwdriver; deciding which space to place the clutter.

   Rate your feelings on a scale of 1–9, with 1 being very negative, 5 neither positive nor negative, and 9 being very positive.

4. *Repeat the visualization* of yourself doing the task for a period of about 5 to 10 minutes. Rate your feelings after the last visualization in the same manner that you did after the first one.

5. *Action Steps*

   A. Set aside a period of time for the task.

   B. Once you are actually in that time period, examine the component parts that you listed under #2 above.

   C. Take the very first step and *break it down even further* into 2–4 smaller steps. For example, if the task is clear clutter off the desk:

      a. decide where the items are to go
      b. decide on what type of containers to put them in
      c. gather the actual containers

D. Begin by doing just the first step in this smaller sequence; then the second, third, and so forth, completing all the tasks in the Beginning/Preparatory stage.

    a.   now rate your feelings from negative to positive.

E. Be aware of how, perhaps, you have gained some momentum and can just keep going.

F. Keep a record of what got accomplished and when.

             Finished   When

G. If stuck, identify the next step, and break it down into 2–4 smaller parts.

H. Continue as in previous section. Visualize again, if necessary.

Financial and Legal Issues

OVERVIEW

This chapter elaborates matters relevant to abstinence control discussed in seminal form earlier (Chapter 8). That chapter's concern was eliminating immediate access to money, building a fence, so to speak, around temptation. The present chapter examines a broader range of financial issues that are essential to long-term stability. Financial concerns are an essential focus of treatment, for they trigger impulses to gamble. Second, the pathological gambling lifestyle frequently leads to legal problems either through neglect of financial obligations or through illegal attempts to obtain money. Therapists must raise client and family awareness over potential legal issues and the need for legal advice. On occasion, attorneys subpoena testimony from the mental health profession, and this chapter will review ways to organize evaluations and reports.

MANAGING FINANCIAL ISSUES

A Hands-On Approach

Depending on a therapist's individual style, a hands-on approach to financial monitoring may already be a staple of the counseling toolbox. In the United States, despite considerable personal financial wealth, astonishing numbers of households have difficulty managing their financial affairs. In a recent economic boom, total household savings actually diminished on average and 53% of Americans reported that they live from paycheck to paycheck. Given that the majority of people enter therapy for relationship issues, it is not surprising that finances are high on the list of conflict areas. Some therapists are comfortable problem-solving with clients around finances whereas others prefer to make referrals.

Therapists who choose to work with pathological gambling, however, will quickly discover that tackling financial concerns is essential to comprehensive treatment. In a study of 146 inpatient pathological gamblers in a private psychiatric hospital (Ciarrocchi & Richardson, 1989, p. 57), 50% were more than $25,000 in debt (excluding home mortgages), 10% between $50,000 and $100,000, and 18% over $100,000 in debt. The NORC study (National Opinion Research Center, 1999) found 10.2% of problem gamblers and 19.2% of pathological gamblers had declared bankruptcy, compared to only 4.2% of nongamblers. Pathological gamblers, thus, are nearly five times more likely to declare bankruptcy. The nonprofit National Endowment for Financial Education (2000) has published a useful guide for pathological gambling patients and their families. This brief compendium and workbook highlights critical issues related to financial management and legal problems for the families of pathological gambling patients. It is an excellent tool for therapists to work with along with their clients.

Identifying and Controlling Assets

The first step in managing finances was discussed in Chapter 8. That consisted in identifying all the potential sources of income in the household as well as external sources, with an eye to turning off the money pipeline. First, patients divert their paycheck to the spouse's or a family member's account via direct deposit or some other means. Next, they surrender all credit cards and eliminate access to loans from lending institutions. Family members may have to document with their local banks a written request, countersigned by the pathological gambler, that forbids loans unless the family member is physically present at the application. Families then identify and restrict the patient's access to all other assets. This includes savings, retirement, stock investments, real estate, and so on. Families also determine the need to change home ownership from joint ownership to the nongambling partner alone.

Once environmental control is in place, families and patients together develop a budget. Many tools exist for developing budgets and are readily accessible. Several free websites offer examples, as do household financial software. Some commercial software companies offer free website budgeting tools as well. A system I've used extensively with clients is a self-help book based on the principles of Debtors Anonymous (Mundis, 1990). It provides an easy one-page budget worksheet along with practical advice and soothing reassurance.

The method I use in session when clients do not bring their own instruments is perhaps the simplest of all. It relies on a single page of 13-column standard accounting ledger sheets that clients can find in any office supply store. Its advantage is that families can not only budget month-to-month, but they can also monitor an entire year's expenditures at a glance and adjust as needed. This is the system we will refer to throughout the budgeting process. Creating a budget is a two-step process. Step one requires obtaining accurate income and expenditure data. Step two involves deciding how to allocate one's financial resources. When expenditures outspend income—usually the case in pathological gambling households—a third step requires problem-solving to manage the shortfall.

Developing a Budget

Ancient Greek philosophers proposed that the unexamined life is not worth living. It can also be financially ruinous. Pathological gambling patients often have no realistic sense of their expenditures. To develop a budget, everyone in the household monitors his or her spending. How? Everyone collects and puts in a single place (envelope, cookie jar, manila folder) *each and every receipt*. Some families pay with check or credit card. This is acceptable as long as the checks are not going into overdraft status and the monthly credit card costs do not add to accumulated debt. The same would hold for purchases and bill paying by mail or Internet. It takes at least one average month of collecting receipts to develop a working budget. Keeping receipts needs to become a way of life as long as the budget remains tight. After collecting receipts, the next step is to develop categories for the expenses. To keep it simple some variation of the following categories can suffice:

> rent/mortgage
>
> heating/air conditioning
>
> telephone, cable and internet
>
> water
>
> real-estate taxes, federal income tax (not payroll deducted),
>   state income tax (not payroll deducted)
>
> alimony, child support
>
> homeowners insurance
>
> household repairs/furniture
>
> vehicle repairs, vehicle insurance, gasoline for vehicles
>
> food/groceries
>
> eating out
>
> clothing
>
> health insurance, medical/dental expenses, therapy expenses
>
> charitable donations, gifts
>
> vacations/travel
>
> tobacco
>
> entertainment

Debts need to be spelled out individually for purposes to be explained later. For example, people need to include each car loan, home equity loan, credit card, bank loan, student loan, and each person owed money, including bookies and loan sharks. The person lists the categories on the ledger or worksheet and writes in pencil the month's expenditures. To develop a working budget, put down fixed known expenses first, for example, rent or mortgage. If clients have not done so, recommend contacting their utility company to establish a fixed monthly payment. Other categories can be estimated (e.g., entertainment) until the data arrive.

Equally important to listing expenses is listing monthly income. Here the categories are usually fixed. Except for people on commission or variable overtime, monthly income is predictable. List each source of monthly income and the amount. The final step involves simple arithmetic, but one that the patient and family have probably avoided until now. Add the expenses and income separately and then compare the amounts. This will at least suggest how much adjusting is required. When a deficit exists, the next step is problem-solving around it (Chapter 13).

Repayment Plan

The repayment plan is crucial for crisis management in early recovery. Ignoring debt payment makes money available to continue gambling. Developing an impossible-to-fulfill plan pressures patients to see gambling as the only possible solution.

Process

When the family has completed the budget above with its various categories, the next step is to separate out gambling-specific debts from all others. A gambling-specific debt is one related to paying off money borrowed from individuals such as bookies, private individuals, loan sharks, or gambling establishments. Next, the family determines how much money is available monthly for each debt. For example, the Smiths have $1,000 a month left for debts. Their nongambling debts amount to $3,000 a month. Further, the amounts owed are uneven. They owe $30,000 each to two banks for credit cards and cash advances, $10,000 on their home equity, $5,000 on their cars. Their monthly payments are $1,000 to Bank A, $500 for the home equity, and $500 for their cars. Gambling debts amount to $25,000, with no fixed monthly payment as yet. To get a ballpark estimate of how to organize repayment, sum up the entire amount, which in this example is $100,000. Then the family figures out what percentage of the total amount each debt represents. For example, Bank A is owed $30,000, and that represents 30% of the total debt. An ideal payment plan would have the family pay Bank A 30% of their $1,000 available funds, or $300 each month. All other payment plans work similarly as a percentage of the leftover monthly income. Ideal repayment plans often remain just that because other forces influence the plan's feasibility. First, Bank A may not want to negotiate down to a low monthly payment. Second, Bank C, which holds the home equity loan, decides the gambler's home is valuable real estate in a bull market and says it will foreclose. Nevertheless, the family has done the necessary calculations and is thus in a better position to negotiate.

Before contacting individual creditors, especially when there is considerable institutional debt, a wise move is to meet with a consumer credit counseling agency. Some are connected with credit unions; others operate independently. They will take the family's financial history and negotiate with lending institutions. They can often reduce or eliminate the interest rates paid on the loan and will consolidate loans into one manageable monthly payment. Even turning debts over to a consumer credit counseling service may not eliminate the need to contact individual creditors. In these cases, the person calls the creditor, explains that the family has fallen on hard times, is committed to repaying the debt, and would like to arrange a reduced monthly payment plan. Creditors are usually open to this process, because reduced monthly payments mean families are less likely to declare bankruptcy.

Gambler Resistance to Repayment Plans

Gamblers Anonymous and clinicians with experience in the field caution about rapid repayment of gambling-specific debts. Gamblers themselves frequently exhibit much resistance to the measured repayment plans suggested in this chapter. Experience has taught pathological gambling patients that keeping credit lines open is necessary to stay in action. In the gambling world, when word gets out that a person is a poor credit risk, it severely curtails gambling. The patient will pay off gambling debts rather than purchase household necessities. The mortgage or heating is less important than the good opinion of a bookmaker. In Chapter 5, we related the story of Myrna, who found $5000 in her husband's pocket after he told her there was no money to forestall turning off the electricity. He responded that he hadn't lied to her because the cash was for gambling. A payment plan that focuses on the family's genuine needs challenges and corrects this mentality. Outstanding debts are a painful reminder of the past, even when patients are sincere in desiring to stop gambling. Rapid repayment, however, creates an illusion of a bailout and may have the unintended effect of opening the door to renewed gambling.

To influence family members to pay off gambling-specific debts rapidly, pathological gambling patients sometimes insinuate that the people they borrowed money from are shady characters who will resort to violence. Parents and other family members are vulnerable to this manipulation and dig into meager resources to pay off loan sharks or bookies. Most people in the field know that reports of violence over gambling debts are greatly exaggerated. Unlike drug dealers, who operate on a cash-and-carry basis, illegal gambling operations need a certain degree of calm and stability to maintain their operations. They have unwritten codes of business conduct that involve extending credit to their best customers. They have little need to draw attention from law enforcement through heavy-handed collection methods. GA members sometimes are willing to contact a bookie or loan shark on a member's behalf saying something like, "George is a compulsive gambler, you'll get paid, but back off until he gets his life in order." They also remind the gambling establishment that George represents a bad business risk to them if it continues to extend him credit. In the small world of local illegal gambling, this can shut down gambling opportunities. Once the gambling-specific and other household creditors are contacted, the family can finalize their budget and begin the process of rebuilding their financial lives.

LEGAL AND FORENSIC ISSUES

Legal Concerns

In a sample of 186 pathological gambling inpatients in a gambling treatment program located within a private psychiatric hospital, 40% reported a criminal arrest (42% men, 8% women), 19% had been incarcerated, and 20% had legal charges pending at the time of treatment (Ciarrocchi & Richardson, 1989). These statistics are even more startling when one considers that this was a stable, middle-class socioeconomic group that still had enough resources to maintain private health insurance for treatment. Data from population surveys show a great disparity between pathological gamblers and nonproblem gamblers with regard to legal issues. The NORC study (1999) reported lifetime arrest rates of 36 and 32% for problem and pathological gamblers, respectively, but 4.5 and 11% for nongamblers and low-risk gamblers, respectively. Lifetime incarceration rates were 10 and 20% for problem and pathological gamblers, respectively, but only 0.4 and 3.7% for nonproblem and low-risk gamblers, demonstrating rates 10 to 20 times higher for gambling disorders than the general public.

The range and scope of these legal issues vary enormously. Typical charges include outright theft, embezzlement, misappropriation of funds, failure to pay taxes, tax evasion, bank or credit card fraud, writing bad checks, mail fraud, forgery, securities violations (handling stocks, etc.), and making false statements on financial reports. Less typical but reported crimes include kidnapping and murder-for-hire schemes to obtain insurance benefits. Assuming that most clinicians are not trained attorneys, giving legal advice falls outside their area of competence and requires referral to competent attorneys. Ideally, one should refer to an attorney experienced in issues related to pathological gambling. Often such expertise is not available, and in looking for referrals one might look to experts in criminal law and addicted populations.

Civil legal issues for pathological gambling patients arise as well. GA and professionals in the field view bankruptcy as a last resort for financial problems. Bankruptcy laws vary according to whether they involve businesses or private individuals. Obviously, this decision requires legal consultation. Families need to discuss in whose name the bankruptcy will be; whether it includes the spouse or only the patient. Consultation will assist the patient and family to decide on which form of bankruptcy: chapter 13 bankruptcy typically reduces amounts owed to creditors but involves a payback plan; chapter 7 wipes out debt but may force the sale of property to pay creditors. Different laws apply outside the United States. Other civil matters include shifting ownership of accounts or property away from the patient. In instances of divorce, family courts may struggle over custody and financial disputes. Courts historically have made inconsistent judgments about pathological gambling patients' rights in property division. Some have awarded spouses a greater proportion of the remaining assets with the logic that they were victims of their partner's irresponsible behavior. Other courts have divided assets equally using the logic that the patient had great financial need because of his disorder (Rose, 1988).

Legal issues can involve the therapist in at least three ways, with each demanding distinct strategies and perspective. The first is when the client has legal issues, is seeing a therapist for treatment, and then decides to submit mental health evidence to the court. The therapist may have made the initial legal referral during the evaluation process and now has to give testimony. Most ethical codes recommend extended discussion with the client regarding appearing in court on a client's behalf. Clients waive their right to confidentiality in those situations, and courts have wide discretion to require therapists to answer all sorts of questions raised by opposing attorneys. Informed consent requires alerting clients to this issue and reflecting together on how this might affect the therapeutic relationship. Clients do not always appreciate that therapists are under oath and required to answer all permitted questions.

The second instance is when assessment reveals that the family, typically the spouse, may have some legal vulnerability (e.g., unpaid federal taxes on a jointly signed tax return, or unpaid taxes on jointly owned property that the pathological gambler sold). These potentially adversarial scenarios are tricky in the sense that the pathological gambling patient may be the primary client, but the therapist feels obligated to alert family members to their potential liability. It is reasonable to encourage the family member to seek legal consultation and document the recommendation. An easier situation is when the family member is the primary client. In this instance, extended discussion of legal concerns is appropriate and essential. The third avenue is when an attorney requests an independent evaluation when the therapist is not the treating professional. This requires a focused forensic report to answer the presenting questions, as discussed in the next section.

Forensic Evaluations

Attorneys have various needs when requesting a forensic evaluation. The needs of prosecuting attorneys differ from those of defense attorneys. Courts acting on behalf of minors in custody disputes differ as well. This section does not intend to cover the range of sophisticated issues involved in forensic examinations. In keeping with the theme of this book, it is meant for generalists who may need to deal with legal issues as part of their overall clinical work. More extensive discussion of legal issues may be found in Rose (1988) and Castellani (2000).

Technically speaking, when a mental health professional submits a forensic evaluation he does so as an agent of the court. Its purpose is to help determine the civil or criminal outcome, but attorneys, as opposed to an independent court-generated request (e.g., custody dispute), are interested in gathering supporting evidence for their position. If the report does not support a position, the clinician should not expect to appear in court or have the report submitted as evidence. A prosecuting attorney may wish to have a report demonstrating that the defendant does *not* have a gambling disorder. A defense attorney may desire proof of the disorder. In family law disputes such as divorce proceedings, the existence or nonexistence of a gambling problem might benefit either party.

Potential Issues

Potential reasons for a forensic mental health report are myriad. In criminal cases, defense attorneys will use any means to demonstrate that their client's emotional condition rendered them either not guilty or, at a minimum, made the act less willful. For all practical purposes, the application of the insanity defense to pathological gambling-related criminal acts is dead. Courts almost always dismiss it, as they do when pathological gambling is offered as a defense for nongambling-related crimes (Rose, 1988). Slightly different from pleading insanity is using pathological gambling as a defense against the person's having *willfully* committed the crime. Rules of evidence vary by jurisdiction, and one jurisdiction (or judge) may accept a pathological gambling defense while another might exclude it. I have testified in two federal courts on behalf of defendants with the same charge (income tax evasion) where one federal judge ruled that pathological gambling did not meet the standards for an acceptable psychological defense when at the same time a judge in the neighboring district ruled otherwise.

In pathological gambling cases, the use of mental health testimony at sentencing is more common than invoking either insanity or reduced willfulness defenses. Here attorneys request the testimony of therapists to demonstrate that their client's behavior was influenced by pathological gambling, thereby mitigating culpability, with the hope of a reduced sentence. Attorneys may also want testimony regarding how invested the client is in treatment to provide the court with proof of rehabilitative capacity. Depending on such factors as the seriousness of the crime and the crowded nature of prison facilities, attorneys can make a compelling case that treatment and lesser punishment (e.g., house arrest with required employment, weekend jail, early parole) will benefit society more. Courts sometimes agree with this logic, particularly if the client has stable employment, family dependents, and a good treatment record. In civil cases, attorneys may consider pathological gambling an important factor in awarding monetary judgments in family law disputes or in business conflicts. Pathological gambling may also be relevant for the professional reinstatement of recovering gamblers to their profession following rehabilitation, for example, attorneys, psychologists, and counselors.

Shortly after the psychiatric community recognized pathological gambling as an emotional disorder in the DSM-III (American Psychiatric Association, 1980), attorneys used pathological gambling as an insanity defense and in some cases won. The authors of the DSM responded in the next version, DSM-IIIR (American Psychiatric Association, 1987) with a "Cautionary Statement," which declared that a disorder in the DSM did not imply that "the condition meets legal or other nonmedical criteria for what constitutes mental disease, mental disorder, or mental disability" (APA, 1994, p. xxvii). It singled out two conditions: pathological gambling and pedophilia. This statement, in my opinion, represented an attempt by the authors to rein in legal use of pathological gambling for determining criminal responsibility. One legal expert on gambling commented on this attempt by asserting, "However, this disavowal is meaningless; the American Psychiatric Association cannot publish a national standard for diagnosing an illness and then say it is not truly setting a standard" (Rose, 1988, p. 243). Lawyers ignored the APA's cautionary statement because they have an ethical responsibility to use every possible legal defense available on their client's behalf. For this reason, clinicians that work with pathological gambling patients should expect to find themselves involved in a client's legal issues.

Report Components

Each mental health professional evaluates the client in light of the specific questions asked by the referring attorney, court, or professional board. Each mental health professional also evaluates the client strictly in terms of his or her level of competence. For example, clinicians need to know if their local jurisdiction permits their discipline to make diagnoses. In an individual state or province, a licensed/certified addiction or professional counselor may not have that privilege, or it may be limited to certain disorders (e.g., substance abuse). If an attorney requests a diagnosis, the mental health professional must make clear that this is within one's professional competence. Similarly, clinicians must abide by the appropriate standards for use of psychological tests or evaluating medical conditions. The comprehensive report, then, will vary slightly according to one's professional discipline; for example, psychiatrists may report on physical findings, and psychologists may use psychological test data. A comprehensive diagnostic report on pathological gambling at a minimum should have the following components:

1. **Identifying information**: name, age, date of report, date of interview, amount of time for interview, and court case number.
2. **Reason for referral**: this describes the legal questions raised and the referring sources.
3. **Materials reviewed**: the clinician describes all materials examined related to the case to demonstrate that he or she has reviewed external sources that may corroborate or challenge the interview data. Some examples might include the various court briefs, indictments, financial transaction documents, previous civil-legal actions, collection agency documents, correspondence between relevant parties, state-federal tax returns, business reports, as well as documents related to gambling winnings and losses. Each document should be

cited separately, for example, "copies of documents pertaining to debt transactions with Trump's Casino (30 pages)."

4. **Statement of whether interview was recorded** on audiotape or other means and client's consent.

5. **Psychological tests** administered or **physical-laboratory tests** administered.

6. **Family history and personal history**: the basic biographical details of the person's life and clinically relevant history.

7. **Mental status examination**: in forensic reports, my preference is to include the data relevant to the presenting questions in this section. As such, it differs from the ordinary mental status section in its much greater elaboration. Specifically, the "content" section is usually several pages long as it reviews in detail the person's gambling history. That section reports all the essential data that applies to DSM criteria.

The structure of the mental status examination, then, is as follows:

    a. general appearance and behavior

    b. flow of thought

    c. mood

    d. content

    e. sensorium

8. **Review of psychological test findings**: each psychologist follows his or her best clinical judgment with regard to choosing the appropriate psychological instrument. In addition to the South Oaks Gambling Screen (SOGS) and/or NODS (see Chapter 5), I typically include a Beck Depression Inventory, MMPI, MCMI, and NEO–PI–R (see Chapter 5). In my experience, attorneys and judges mistakenly believe that a personality test should somehow "pick out" pathological gamblers. We saw in Chapter 3 that the MMPI, for instance, cannot discriminate substance abuse from pathological gambling. This sometimes leads to lengthy questioning in court as to whether pathological gambling is truly a disorder if it cannot be picked up separately on a psychological test. The psychologist needs to explain that the purpose of a specific psychological test and diagnostic criteria for a specific condition are not always coterminous. For example, the Beck Depression Inventory tells a clinician how many depressive symptoms a client has, but separate criteria exist for the diagnosis of major depressive disorder. There *are* criteria for pathological gambling: they exist in the DSM. That is what the clinician uses to determine a diagnosis. Psychological tests answer other questions regarding the person's emotional state that permit putting pathological gambling, if it exists, within the context of a comprehensive personality evaluation. They may be specifically useful for ruling out issues that may complicate rehabilitation, for example, the presence of a thought disorder, antisocial personality disorder, or substance abuse.

9. **Review of physical-laboratory test findings**.

10. **Diagnostic conclusions**: this section represents the bottom-line for all concerned. Since gambling is the referral question, I begin with noting that the DSM requires matching five of the following criteria. Then I list each of the 10 criteria in order along with my impressions, for example, #1: *person is preoccupied with gambling*. Thereafter follows all the data from the content section that either support or fail to support matching this criterion. The report reviews each of the criteria in this fashion and reaches a conclusion regarding the presence or absence of pathological gambling. In addition to pathological gambling issues, the report also notes all other significant mental health issues and diagnoses, although the exact matching method with each DSM criterion is not necessary since they are not the major focus of the referring question. It is also appropriate to make treatment recommendations as warranted or to comment about what gains, if any, may have occurred with current or previous treatment.

A report structured in this manner, then, makes clear its conclusions along with the data used to derive the conclusions. Appearance in court is the forum for describing the report orally along with its rationale. Mental health professionals need to remember that most legal hearings are adversarial processes, and one or all of the parties may challenge the findings. Professional reinstatement hearings are more free-form, with board members and attorneys asking questions. They direct questions at the quality of the person's recovery. When we testify, it is important not to claim more than we can know. We cannot predict abstinence or relapse with absolute certainty. We can only judge the future according to degrees of certainty: for example, highly likely, highly unlikely.

A major breakthrough in professional reinstatement is the acknowledgment that pathological gambling admits of rehabilitation in a similar manner to substance abuse. Professional boards, particularly those dealing with attorneys, usually exclude for life individuals who commit acts of "moral turpitude." The District of Columbia Bar, for example, admitted back to practice an attorney who served time in federal prison for failure to pay income taxes and who had been disbarred for five years. Review of the case concluded that the crime was directly related to pathological gambling and that with evidence of rehabilitation the attorney could be readmitted to the practice of law. Ordinarily, an attorney who had committed a felony would receive a lifetime suspension. One of the few exceptions was offenses related to substance abuse followed by extensive rehabilitation. This was the first instance, to my knowledge, of treating crimes related to pathological gambling in a similar way to crimes related to substance abuse. Other state bar associations have followed suit, reinstating attorneys following suspension and gambling treatment rehabilitation when misconduct was integrally related to pathological gambling.

CHAPTER

14

Couples and
Family Treatment

Research on the long-term well-being of people recovering from addictions has demonstrated the crucial impact of healthy family environments (Moos *et al.*, 1990). In light of the high treatment dropout rates in pathological gambling research studies, it is interesting that no study to my knowledge has incorporated relationship counseling as a modality to improve retention.

This chapter addresses two broad areas related to family issues. The first focuses on effective treatment for pathological gambling patients by including partners and family members. The second focuses on how clinicians can help family members and partners who seek treatment for their own needs. Little research exists on specific family treatment, but marital status and family life satisfaction are related to gambling abstinence (Hudak *et al.*, 1989). The extensive international system of mutual-help groups available for substance abuse family members far surpasses available resources for gambler's families. At this time, in the entire state of Maryland only three meetings exist in the official literature of GamAnon.

This chapter discusses several topics. First, it examines typical family scenarios and the different perspectives of patients and family members. We follow this with a review of research on family issues. Next we reexamine treatment strategies discussed in other chapters that lend themselves to a couples format. The next two topics represent the clinical heart of family work. One relates to family strategies in cases where the pathological gambler is the primary client and following that we examine methods for working with family members as the primary client. Finally, we take up countertransference issues. Countertransference often arises when the effects of pathological gambling are clearly seen on the family.

FAMILY SCENARIOS

Three typical scenarios develop in the families of pathological gamblers. What is striking is how each scenario can develop whether or not the person actually stops gambling!

Scenario 1. The family/partner eventually accepts the gambling member with little loss of intimacy. This may follow a long period of coming to terms with the gambling behavior, or it may happen rather quickly. If the gambler is abstinent, this facilitates more rapid healing of family issues. In other cases, family members minimize the financial damage and maintain intimacy despite continued gambling.

Scenario 2. The family/partner develops a relationship with the gambling member that constitutes a parallel existence but is emotionally cold. In these situations, the family/relationship does not recover emotional closeness, but all parties choose to maintain some level of interaction. To outsiders, the family gives the appearance of functioning as a unit but tacitly or otherwise it has minimal expectations around intimacy. If the gambling continues, family members protect themselves from the financial devastation and coexist with the gambling member.

Scenario 3. Family/partners remain together, but intense conflict characterizes the relationship. Whether or not the gambler is abstinent, family members remain chronically angry.

Since families are dynamic systems, these patterns may change over time or intermingle. Sometimes relationship patterns move from rage to cold indifference or vice versa. If the gambling persists, even the most accepting partner's emotional state will shift.

PATHOLOGICAL GAMBLING PATIENTS AND FAMILIES: DIFFERENT PERSPECTIVES

The resiliency of many families is often remarkable. When they stay together, families of pathological gambling patients often have great energy even under chaotic circumstances. In this way, they resemble the patient's excitement-seeking. The long-term realism and tough-minded approach of spouses also stands out. A patient in recovery for 8 years found a job in the same company as his wife. I asked the wife if she thought this would help the family save money because now they could all be under one person's medical benefits. Her reply had a hard edge as she informed me she would never put herself or her children in a situation where her husband could damage their welfare with a relapse. She vowed to maintain family coverage in her plan, and he was welcome to pursue individual coverage for himself.

The Pathological Gambling Patient's Emotional and Behavioral Experience

Early treatment experiences tend to differ from late treatment or stable recovery phases. During active gambling, the chaotic lifestyle of the gambler creates havoc in relationships. Furthermore, gambling is only one impulsive behavior that can sabotage relationships. In addition to financial problems, gambling patients have significant emotional and physical health problems (Lorenz & Yaffee, 1986). To make matters worse, the same study reports that 23% of the pathological gamblers sampled ($n = 206$) had affairs during their active gambling period, and 14% had affairs even during the recovery phase. It is not surprising, then, that pathological gamblers in treatment report high divorce rates. One study found that 35% were divorced, separated, or remarried—rather remarkable given that the mean age was only 38 and the modal age 26 (Ciarrocchi & Richardson, 1989; *n* = 177). Clinicians, therefore, should expect to find an array of relationship problems in early treatment.

Pathological gamblers themselves report a variety of marital difficulties. In the sexual sphere, 49% of GA members reported that the sexual relationship was unsatisfactory for both partners during active gambling and remained so for 19% following gambling abstinence (Lorenz & Yaffee, 1986). The same study reported, not surprisingly, that around 80% reported difficulty communicating their feelings to their spouses and 60% reported inability to resolve marital conflicts. A second feature of pathological gamblers' defensiveness is hypersensitivity to criticism. Gamblers experience recovery as an enormous mountain. They derive satisfaction from conquering it and are aware of what it cost them to climb it. Partners, as we shall see below, operate on a different timetable. Consequently, patients tend to react stridently to families' reminders of past behavior. Patients experience this as an unfair shot. After all, aren't they abstinent? Haven't they done everything possible to improve the situation? Didn't they turn over all the finances? Work extra to pay off bills? The end result is that they believe that "I can never do anything to please her." This leads to a belief that no amount of effort is sufficient. The patient may isolate or try to prove he is admirable and his partner ungrateful. Naturally, partners defend themselves by reminding patients of the suffering they caused. When this pattern escalates into chronic conflict, it destroys motivation to improve the relationship and creates an incentive to withdraw emotionally and physically.

The Partner's Emotional and Behavioral Experience

Narcissism exaggerates patients' defensiveness, thereby reducing their ability to have empathy for their partners. Exaggerated optimism, which is a needed illusion for many to continue gambling, is closely linked to a sense of entitlement in relationships. Entitlement, of course, does not facilitate intimacy. An even darker side to entitlement and exaggerated self-esteem is its link to violent behavior. Roy Baumeister has made a convincing case for threatened egoism as one source for violent behavior (Baumeister, 1997b; for a review, see Baumeister *et al.*, 1996). If clinical observations on the high rate of narcissism for male pathological gambling patients are accurate, then we could predict high rates of domestic abuse in pathological gambling families. One report found that 50% of female spouses and 10% of their children reported physical abuse from the male pathological gamblers (Lorenz & Shuttlesworth, 1983).

The core conflict between pathological gambling patients and partners centers on *a developmental time lag in the recovery process* for the gambling-afflicted trauma. Social cognitive psychology maintains that trauma shatters basic assumptions in people's worldviews (Janoff-Bulman, 1992, 1999). Assumptions typically shattered in trauma include: (a) the world is a good place, (b) people get what they deserve, and (c) I have self-worth. Social cognitive theory maintains these assumptions are fundamental to peoples' beliefs about the way the world operates. There is hardly a daily activity we engage in that does not assume one of these beliefs. I would never have walked, drove, or taken public transportation to work today if I did not assume I would get there alive. To make *that* assumption, I needed to make other assumptions about the world [tornado will not come], people [they would drive rationally], and things [the ground will hold my weight]. If someone is a robbery or earthquake victim, fundamental beliefs unravel. Furthermore, shattered assumptions attack my self-worth; if bad things happen to me, what does it say about me? Unfortunately, one of the ways we make sense of trauma is to blame ourselves. If I am to blame, at least there's an explanation for this terrible event. The trade-off, however, is that I lose self-worth in exchange for seeing the world as meaningful. Ironically, we can tolerate negative self-views more than a disordered world.

Returning now to family life, we can understand the developmental lag in coping with gambling-afflicted trauma. Obviously, recovery means gamblers must change their worldviews. The cognitive distortions described in previous chapters are now seen as faulty. If the world does not work the way I believed it did, this undermines other fundamental motivations and approaches to life. If the data overwhelmingly demonstrate that I am not a lucky person, what does that mean? Who am I really? How did this come to be? What is the exact nature of the world? How do we get to our goals if not this way? If I didn't get what I deserve, what does this say about me? About the notion of a just universe? Recovery requires processing these and similar questions. Treatment addresses these concerns and rebuilds alternative assumptions about the world and one's self-worth. Pathological gambling patients, however, have one enormous advantage their families do not. The gambling-inflicted traumas occur gradually for them. As we noted in the chapter on motivational enhancement, people can spend several years in the contemplation stage reflecting on the necessity of change. They continually process and reprocess available data before deciding to change.

Families, on the other hand, frequently sense something is wrong, but the deception inherent in pathological gambling leaves them unclear as to the degree of the problem. When the gambling problem is revealed, it shatters family members with its scope. Furthermore, they must process this on the run, so to speak, because at this point they are usually in crisis. No Red Cross worker shows up at the door, no insurance agent arrives with a check to begin the rebuilding process, and nobody from social services delivers a list of free day-care services.

Research confirms both gambling-inflicted stress as well as a developmental time lag in the recovery between problem gamblers and their partners. A series of studies used the Family Environment Scale (FES; Moos & Moos, 1981) to compare perceived family relationships of pathological gamblers and their partners. The FES is highly predictive of overall life functioning in addicted individu-als and their families (Moos & Moos, 1984). The authors standardized the scale on a large normal population for ten areas of family experience. A weakness of previous family research in pathological gambling is the use of nonstandardized instruments. Although such studies can identify family-life problems, we cannot draw conclusions about their severity compared with either normal families or those with other clinical conditions.

A study of 15 hospitalized pathological gambling patients and their spouses found that both groups reported less cohesiveness, personal independence, and intellectual–cultural orientation than normal controls on the FES (Ahrons, 1989). Furthermore, on a standardized symptom checklist spouses reported the same level of emotional distress as their hospitalized partners! A larger study of hospi-talized pathological gamblers divided them into alcoholic ($n = 34$) and nonalco-holic ($n = 33$) groups (Ciarrocchi & Hohmann, 1989). Male alcoholic gamblers reported significantly greater conflict and decreased personal independence on the FES than normal controls, and male nonalcoholic pathological gamblers reported less independence and intellectual–culture orientation. Neither pathological gam-bling group differed significantly from each other or the comparison alcoholic nongambling group.

These studies indicated that both pathological gambling patients and their spouses report significant family distress during early treatment, and wives exhibit levels of emotional distress equivalent to their hospitalized partners. What happens in family environments following recovery? Male members of GA for less than 2 years described their families as having significantly less independence, less intellectual–culture orientation, and less active-recreational orientation than normal families (Ciarrocchi & Reinert, 1993). On the Family Relationship Index, a composite index of distress derived from the FES, these short-term GA members reported significantly more family distress than long-term GA members did. Long-term GA members, interestingly, reported signifi-cantly *less* conflict and *greater* moral-religious emphasis in their families than normal members. Wives of GA members who were GamAnon members had a different pattern. *Short-term* GamAnon members, like their GA counterparts, reported significantly less independence, intellectual–cultural orientation and active-recreational orientation than the normal control group. Unlike their GA counterparts, however, *long-term* GamAnon members reported significantly *less* intellectual–cultural orientation and active-recreational orientation than the nor-mal control group.

In summary, long-term GA members perceive no greater distress than normal families in eight relationship dimensions and less conflict and greater moral-relig-ious emphasis compared with normal families. Together, this suggests that long-term recovery (more than 2 years) leads to perceived positive family environments for male problem gamblers in recovery. Wives of GA members gave a different account. Even when their partners had been in recovery 2 or more years, spouses reported significantly less relationship satisfaction than people in the general population.

Core Themes in Partners

Examining core themes that relate to the traumatizing shattered assumptions may provide useful leads for clinical intervention.

Trust

Just as trust is considered the primary developmental stage acquired in infancy (Erikson, 1963), trust is primary in relationships. Discovery of the inner and outer worlds of pathological gambling creates enormous mistrust. It violates the person's belief that the world is benevolent. In pathological gambling families, the assumptions of stability change instantly. Checking and savings accounts no longer exist; your spouse has intercepted your mail; you owe a fortune to the IRS (and it's in both your names); the mortgage is behind several months; your spouse collateralized your car on a loan; and this is the end of private school for your children. One emotional reaction to this mistrust is chronic anxiety and worry. Spouses enter into a perpetual mode of waiting for the other shoe to drop. For defensive purposes, they elevate suspiciousness to new heights. Everything their partner says, does, describes, promises, or fails to do becomes one more example of basic deceit. The smudge on the envelope means he's tried to open the mail. The click on the other end of the phone means the bookie's calling; getting stuck in traffic requires verification from the state police, and so on.

Fairness

The world not only ceases to be benevolent, it ceases to be just. Prior to the trauma of discovery, partners may have believed, as most do, that on average people tend to get what they deserve. Justice and control are important assumptions we make to ward off the scary idea that pain and suffering strike randomly (Janoff-Bulman, 1992, p. 9). Realizing the full impact of problem gambling, however, leaves no room for doubt that the world is unfair. Numerous afflictions now descend on innocent spouses and children. Bouts of rage rise and fall like waves in the ocean. Family members see reminders of their victimization everywhere: the neighbor's new car, turning down the invitation to eat with friends, needing to work overtime, and so on. Family members are often not conscious of the triggers for their bad mood, so automatic is the process. Recovering gamblers who work at being empathic may respond supportively at first to these anger reactions. When the reactions continue undiminished, the patient asks, "Why can't you just get over it? It's been three years." Such questions confirm the partner's belief that "he just doesn't get it."

Self-Esteem

To make the world work, a positive sense of self is crucial. With no self-confidence, we would undertake little beyond mere survival and not enter into social relationships at all. Trauma seriously wounds self-worth. People often blame themselves for the event. "If only I had not been alone with him." "Why did I move to that neighborhood?" "I should never have let her use the car." Personal blame seems to arise out of our need to make the world orderly and rational. Blame helps make events appear less random. People blame others for the same reason. Rather than see rape as random, some find it more coherent to describe the victim as immoral. In pathological gambling families, partners often flagellate themselves for "not seeing this coming." They describe themselves as naive, wimpy, or weak. The events happened because they had their head in the sand.

In summary, each person in the pathological gambling relationship has unique perspectives. Although many clinicians have called attention to families' needs, a trauma-recovery model explains the nature of the family's feelings, attitudes, and behavior. It also explains the lengthy recovery process attested to by clinicians and families alike (Darvas, 1981). This clinical model assumes that the slower recovery time for families and partners relates to the greater unpredictability and uncontrollability they experience in the event versus what the pathological gambling patient experiences. Emotion theory (Barlow, 1988) gives unpredictability and uncontrollability a prominent role in psychological disorders, providing a further explanation for the extreme emotional distress found in these households.

In the next two sections, we describe two approaches for reducing emotional distress in families. The first involves couples approach where both parties work together and a second individual approach that works with the family member alone.

COUPLES THERAPY FOR PATHOLOGICAL GAMBLING

The first goal of couples therapy relates to supporting the patient's desire to stop gambling. Couples therapy accomplishes this through: (a) developing environmental controls (Chapter 8), (b) working together for financial recovery

(Chapter 13), (c) handling legal issues (Chapter 13), and (d) providing a forum for the partner to ask questions, ventilate, give feedback on the gambler's behavior, and obtain emotional support. Individual chapters have pointed out how clinicians can accomplish these goals with partners.

Beyond these task-oriented goals, however, couples need to heal relationship wounds. As described above, deception creates longstanding mistrust. Worse, pathological gamblers develop habits that are destructive to intimacy. These include looking for quick solutions to problems, avoiding negative emotional events, hiding vulnerable parts of themselves, saying what they think people want to hear, and confusing feelings of excitement for intimacy. These patterns do not die overnight; they linger and create barriers to intimacy. Similarly, partners develop defensive maneuvers that also create intimacy barriers. These may include maintaining a high index of suspicion, creating an independent emotional existence, staying angry for fear of being taken advantage of, and striving for total emotional control to cope with their chaotic environments. In my view, only broad-based relationship therapy can address these needs. Many families stay together out of economic need. Too often, the gambling experience destroys any expectation of intimacy for either partner. As a result, they coexist with varying degrees of tension, depending on the solutions they select.

An interminable array of therapies exists for couples. Is any one well suited for pathological gamblers and their partners? Unfortunately, we have no direct research to answer that question. My own belief is that only an approach that emphasizes tolerance and acceptance can repair the damage inflicted by this disorder. Recently, two prominent behavioral marital therapists developed such an approach following their disappointment with standard behavioral marital therapy. They found that couples abandoned quickly the precise, clearly operationalized strategies so painstakingly taught. Through data analysis, they independently found that emphasizing behavioral change could go only so far. People have limited capacity to change, yet successful intimate relationships exhibit a high degree of tolerance. The researchers joined together to create a couples therapy that focused on the paradox of acceptance and change, that is, we are most inclined to change when we feel accepted. Further, they concluded, instead of an array of artificial communication techniques, wouldn't it make more sense to teach people strategies that felt natural?

The result was an empirically based couples therapy that they called Integrative Behavioral Couples Therapy (IBCT), which tries to mirror what happens in successful relationships. Their model seems ideal for the healing required of pathological gambling families, and I have incorporated it with adjustments to these couples. The model is described in a lengthy treatment manual (Jacobson & Christensen, 1996) and in a clearly written self-help book (Christensen & Jacobson, 2000). Research has validated its efficacy (Jacobson et al., 2000), and the approach is currently part of 5-year government-funded outcome study.

MODEL OVERVIEW

This chapter does not describe every aspect of IBCT that might be useful, but it provides the context for gambling-specific interventions. We assume here that focusing on relational issues comes *after* addressing the more immediate goals described in this book. Unless the gambler has made some commitment to change and the family has strategies in place to contain the damage, the finer points of enhancing intimacy will go nowhere.

In IBCT, the clinician moves first toward developing a meaningful formulation of the problems in the relationship. This formulation becomes the heart of acceptance and change, so it is especially important to take the necessary time to get it right. Assessment begins by asking the couple to describe their courtship history during a joint interview. This usually creates a positive atmosphere with humorous tales of who hit on whom, and so on. Each partner shares what attracted him or her to the other person. This is relevant because the nongambling spouse often found qualities attractive that were intricately connected to the gambling behavior.

Following this conjoint session, the clinician meets individually for one or two sessions with each partner. The purpose of these interviews is to assess each partner's relationship history, family background, and other influences on their current expectations about relationships. Questions addressed include what is the ideal degree of closeness for them and the ideal degree of control in a relationship. This interview can also screen for issues related to sexual infidelity, domestic violence, or previous abuse that people might hesitate to reveal in a joint session. Out of this material, the clinician derives the formulation that situates the major tensions for the couple that derive from the gambling experience. The case below will illustrate one such formulation, but we need to examine how the formulation fits in with the overall therapeutic goal. IBCT minimizes blaming in its goal of helping couples achieve tolerance and acceptance. A core strategy is *empathic joining* around a problem or making the problem an "it." Adapting that model to the pathological gambling situation, we want to help couples view the gambling as an "it." Even though personal responsibility is emphasized for motivational enhancement (Chapter 7), that aspect is temporarily bracketed to focus the couple on joining against a common enemy. This constitutes "building a relationship around the problem" (Jacobson & Christensen, 1996, p. 103). Following these initial assessment sessions, the clinician provides the couple with feedback in a session that outlines a formulation with its implication.

Case Illustration

This case illustrates both the generic methods of IBCT and its specific application to treating pathological gambling in a couples modality.

Background. Franco and Maria were Americans of Puerto Rican heritage who had been high school sweethearts but came from different socioeconomic backgrounds. Maria's family had settled in the United States because her father's international consulting business moved its headquarters from San Juan. Franco himself came from a divorced working-class family that lived in a lower-middle-class urban neighborhood. Franco never used drugs but noted that 20 of his 24 cousins were drug addicts. Maria and Franco had become "best friends" in high school, but as romance developed they essentially dated no one else. They married when Maria finished college. Following college, Maria took a well-paying job as a systems engineer while Franco apprenticed as an electrician after high school and now was self-employed. Franco was industrious, hard working, and resourceful, but Maria's wages were roughly 2½ times his. The couple desired to start a family but was unsuccessful due to Franco's low sperm count. When the couple married, they joined Maria's family church, the Roman Catholic Cathedral parish, in which her family was heavily involved socially and spiritually. The congregation was active in the Hispanic community, but the emotional atmosphere was rather formal and traditional. Franco's family worshiped in a storefront charismatic church in his neighborhood that was close-knit, warm, and culturally connected to the Puerto Rican community.

Gambling history. Franco gambled actively for 17 years starting at age 14 until he was 31. He dabbled in several types of gambling, but the racetrack finally did him in. Unlike many pathological gamblers, Franco rarely lied to Maria about his gambling. He seldom informed her in advance of his binges, but if she asked him his whereabouts he replied honestly. He even told her what amount he had lost or won. As the losses mounted, Maria put her foot down and insisted he do something about his problem. She took as complete control over the finances as she could. He attended GA and was abstinent for almost 4 years prior to the relapse that precipitated his entering treatment. For the past 6 to 9 months, Franco had gone to the track on average twice a month losing about $500 each time. The thorn in their relationship, however, was Franco's infidelity with an 18-year-old woman in his old neighborhood that began when he took on a construction project there. The woman had two children, one a newborn (not Franco's), and she herself had a serious drug problem. Maria was fully aware of the relationship, but Franco maintained there was no physical relationship between them. When they entered treatment, Maria and Franco were still living together but separated shortly thereafter when Franco requested time to "get my head together." Each partner stated they wanted to work together as a couple to see whether they could salvage their marriage.

Personal attractions. In an early session, IBCT asks the couple what they were attracted to in each other. Franco stated he was attracted to Maria because she was smart, pretty, and caring. She would do anything for people.

Furthermore, when she was around he always felt wanted and needed. He found her voice soothing and sweet, and, best of all, they were always friends. Maria said she was attracted by the fact that they talked about everything together. She found Franco different, a man who knew what he wanted, and a man who was confident in being his own person. She found him real, not phony. In addition, he really cared about people and went out of his way to help others.

Differences. IBCT maintains that for distressed couples differences trigger attempts to change the other person that in turn spiral out of control when the partners resist such efforts. Franco was an extremely hard worker, willing to put in long hours for extra pay. Maria was even more extreme in her workaholism. Franco hated that they seemed to have so little time for each other. Social life, in his opinion, was geared toward larger family gatherings, with no down time as a couple. They had not taken a vacation in 2 years despite having adequate finances. He also felt that Maria had not only taken control of the finances. but also every other area of their life together. She took charge of socializing, buying gifts for family and friends, deciding when to try to get pregnant, responding to her parents' social demands, and even where they worshipped. Maria, for her part, felt horribly wounded by Franco's romantic attachment to this young woman. She felt that after 20 years of friendship Franco had let her down. She always believed in his strength, for example, his ability to give up gambling, but now she didn't know what he could manage. She wanted to believe him but didn't know if she could trust anything about him—from his gambling to his extramarital relationship.

Formulation. When the assessment is complete, IBCT moves to the therapist's formulation of the couple's issues. In the formulation, the therapist provides the couple with a nonjudgmental explanation of how things got to be the way they are. This formulation is presented tentatively as a flexible hypothesis, and the therapist invites each partner to give feedback as to its accuracy and adjusts as necessary. In accepting the formulation, the couple has a tool whereby they can empathically join together, so the problem becomes an "it" instead of a "him" or "her."

Therapist's formulation. "First, I would like to review the ground we've covered so far. In the first sessions, we reviewed the history of your relationship, how you met, and your own family backgrounds. We also looked closely at how each of you thought the problem between you started. I want to thank both of you for your honesty and openness up to this point. I certainly have no way of being helpful without your truthfulness. Also, no matter where things go from here, I want to commend both of you on your commitment to each other; the fact that you both still hope to make things work despite your difficult circumstances is a tribute to the strength of your relationship.

"Now let's look at how things have gotten to be the way they are. Let's start from the fact that each of you was attracted to the other for some qualities that were similar but some that were quite different than your own. Franco, you saw in Maria and her family a stability that was unlike your own experience. Your mother has been divorced four times, but you saw in Maria someone who would be extremely responsible. You knew she would work hard to provide for her family and would be super-conscientious. Her father was able to help you both out financially when you were younger, and that allowed you to buy a home, and now you're at the point where you can afford a nicer place. Maria, for you Franco was confident, caring, a confidante, and someone who was his own person—unique and not ashamed of whom he was. He appreciated what your father accomplished, but he could stand up for himself, too. None of these issues was a major hassle in the early part of your marriage. However, when the gambling got out of control, things changed. Out of necessity, Maria took charge of many family responsibilities. You both agreed that she needed to have total control over the finances: your checking and savings accounts, retirement fund, paying bills, budgeting, and so forth. Franco's role in these matters diminished."

Postgambling effects. "But those weren't the only areas that he saw his responsibilities and control lessened. He began to believe that he was no longer needed, and being close in a relationship for Franco means feeling needed. He looked around and saw that this competent, intelligent woman that he was thrilled to know early on was now totally autonomous in his mind. You both even discussed a sperm donor at one point to get pregnant, thereby eliminating even his biological paternity. To Franco, it seemed like Maria was in charge of everything that mattered even going to church. At the time, Maria was working harder and harder. It seemed to Franco that there was no time for the relationship—seldom having downtime, rarely going out alone, and almost never taking vacations. But Maria was stunned by what Franco's gambling had cost the two of you financially. She realized that if she didn't take control quickly economic disaster would strike. Many of the areas she took control of naturally flowed from regulating the finances. Whom you bought gifts for, how much you spent, and how often you went out became intricately tied up with the budget. Maria felt that this was a tremendous burden that she shouldered alone. Her family knew about the gambling problem, but she did not want to go into details with them because she wanted them to respect Franco. Her father had a good relationship with him, and she didn't want to endanger it. Sure, Maria was working extra hard. But your goals together had always been that she would work hard early in the marriage and by paying her dues accumulate substantial savings to be a stay-at-home mom for several years. This was something both of you valued, but your savings took a hit from the gambling, and the only way to achieve that goal was for her to work extra hard. Which leads us finally to Franco's relationship with Rita. Superficially, there could not be a greater contrast between Rita and Maria, yet the one thing that the relationship provided for Franco was a feeling of being needed. Certainly, Rita is extremely needy. Naturally, for Maria this relationship is deeply hurtful and leads her to conclude that once again Franco has let her down. She feels her former confidante is no longer trustworthy, and with his return to gambling she needs to be even more independent."

Polarization vs. acceptance. "I think it's easy to see how each of you tried to find a way out of this situation. Each of you tried to change the other. Maria, you wanted to count on Franco but felt you had to take control of things; Franco, you wanted to be your own person and feel needed, but you began doing that by gambling and developing an attachment to another woman. When each of you tried to get your needs satisfied, this started a vicious cycle of demanding change and digging your heels in. I want to emphasize that there's absolutely nothing wrong with the needs each of you has described. How each of you described your need for closeness and control is legitimate. As far as I know, none of your needs is against the Ten Commandments. On the other hand, probably neither of you would want to fight to the death defending your needs to the extreme. Maria, you've already described how burdensome and lonely being in control is. Franco, you've described how guilty and confused you feel about your other relationship. What we can begin to do here in our sessions together is pay attention to how this formulation, which I've written out for both of you, affects your interactions. I'm not going to tell you which changes, if any, you should make; but perhaps if you step back a little you will each see what you are doing to try to change the other person, and what the other is doing to try to change you. That perspective may help you be a little more understanding and accepting of each other, and *then* you may want to consider changes."

Questioning the couple. "In fact, if things were to improve between the two of you, what changes might you personally have to make, ones that you would have to take responsibility for?" Franco volunteered that certainly he had to stop seeing Rita; although he was confused emotionally about seeing her, he knew in his head it was a bad thing. And, even though he could not promise he would stop seeing her today, he knew he had to do it if he wanted to save his marriage. Maria admitted she was so focused on trying to have a baby that she hadn't heard Franco. She knew that controlling things worked well for her but realized it was unreasonable to decide everything in their relationship."

Following the formulation, the therapist points out that they would be paying close attention to four kinds of therapeutic conversations (Jacobson & Christensen, 1996, p. 110). First, they would regularly discuss the differences between

Maria and Franco as noted in the formulation. This continual reflection reinforced their standing back and viewing the problem as an "it." Second, they would discuss upcoming events in light of their differences to prime themselves to anticipate potential conflicts. Third, therapist and couple together would process recent negative events in light of this formulation. Empathic joining tends to diminish the level of negative feeling surrounding unpleasant exchanges. Finally, processing positive events reinforces how each couple actively contributed to the experience through tolerance and acceptance of the other's difference.

IBCT's advantage in this case and others is how it can incorporate both gambling and other significant relationship issues into a coherent whole. Even if the therapist has no interest in working exclusively within an IBCT framework, the outline provided here is fruitful for the issues that arise in gambling recovery. IBCT also provides a means to help spouses manage anger that regularly wells up even in relationships where partners are committed to recovery. We cannot delineate in this brief exposition all the potential uses of IBCT in couples work with pathological gambling, but interested readers may find in the references other useful strategies, such as looking for underlying positive emotions in the hard, negative emotions. Before leaving IBCT altogether, I have adopted one other technique in couples therapy for pathological gambling. This is known as "disarmament," a strategy discussed in Chapter 8.

In IBCT, once each partner clearly understands their own and their partners' expectations, each tells what they are likely to do to set off the other's hot buttons. This is a playful exercise with the serious goal of developing distance from one's emotional triggers. I have adapted this by inviting pathological gamblers to share all their "tricks of the trade" if they wanted to deceive their partners and resume gambling. They tell their partners what exactly they should look for if the gambling resumed. These include personality features (e.g., becoming distant, or acting too caring) and behavioral characteristics (spending a long time reading the sports page, increased number of phone conversations, etc.). Before inviting the pathological gambler to disclose this information, I inquire as to how motivated he or she is to stop gambling. When they say they are fully committed, I ask if they would be willing to share all their trade secrets that allow them to deceive others so as to close off as many avenues to relapse as possible. Some initially hesitate, but usually the logic of this approach convinces them to be open with their partners. The disclosures often reveal many unknown features to partners and therapists alike. It helps partners to gain self-confidence in knowing more precisely what to look for should the partner relapse. It also provides the couple with a database for communication between them when the partner notices a problematic reaction in the other (see Worksheet 8.3).

WORKING WITH FAMILY MEMBERS ALONE

Conjoint therapy at times is unfeasible. Some patients have no desire to stop gambling. Others stop gambling but choose not to work on the relationship, and some partners feel that their primary need is to work on themselves. Family members may seek therapy in such instances. This section explores therapeutic strategies that would directly help family members themselves. It also assumes that the family members' emotional stability can at least indirectly benefit the pathological gambler. A frequent issue that brings a spouse or partner into therapy is seeking help with the decision to stay in or leave the relationship. In those situations, a major goal, in addition to helping the partner sort out his or her decision, is *the empowerment of the family member*. This position assumes that no one can meaningfully decide to maintain a relationship when they perceive themselves as having no choice. A typical scenario is for a wife to enter treatment when the family is essentially bankrupt. She has no information about their financial situation, has potential tax problems, and is unemployed with small children. In these cases, the first goal is to enhance autonomy by developing financial and emotional independence for her and the children.

Coping with Negative Emotions

In this section, we use cognitive processing to assist intimate partners and other family members in managing extreme feelings that arise. Outlined below are several common core themes. However, these themes are best *elicited*, rather than *imposed*, by the therapist.

Anxiety is normative in pathological gambling families. In our culture, money remains the means to life stability at the level of survival and plays an important role in people's social identification. Sudden loss not only causes apprehension about the future; it also strikes at a person's sense of self. Children who once thought of themselves as secure now wonder if parents can meet their needs. Children may ask, "Mommy, are we poor now?" Intimate partners describe a trauma-like numbness when the financial devastation becomes clear. They fear for themselves, their children, and the future. Older couples may react with even greater shock given the lack of time to recoup their losses or if on a fixed income.

One set of strategies involves *action* strategies. Chapter 12 recommended problem-solving under the principle that it's better to throw a bucket of water on a fire than to process your feelings about it. Similarly, the environmental management strategies discussed in Chapters 8 and 13 will also lead to enhanced self-efficacy. A second set of strategies helps people manage the worry itself so that it doesn't spiral out of control. These strategies fall into two types. Worksheet 10.1 illustrates a cognitive processing method that partners can use to manage fears or worries. Clients examine how they will cope with their current concern to determine whether they are: (a) over-predicting negative consequences, or (b) viewing the situation as a catastrophe they cannot cope with. It is a straightforward cognitive approach wherein clients list evidence for and against the idea and also concretely examine their resources for managing the situation.

A second method aims at eliminating ruminating over the worry. Perhaps they've tried cognitive processing, but it has not turned off the worry. In this case, sheer exposure by writing out the worries and staring them down for an extended period often reduces the duration and intensity of the intrusive thoughts. A related approach is to put off thinking about the problem until a set time in the future (worry time). The essence of exposure is to list all the worst possible aspects and read it over and over. Clients can also read the worries into an audiotape or into their computers and replay the worry for long periods (e.g., 30–45 minutes). Writing out the worries and other exposure techniques are particularly useful when people cannot sleep because of ruminating (Pennebaker, 1990).

Anger is often so dominant an emotion that an extended discussion is in order. Anger normally occurs when people feel taken advantage of—a legitimate reaction in pathological gambling families. In my experience, however, anger lingers in pathological gambling families well into recovery to a greater extent than noticed in other types of addiction. Based on clinical observations, hanging onto anger seems to serve several functions. Letting go of anger would make it too easy on the pathological gambler. "If I let him off the hook he gets away with everything." Guided discovery often unearths the belief that family members feel obligated to be the punishing agent. Sometimes they resent the patient joining GA or developing a belief in the disease model of pathological gambling. They believe that seeing pathological gambling as a disease exonerates the patient. "I was just sick" is what the family members think they are hearing, and they find this deeply disturbing. They feel the gambler's getting all the attention. "We're the ones who are the real victims," they protest.

A second reason for hanging onto anger is a realistic one. With no guarantee that a relapse will not occur, forgiveness may not make sense when one is in a position to be re-victimized (Exline & Baumeister, 2000). For some family members, then, anger provides motivation to keep up their guard and not be as naive as the first time. Anger can also provide powerless people with the energy needed for their own empowerment. The substantial losses family members experience also contribute to anger. The list is endless: material possessions, confidence in the future, trust in how the world operates, trust in the person you've committed your life to, your social circle with its forms of entertainment, and your ability to provide security for your children. Two extremes should be avoided. The first is the "let-it-all-hang-out" school of therapy. Based on a "hydraulic" notion that anger must be expressed so the person does not suffer emotional harm, some advocate repeated efforts at "getting in touch with your anger." Empirical evidence points to the deleterious nature of anger reinforcement both physically and emotionally (Tavris, 1989; Tice & Baumeister, 1993). The second extreme is premature attempts at forgiveness, as the following case illustrates.

> Miriam's husband revealed to her a month ago that he had lost a third of their retirement savings gambling in the stock market on options. Recently retired herself, she saw little hope of recouping their losses despite the fact that Ben continued to work. She was paying a high price for her constant rage in the form of continual migraines and intestinal upset. Around her High Holy Days, she stopped in the synagogue reading room and found several pamphlets on forgiveness. She escaped for 3 days to the mountains to read and reflect on the future. The pamphlets convinced her that to obtain peace of mind she would have to forgive her husband. She called him up, they met, and had a long discussion around forgiveness and reconciliation. Ben, who had been most contrite all along, thought he saw evidence of peace returning to his wife. After returning home, they received a holiday letter from friends, who talked about how they were settling into retirement and about to embark on their dream journey to Israel and other sites on an around-the-world tour. Realizing that she could never fulfill her similar dreams, Miriam cried uncontrollably for the next 2 hours. She felt like a miserable failure for succumbing to her rage against her husband.

Miriam's experience demonstrates that, although anger damages people emotionally, the motivation for reducing anger should not become another source of defeat. Miriam believed she could turn off her anger like a switch by focusing on forgiveness. Although there are emotional benefits from forgiveness (McCullough *et al.*, 2000), it is not helpful if the person feels worse about her inability to forgive. Miriam unintentionally re-victimized herself. Given all these reasons for hanging onto anger, coping with it requires clinical acumen. As in most therapeutic endeavors, awareness must be the first goal. Guided discovery can elicit the motivational sources for people's anger. Anger can diminish when people gain insight into its source. Eventually, when Miriam saw she was taking responsibility for punishing her husband, she came to two conclusions. She already had her hands full cleaning up the gambling mess without taking on added responsibility for meting out punishment. Second, her husband would have to answer to himself for what he did.

Before undertaking any anger reduction interventions, it is essential to clarify motivations for reducing anger. The case of Miriam illustrates how women in particular are vulnerable to attempting therapeutic changes that could reinforce self-defeating beliefs and emotions. Her focus on forgiveness is entirely other-directed in this case. Being a dutiful spouse and religious person required, in her mind, emptying herself of any negative feelings toward her spouse. Yet when the unrealistic nature of this strategy became evident, she saw herself as a failure. To avoid re-victimization, it seems much wiser to proceed by asking the family member, "How will it benefit *you* to decrease your anger? What would *you* get out of it in terms of making your life better?" If the client can answer this in a positive way, the therapist can both prevent re-victimization and ensure a positive motivation. This also gets across the central point in working with family members: you are the primary focus here. Too great a focus on the welfare of the pathological gambler will blind you to your own needs and consume the energy required to manage your affairs.

Interventions for each of the core themes described above, therefore, proceed somewhat differently. For those who believe they need to be the punishing agent, a series of questions may help shift perspective. "Is that a necessary role for you? Is it a realistic one? Is carrying out that role fit in with the kind of person you see yourself as?" Occasionally, therapists may discover that a partner's chief interest, even years after the event, is to literally dance on the person's grave. In such cases, when no incongruence of values exists for the family member, the only approach is to have the person examine the costs and benefits of remaining vindictive. Even that approach may yield a continuing desire to remain angry, and therapists can only point out the cost of this approach.

People who believe that anger is their only source of energy for what they have to do may be invited to explore this belief further, answering such questions as "Can you think of some accomplishment or life goal that had some motivation *other than* anger as its driving force for you?" People may benefit from a cost/benefit analysis as a motivational enhancement tool (see Chapter 7). Intervention strategies related to not being taken advantage of are more complicated. One strategy that can avoid the extremes discussed above can emphasize the health and emotional benefits from forgiveness and that forgiveness may be congruent with the client's spiritual outlook. However, client and clinician must be aware that it is not possible to sweep powerful emotions under the rug, and even forgiveness will not immediately eliminate negative feelings toward the person. Here again, the client should tell the therapist why giving up anger is in the *client's* best interest.

Those who choose to work on anger reduction should also explore ways to prevent being taken advantage of. Some questions could include the following: "It seems like anger keeps you on your toes but is it possible to have some other reason for staying alert?" "Could logic and planning be one way to prevent gambling setbacks?" Once the client agrees that anger is not a necessary emotion to stay alert, then the cognitive processing strategies suggested here could come into play.

Anger related to intense feelings of loss represents a challenge because such processing often transforms anger to sadness. People stay angry because it's less painful than feeling sad. "If I let go of my anger," reasons the family member (not usually consciously), "then I will be overwhelmed by the loss I've suffered." Rather than trying to challenge the client about the truth of this insight, the better strategy is reflective listening with large doses of empathy statements around his losses. Gradually, clients develop safety within the trusting therapeutic atmosphere to disclose their pain over these losses. In this way, clients learn that anger is a natural reaction, but the greater pain is over the many losses.

The final core theme in negative emotional responding for family members is one related to self-blame for ending up in their situation. Self-blame can cover a wide territory. It ranges from the specific—"I should have noticed something wrong"—to the general—"Why did I marry this person?" Some family members blame themselves for being unaware; others for not taking action when there were warning signs. The degree of blame also varies. One may feel some responsibility; others may feel totally responsible. Clients respond well to reading the diagnostic criteria for pathological gambling (Chapter 5). Here the therapist emphasizes that lying and deception are part of the disorder's diagnosis. It is even useful to point out that the criterion mentions lying to one's therapist, indicating that the pathological gambler can deceive even supposed experts. A discussion around deception and lying reduces family members' over-responsibility.

When this intervention is insufficient, more formal cognitive processing may help. Using a standard cognitive therapy worksheet (i.e., Worksheet 10.1), Phyllis analyzed her belief that she was the major contributor to her husband's disastrous gambling history. Her reasons for believing this were: "If I had been more loving, he wouldn't have needed to gamble. If I hadn't been lazy and let him take care of the finances, we wouldn't be in this situation. These things don't happen to competent people." Phyllis examined the evidence for and against these beliefs. For the first belief, she noted that her husband divorced his first wife *before* he began gambling, so marital dissatisfaction did not *require* that he gamble. In the second instance, it was true she had given Sam free reign of the finances. But was her explanation correct that she was lazy? In her discussion with her therapist, Phyllis revealed that finances were his *only* household responsibility and that she turned them over only when she was exhausted from doing all the cleaning, working a full-time job, and having primary responsibility for the children. With regard to the notion that these things didn't happen to competent people, Phyllis admitted that some of her GamAnon peers struck her as being quite competent—one was a corporate executive whose spouse was a pathological gambler.

Finally, when processing realistic events, such as not responding to warning signs, cognitive therapy invites people to examine the *character* conclusions they make about themselves. Even if they were asleep at the wheel, does this make them bad? Furthermore, does this make them deserving of the treatment they received? Did this *make* the pathological gambler lose control? And even if somewhat culpable, on a scale of evil how does their behavior compare to, say, Hitler?

This section makes clear that helping family members is an important therapeutic goal for both pathological gambling patients and family members themselves. Even when there is little hope for the gambling patient, therapy can enrich the family and open their eyes to additional life choices.

COUNTERTRANSFERENCE ISSUES

Before leaving this topic, a few words are in order about what makes family work a challenge—the issue of countertransference. Countertransferential feelings and attitudes can impede our effectiveness in working with family members and gambling patients, thus warranting periodic self-reflection. In no particular order, I have listed some of the common themes observed from supervising gambling counselors.

Anger at pathological gambling patients arises when therapists see the devastating effects of the disorder. This anger may lead to colluding with the family's desire for revenge. Patients' narcissism affects therapists differently. Sometimes it is repulsive, and therapists are inclined to show clients they are not so special. In working with gambling patients in front of families, therapists might be inclined to demonstrate their superiority or put down the patient. Sometimes narcissism intimidates the therapist. The first statement of Alex, the patient in the precontemplation stage described in Chapter 7, was, "So what is it you can do for me?" In these cases, some therapists try to prove just how competent they are and thus afford patients the expertise they feel entitled to.

When therapists feel strongly negative toward pathological gambling patients, they may encourage separation or divorce. Despite the pain and suffering involved, many families choose to stay together and therapists may feel frustrated by this decision. Finally, when patients cannot maintain abstinence, it is natural to question one's competence as a therapist. We may want to terminate therapy because it seems like it's going nowhere, or we may want to stop seeing families because it's upsetting to see their pain. Therapeutic support is needed for both family and pathological gamblers at these times.

Not all therapist reactions are negative. They may not only feel compassion for pathological gamblers and their families; they may also feel a great deal of attraction. Many gamblers have interesting, even entertaining personalities. Their lives can even be more exciting than the therapist's! They marry accomplished and exciting people. Their children are often bright, verbal, and suffering. Therapists can become quite fond of them and their families, and be motivated to help. In itself, positive attraction can help therapists persist, and this is beneficial as long as they monitor inclinations to cross boundaries or form inappropriate therapeutic alliances.

Spirituality, Virtue, and Character

A Model for Therapist Collaboration in Long-Term Growth

RATIONALE FOR CHAPTER

Multiple forces necessitate therapists developing an understanding of the role spirituality plays in the well-being of pathological gambling patients. In the 12-step tradition, spirituality has a venerable history (Kurtz, 1999), and is at the heart of its various manifestations, including GA. From the therapist's perspective, spirituality represents a language system for many clients who participate in mutual-help programs. Spirituality is a metaphor that relates to the client's worldview, and metaphors are crucial motivators that advance healing (Meichenbaum & Fong, 1993). Therapists who remain ignorant of this language system have less access to their client's inner world of meaning (Rogers, 1951), fail to take advantage of these powerful metaphors, and leave barriers to empathic understanding.

Second, ethical demands have increased in the past decade to recognize the important role diversity plays in clinical management. The standards of every mental health profession require its members to pay heed to how diversity influences assessment and treatment. Clinicians are not always aware that ethical codes identify religion as a form of diversity along with ethnicity and gender variables. In short, ethical standards tell us that religion is a multicultural issue. The DSM itself provides an additional perspective on diversity. Since 1994, the DSM has emphasized the crucial role understanding diversity plays in the diagnostic process (APA, 1994, Appendix C). Diversity influences diagnosis in at least three ways: (a) prevalence and manifestation of various disorders within certain cultural groups, (b) how the differences between client and therapist may impede accurate symptom understanding and diagnosis, and (c) how cultural differences may affect the course of treatment itself. The DSM requires clinicians to attend to these issues in each assessment and note their potential influence. With ethical codes and the DSM focusing clinician attention on religious diversity, clinicians who fail to document the role of spirituality for the individual are open to accusations of ignoring professional standards.

A third reason for including issues related to spirituality, virtue, and character is the link between self-regulation and well-being. As emphasized throughout this book, self-regulation has many benefits for psychological functioning. Research indicates that self-regulation is related to school and professional achievement, marital stability, longevity, well-being, and physical health. Each is an important marker of addiction recovery and desirable in itself for emotional stability. Although spirituality is not an essential ingredient for working on character or virtue, the two can be integrally linked. Many derive their motivation for good conduct from an overarching spiritual perspective that should facilitate its attainment.

A fourth reason for including spirituality is that the complexity of the issue requires providing guidelines to clinicians for navigating its promises and pitfalls. Religion and spirituality are such vast topics that no single person could hope to bring a comprehensive understanding to the total range of cultural issues across all institutions and spiritual systems. In the United States alone, one source lists 1,730 "primary religious bodies" (Paloutzian, 1996, p. 7). Primary religious bodies refers to denominations, churches, or sects. This does not include the many variations in other countries of major groups such as Buddhism, Hinduism, Islam, or smaller New Age groups in the United States and elsewhere. Only the proverbial genius or madman would assert having a comprehensive understanding of the potential multicultural issues across all groups.

This puts the clinician in a dilemma. On the one hand, ethical codes require assessing diversity issues as they pertain to religion or spirituality. On the other hand, therapists face a bewildering array of religious or spiritual manifestations. The therapist may not only have a dissimilar religious background from the client; he may not possess a sympathetic view of religion generally. Psychologists as a group are not representative of the United States population as a whole in terms of membership in religious organizations. They are more likely to view themselves as agnostic, atheist, or nonbelieving than the general public. They are also, in the words of sociology, "religious apostates," that is, they are more likely than the general public to have left the religion of their family of origin (Bergin, 1991). These differences do not suggest that psychologists or any group of mental health professionals are unable to be empathic and nonjudgmental, but they point to what one psychologist has labeled a "religiosity gap" between clients and therapists (Bergin, 1991). Such differences can fuel countertransference and require exploration.

Finally, for the reasons cited to this point, a good case can be made for *avoiding* religious and spiritual topics in therapy. Mental health professionals, according to this argument, are not trained as pastors, spiritual directors, or religious advisors and ought not operate outside their own area of competence. Professional ethics require us to "first do no harm." Religious or spiritual interventions are ill advised by persons without training. If therapists are to err, they are better off committing sins of omission than commission. A respected alcoholism clinical researcher, Barbara McCrady (1998), made a persuasive case for this position. In discussing whether therapists should intervene in a client's spiritual framework, she questioned to which spirituality should one direct the client. Should it be toward the client's, the therapist's, or some third "more adaptive" spirituality? Her question raises the equally compelling possibility that far more damage could occur from loose-cannon spiritual interventions than respectful silence.

This chapter attempts, therefore, to assist clinicians by providing a model that can locate client's spiritual concerns within some type of multidimensional religious space (Miller, 1998) from which therapists can feel knowledgeable and comfortable about their clinical decisions. It does not propose to make therapists experts in religious studies or change their occupation to spiritual advisors. It provides a model that can explain *how* and *whether* a client's specific spiritual issue falls within the purview of a mental health professional's competence.

To accomplish this, the chapter has four goals:

1. From the perspective of clinical science and practice to define the terms religion and spirituality.

2. Provide a generic model to understand as broad an array of religious and spiritual experience as possible, thereby giving clinicians an anchor-point to incorporate future descriptions of these phenomena.

3. Describe which aspects fall under the purview of clinical practice.

4. With this foundation, make clinical applications to the more common spiritual issues seen in pathological gambling recovery.

RELIGION AND SPIRITUALITY: MODEL AND DEFINITION

The psychology of religion has made significant advances in developing empirical methods to enhance our understanding of this universal human disposition. To date, the field has not settled on a single definition of religion or an agreed-upon model. Nevertheless, there is consensus that religion and spirituality represent a multidimensional construct that includes cognitive, affective, experiential, motivational, and behavioral features (Hood *et al.*, 1996; Pargament, 1997). Although this chapter could have employed any of the models proposed in the aforementioned reviews, I have chosen a phenomenological model for understanding religion and spirituality that also employs a multidimensional approach (Cannon, 1996). This model, taken from the field of religious studies, catalogues the full range of religious or spiritual experience into six aspects. This generic model allows one to anchor disparate experiences into a longitude and latitude within multidimensional religious space (Miller, 1998). It maintains neutrality about the value of any particular religious system—an essential requirement for clinicians functioning in a pluralistic society. Religions differ from each other not only in terms of their content regarding these six ways but also by the degree of emphasis they give to any one domain. As a result, we can more clearly define religion and spirituality and point out the clinical interface.

The fundamental assumption behind this model is that all religions have a perspective about what constitutes *ultimate reality*. Ultimate reality emerges within a religious tradition when it grapples with the problem of meaning or, more specifically, the problem of evil (Cannon, 1996, p. 27). Meaning tends to be a problem only in its absence (Baumeister, 1991b). Each way of being religious takes a slightly different approach to ultimate reality. The model does not assume that this ultimate reality exists, is the same for each religion, or represents the common quest for all religions. Although each way is distinct, they are interrelated and often difficult to distinguish in their concrete expression.

Six Ways of Being Religious

We begin by briefly describing each of the six ways. From this overview, we attempt to define religion and spirituality before exploring how therapists can use this model clinically.

The Way of Sacred Rites

Religions use various symbol systems in ritualized ways in order to orient themselves to ultimate reality. "All religious rituals symbolically make reference to the *realities* found within the *other world* of the religion and represent some kind of acknowledgment of, interaction with, or participation in those *realities*" (Cannon, 1996, p. 54; emphasis in original). These symbol systems include art, sacred rites, architecture, religious garb, and the like.

The Way of Right Action

Religions typically have codes of conduct, but unlike conduct prescribed when orienting oneself to the *other world* (way of sacred rites), right action is oriented toward *this world* according to the requirements of ultimate reality. Is it an eye for an eye, or turn the other cheek? Are divorce or polygamy permitted? Should I give to the poor, or should they help themselves? All religions typically maintain that their codes of conduct represent "*the way things are ultimately supposed to be*" (Cannon, 1996, p. 56; emphasis in original). In other words, when we act properly, we do so not for the sake of the social order or to ensure domestic tranquility, but we are conforming ourselves objectively with the ultimate principles of existence.

The Way of Devotion

This way emphasizes the affective component in being religious. "The way of devotion specifically involves cultivation of a personal relationship with *ultimate reality*" (Cannon, 1996, p. 58; emphasis in original). In this relationship, people may feel in awe and dependent on ultimate reality (Otto, 1950) and desire an experience of trust and surrender. For practical purposes, the ways of right action and devotion will constitute the majority of what passes for spirituality in the therapeutic context.

The Way of Mystical Quest

People who pursue this path seek to move ultimate reality from the back burner of unconscious experience to that of direct consciousness. It involves methods and meditation forms for people who want to experience ultimate reality directly for the sake of union with it. People on this quest often lead ascetic lives, believing attachments to material and egocentric desires impede union. Such individuals have left lively historical records that are masterpieces of self-regulation strategies that are still instructive today. It would be unusual for pathological gambling patients in the early stages of recovery to have an interest in this spiritual dimension.

The Way of Shamanic Mediation

From the perspective of Western culture, this represents the most unusual expression of religious experience. This way operates when people feel totally overwhelmed by life's challenges, for example, major illness, destitution, severe trauma or loss. In shamanic mediation, an individual or religious leader attempts to make contact with the *unique powers of the other world* in order to rectify the person's lot. Two practices that persons in our culture may have familiarity with involve religious healing and exorcism. In the first case, the healer or sufferer attempts to harness the power of the ultimate reality to remove the sufferer's physical or emotional distress. Something similar happens in exorcism, except that the exorcist mediates the power of ultimate reality to force out the personalized evil force (e.g., the devil) believed responsible for the suffering.

The Way of Reasoned Inquiry

Each religious or spiritual system assumes the existence of an ultimate reality toward which the other five ways of being religious are oriented. In the way of reasoned inquiry, people use various cognitive methods to understand the existence, nature, and form of their ultimate reality. Primary religious bodies codify these cognitive exercises into *theologies* or some other systematic form of reasoning. Less formal spiritual systems also engage in this process to the degree that they use intellect to comprehend the ultimate nature of things or discursive reasoning to arrive at truth. Completely private, individual spiritualities that are not socially shared also participate in reasoned inquiry to the degree the individual engages her intellect in the process.

Interrelationship of the Six Ways of Being Religious

Several features of this model require comment. The six ways of being religious are interrelated. A particular religion/spirituality may participate in all six ways. If I come to understand the nature of ultimate reality (inquiry), I may then be motivated to want to relate to it (devotion), and harness its energy (shamanic mediation), and so on. Various religions/spiritual systems may emphasize or deemphasize a particular way of being religious. A Quaker prayer meeting looks dramatically different from an Eastern Orthodox Easter liturgical service (sacred rites), yet each is oriented toward a sacred space. People may be disposed to certain religious/spiritual forms on the basis of their individual personalities. A study of personality factors in different groups of Christian clergy found higher rates of obsessive-compulsive personality indicators in Roman Catholic clergy compared to Methodist and Lutheran, whereas the Protestant clergy were higher on histrionic indicators (Hoolighan, 1991).

Religion and Spirituality Distinguished

With these six ways of being religious as our backdrop, it is now somewhat easier to distinguish these phenomena. Religion is an organized social system regarding ultimate reality with a body of beliefs and practices. It differs from communism in that religion's ultimate realities involve *other worlds*, whereas for communism and other "isms" ultimate reality exists exclusively in this world.

Spirituality, as Miller and Thoresen noted (1999), is like personality—it resides in the person. Popular writers in the addiction self-help field and elsewhere are almost evangelistic in their fervor for separating religion from spirituality. Their motivation for this emphasis is sincere, for they recognize that many addicts grew up in households where religion represented "toxic faith," so that any mention of organized religion triggers avoidance. The danger in this emphasis, however, is twofold. First, it may lead people in recovery to start their spiritual quests needlessly from ground zero, when reacquaintance with their own experienced tradition may be adequate. Second, it may privatize spiritual experience and sever it from the benefits derived from social connections in a believing community (Pargament, 1997).

Therefore, I prefer a more integrated approach to spirituality and religion. Spirituality represents the individual's attempt to relate to his or her ultimate reality in the six ways outlined above. A person's spirituality is religious if the ultimate reality constitutes an "other world" and/or if it follows the tradition of a primary religious body. The puzzle is what to call meaning-systems that represent "this world" (e.g., nature, environment, an all-connecting force). Some would prefer that these meaning-systems not be called spiritual; others advocate the opposite. For our purposes, we do not need to convert clients to our definitions. We can allow clients to call it whatever they choose to. We need to ascertain as clinicians how the person's spirituality *functions*. Is it capable of being a force for growth? Can it lead to transcending their impulses for immediate gratification? If yes, then it has therapeutic potential.

In summary, then, spirituality is a multidimensional cognitive, affective, experiential, motivational, and behavioral cluster of practices directed toward understanding and relating to ultimate reality, with ultimate reality usually involving an "other world" in addition to encompassing "this world." Spirituality may or may not exist in the context of organized religion, but participants in organized religion engage in spiritual practices to some degree. A related concept in spirituality and psychology of religion is spiritual transcendence (Piedmont, 1999). "Spiritual transcendence refers to the capacity of individuals to stand outside of their immediate sense of time and place to view life from a larger, more objective perspective. This transcendent perspective is one in which a person sees a fundamental unity underlying the diverse strivings of nature and finds a binding with others that cannot be severed, not even by death" (Piedmont, 1999, p. 988). Piedmont has operationalized this construct into three components through his Spiritual Transcendence Scale: universality, prayer fulfillment, and connectedness. The concept of spiritual transcendence may have clinical relevance, for it represents a motivational aspect for moving beyond oneself and one's limited immediate horizon. As we shall see below, the 12-step tradition sees moving beyond oneself as the crucial enterprise in addiction recovery. It may also be relevant to self-regulation in that self-regulation failures have been referred to as failures in transcendence (Baumeister *et al.*, 1994). In other words, a spiritual frame of reference may decrease impulsivity by orienting people to realities beyond some immediate desire for gratification. Piedmont also reviews empirical evidence that lends support to the idea that spirituality may represent a personality trait.

THERAPEUTIC INTERFACE WITH SPIRITUALITY

The Therapist and the Ways of Being Religious

Given this model for understanding religious-spiritual experience, it is possible to clarify now what falls properly within the scope of therapy and what does not. The ways of sacred rites and shamanic mediation are relevant at the assessment level. People's level of involvement in these experiences contributes to understanding their culture. Participation in sacred rites identifies significant social groups for the client. These groups may have potential as supports or buffers against psychological symptoms. Depressed, lonely people may feel better when others in their religious group reach out to them. Assessment is required, on the other hand, when these groups represent significant sources of conflict or suffering as recognized in the DSM code "Religious or Spiritual Problem" (APA, 1994, p. 685).

Following such assessment, the implications for the client's participation in religious activities should be discussed respecting the client's viewpoint. When it appears that significant conflict exists, the impact on the client is discussed along with various remedies. Rather than challenging the client's viewpoint, a respectful approach is to suggest setting up behavioral experiments that allow the client to evaluate several outcomes. Clients could evaluate participating and not participating, participating with group A and with group B, participating with outlook A and outlook B, and so on. Although spirituality is intensely personal and sensitive, so are many other value-laden topics that therapy tackles, for example, politics, sex, and divorce. We can use the same respectful strategies for spirituality that we use for these topics as well.

Shamanic mediation involves evaluation as a multicultural issue at a minimum. A cancer victim's expectations for visiting a New Age healer rather than, or in addition to, receiving chemotherapy merits discussion. Similarly, the meaning of parents taking their misbehaving 6 year old to an exorcist warrants dialogue. It is outside the scope of the therapist's competence, in my opinion, to render judgments on these issues or to recommend them; but it is certainly within the scope to explore their implications for the client's emotional well-being.

The ways of devotion and mysticism require assessment as well. Pathological gamblers who participate in organized religion will commonly have devotional practices. They often blend with their sacred rites various practices, depending on the denomination. But people may also have private devotional practices. Assessment is useful because many find that these practices relieve anxiety or depression during stress and suffering. Mysticism is uncommon in my experience with pathological gambling. In treating clergy with gambling problems (Ciarrocchi & Wicks, 2000), I have seen an occasional person with a mystical bent, but only after considerable time in recovery. I would suggest evaluating these practices similarly to the ways of devotion.

The way of understanding is less often a topic in therapy than sacred rites, devotion, or conduct. Assessing a person's philosophical or theological viewpoint is relevant when it appears linked to cognitive, affective, behavioral, or motivational impairment. A gambler who believes she must confess openly to someone she stole money from could bring serious personal harm to herself. Discussion might lead to alternative choices that could honor the spirit of the rule. From experience in treating people with religious obsessions (Ciarrocchi, 1995a,b, 1998), it is apparent that people often misconstrue their religious group's theology, thereby causing considerable suffering. When a therapist suspects that this is the case, consultation with a religious leader from the client's denomination is advisable. Once again, as suggested above, direct challenging of the faith-system is unethical, in my opinion, for it is both (a) outside the competence of most mental health professionals, and (b) intrusive. Rather, the strategy of behavioral experiments described previously appears less invasive, yet allows for a method to consider alternative faith-viewpoints.

The major thrust of this chapter, then, is on the way of right action. Just as motivational enhancement incorporates client values (Chapter 7), values define behavior that is deemed moral. People with or without a spiritual viewpoint acknowledge morality. I may not believe in God, but I will condemn slavery. Pathological gambling often leads people to engage in immoral behavior whether defined by their own or society's standards. Recovery involves a resettlement, so to speak, into the land of morality. Most spiritual traditions maintain that a lifestyle that is indifferent to certain moral standards (e.g., continual lying) probably corrodes moral conduct in other areas as well (e.g., sensitivity to helping others). If virtue is a skill and the virtues have unity, as the ancient Greeks maintained, pathological gambling often causes atrophy of several virtues and weakens the ability to develop them. Restoring moral behavior thus becomes a relevant therapeutic goal both for personal self-regulation and as the foundation for participating in the social community.

From this point on, we rely on the term *spirituality* to refer to the individual's attempts to relate to their ultimate reality whether it derives from a formal religious tradition or not. In this section, we provide an orientation toward the six ways of being spiritual for the therapeutic context.

Spiritual Assessment

Assessment provides the foundation for any therapeutic interface with the person's spirituality. By assessment, I am not referring to formal psychometric instruments, although they are not precluded. A huge array of instruments exists for measuring various aspects of religious and spiritual behavior (Hill & Hood, 1999, with a second volume in preparation). Some have excellent psychometric features, but no single measure encompasses the six ways of being religious. Measures of spirituality have two inherent problems at this stage in their development. The first is to what degree the measures overlap with each other and the second is the degree to which they represent the "religification" of nonreligious psychological variables, for example, personality (Piedmont, 1998). Also, measures that are useful for research purposes often have little clinical utility. For these reasons, the wisest course, at this time, is for each therapist to conduct an individual clinical assessment loosely based on the six ways of being spiritual.

I have provided a series of brief open-ended questions to explore these areas. The clinician can choose questions that are relevant in a given case and follow up on areas of ambiguity. This chapter assumes that spirituality is not the first therapeutic focus in pathological gambling recovery. Spiritual issues are explored in-depth once the crisis is over and the client desires to look toward longer-term goals. Practically speaking, then, clinicians may already know a great deal about their clients even with respect to their spirituality. Indeed, the initial assessment would have inquired as to the importance of spirituality in the client's life, thereby providing data even at that early point in treatment. The questions are not exhaustive but represent a starting point.

Assessment Questions

1. What role, would you say, spirituality plays in your life?
2. Was this always the case? [if not] How do you feel about this change?
3. What role did it play in the household you grew up in?
4. Is your spirituality part of an organized religious body?
5. Do you attend religious services? How frequently? What do you get out of attending those services?
6. [if person attends religious services] Do you socialize with people in your congregation? How would you feel about increasing your level of social contact with them?
7. Do you pray? In what ways? When and where? Why is it important for you to pray?
8. What kinds of spiritual experiences have you had that you recall as being very powerful? [when client is not clear] For example, feeling a sense of oneness with all the universe, or at harmony with

everyone or everything in the world? Perhaps having a sense that God or a higher power was speaking directly to you. [clarify that these experiences do not arise under the influence of drugs/alcohol]

9. Do you enjoy reading religious or spiritual literature such as the Bible or books to help you feel closer to God? Or your higher power? Can you recall an example?

10. Do you see any connection between your personal moral conduct and your spiritual beliefs? In what ways? Aside from your gambling itself, which character flaws do you believe you have to change? Which virtues do you need to develop to feel better about yourself morally?

11. What effect, if any, did your gambling problem have on your spirituality? In which areas? What, would you say, are your regrets about this?

12. What role, if any, do you think spirituality could play in your recovery process? What kind of changes would you have to make for it to play that role? Would you be interested in using your therapy sessions to keep an eye on your change plan?

13. [for those attending GA] In addition to helping you stay abstinent, how can GA assist you in attaining your spiritual goals? Have you shared this desire with your group, sponsor, or individual members? What would be the best way to involve yourself in GA to attain the necessary support for your spiritual goals?

The questions limit themselves to typical spiritual experience, yet question #8 about powerful spiritual experiences invites clients to share more unusual experience that may fall under the realm of mysticism or shamanic mediation. These questions are neutral to avoid imposing any value judgments about spiritual experience, yet comprehensive enough to meet ethical guidelines for including religious diversity in a multicultural evaluation.

Assessment Conclusions

Following this evaluation, clinicians should have enough data to orient the person's spirituality within the overall treatment plan. Specifically, the evaluation should have accomplished the following goals:

1. Legitimized spirituality as a relevant topic in therapy.
2. Clarified what aspects of the client's spirituality do not fall within the range of the clinician's area of expertise.
3. Identified what aspects of the person's spirituality support gambling recovery.

4. Determined to what degree spirituality can provide motivation for making the required behavioral changes related to recovery. This point may play a crucial role in implementing motivational enhancement strategies (Chapter 7). One of the most powerful motivators for change is the person's value system—yet, I suspect, one that clinicians neglect because of concerns about imposing values. Spirituality can play a vital role motivating people away from self-centeredness and immediate gratification.

Self-Centeredness: The Primary Spiritual Enemy

In the 12-step tradition self-centeredness represents the primary character flaw that motivates addictive behavior. "Selfishness—self-centeredness! That, we think, is the root of our troubles ... [T]he alcoholic is an extreme example of self-will run riot" (AA World Services, 1976, p. 62, cited in Reinert, 1998). From this conceptualization of alcoholic development, the 12-step tradition placed much emphasis on methods to move the individual beyond self-centeredness. At its core is the notion of "surrender." Surrender overcomes self-centeredness in at least two interesting ways. First, the person surrenders to a higher power, acknowledging that she is not the center of the universe but is oriented to a larger ultimate reality. Second, the person surrenders in the sense of admitting powerlessness over drinking and giving up attempts to control the uncontrollable.

From a completely different starting point using the insights of social psychology and historical reflection, excessive self-focus has also been targeted as a major source in self-regulation failure (Baumeister, 1991a, 1997a,b). This analysis starts with the changing nature of the understanding of the self in Western culture from the time of the Renaissance. Up until that point, people largely defined themselves in terms of the social networks and roles that embedded them. With the social changes brought on by scientific, industrial, and religious upheaval, people's roles and social networks became fluid. This created a "crisis" for the self in that it no longer represented a given, and each person must construct what it means to be or have a "self." As a result, modern society is beset with "identity crises" (Erikson, 1968) or other syndromes that represent people's quest to solve the problem of the self.

The premise for self-regulation failure from this analysis is that so much focus on the self creates psychological burdens for people. They spend enormous amounts of energy focusing on the self attempting to discover whether or not their self-views match their expected goals or accomplishments. Because the entire culture shares the centrality of the importance of the self, everyone engages in a continual self-evaluation process, particularly in reference to how well we compare to others. It is natural, then, that people will be motivated regularly to "escape the self," meaning escape the burden of constantly worrying about "how am I doing?" In this analysis, some forms of escape are psychologically positive or neutral, but others are negative. Baumeister (1991a) summarizes in considerable detail how self-regulation failure is a common outcome of this process, one that also may lead to addictive behavior (Chapter 4).

A further aspect of Baumeister's analysis has particular relevance for spirituality. With the decline of shared religious/spiritual and cultural worldviews, people needed to develop some type of value base for themselves. Why, for example, should I behave in the ways I do? If the ruler no longer represents the will of God, what is the meaning of political structures? If the Bible is a myth, what becomes the basis of human activity? In this analysis, a value is something that does not need to justify itself (Baumeister, 1991b). But if religion does not justify my behavior, what does? Baumeister posits that what happened in Western culture is that the self became the plug for this value-gap. We drifted from the ancient Greek notion of Protagoras that man is the measure of all things, to man is the center of all things. To complete this analysis, however, modern society demonstrates rather clearly that the self isn't up to this project. It's simply not big enough. When people believe it is, they usually overreach, and this awareness leads to self-defeating escape behavior. Others are frightened by having to fill this gap, and through excessive self-focus become socially anxious and take the safe way out. They thus see themselves as failures and also escape by means of self-destructive behavior.

Self-regulation theory, then, provides a psychological basis for understanding the 12-step tradition's focus on self-centeredness. One caveat is in order. In keeping with our review in Chapter 4, self-centeredness may refer to excessively high or low self-esteem. High-self-esteem individuals who are narcissistic and entitled fail by reacting to threats in ways that attempt to prove themselves. Decreases in narcissism occur in the course of addiction recovery (Reinert, in press). Low-self-esteem people are self-centered in the sense that their self-focus results in excessive performance concerns, and cause self-fulfilling prophecies. They unwittingly create the very social rejection they fear (Wells, 1997). Approaches to healing self-centeredness, therefore, must differ depending on which version the client is susceptible to—a topic to be discussed below.

Healing Self-Centeredness Through Virtue

Mental health professionals do not have expertise as spiritual counselors, but they have much to contribute to a client's self-selected goals for moral conduct. Through their understanding of behavioral science, they can support, guide, and provide feedback for the changes clients desire. This section reviews three approaches to right action or moral conduct with a view toward integrating their insights in the service of self-regulation. The first approach reviews virtue from the standpoint of Greek philosophy, which introduced the term into our ethical system. Returning to this original source can show us how early ethical thinking situated the way of right action into a moral framework. The second approach reviews virtue from the standpoint of ancient spirituality, particularly the early

Christian ascetics who lived in the Egyptian desert and who had a profound influence on later monasticism and spiritual practices. The third approach is self-regulation theory, which attempts to incorporate virtue as a relevant construct for modern psychology.

Aristotle and the Role of Virtue

To Aristotle and his followers, virtue played a central role in achieving happiness. Their confidence in knowing reality may not sit well with the modern mind, but for them human nature was an objective fact that we could understand. They believed, further, that we could know that happiness was the end (*telos*) for human nature and that virtue was the path to happiness. More relevant for our discussion than these epistemological assumptions are the various insights on virtue within that system.

First, Aristotle provided a catalogue of virtues that is reasonably similar to the modern catalogue. Second, he believed that virtue was a "mean between two extremes." By this he understood that a virtue stood between two excesses or vices. Generosity, for example, stands between the vices of prodigality and stinginess; pride stands between vanity and excessive humility. What may surprise those who believe modern psychology discovered the importance of emotions is how Aristotle's view held that emotions play a central role in moral conduct. He did not mean, as we might, that emotions create strong impulses *against* moral behavior. First, he maintained "that our instinctive emotional reactions can be the source of ethical principles" (Robinson, 1995, p. 57). Emotion is the first feedback system in judging the morality of an act. Second, virtue involved "an acquired tendency to experience certain feelings when confronted with certain situations ... [and] such a tendency is precisely the kind of thing a virtue is" (Robinson, 1995, p. 58). Moral conduct requires that we train ourselves to have the *right kind of emotions*. Aristotle did not advocate, as other ethical systems did, that we become indifferent to our feelings in order to control them. Virtue, being a mean between two extremes, does not mean it is passionless. Consider pride as a virtue. Winning the Nobel Prize should lead to feeling enormous positive emotion. I should still fall between the extremes of conceit (vainglory) and excessive humility (self-deprecation). Virtue means feeling the *right amount* of emotion that fits the occasion (Robinson, 1995), but the right amount at times may involve great intensity.

Third, Aristotle maintained that there was unity among the virtues (Annas, 1993). One source of that unity is that virtue requires a kind of intelligence called practical reasoning. Practical reasoning sorts out whether an act is right or wrong in the given situation. If my practical reasoning is attuned to figure out what generosity would mean in this case, chances are it can also sort out what honesty means in another. Each virtuous act helps sharpen my practical reasoning. "Each virtue, then, contributes to my overall good" (Annas, 1993, p. 75).

Finally, virtue is person-driven, not rule-driven. The ancient Greeks did not focus on rules to the extent that modern ethical systems do. They believed ethics should answer broad questions such as "What sort of life should you live?" (Socrates), or "What sort of person should you be?" (Aristotle). Virtue was a habit that disposed a person to act in ways that would lead to happiness. Vice was its opposite. Rules, then, had their place, but "rule-following on its own will not get you very far in moral progress, unless you understand the point of the rules" (Annas, 1993, p. 99). And the point of the rules was to acquire virtue.

Ancient Spirituality and Virtue

The second virtue-approach we examine is early Christianity's attempt to incorporate a virtue system within practical spiritual practices. The desert had great spiritual significance for Jews and Christians in the centuries before the birth of Christ and for several centuries thereafter. Many spiritually minded men and women retired to the desert to reflect on what type of life they should live in relation to their new faith. Many went out to live alone as hermits, but some joined like-minded persons to form monastic communities of men and women. The wisdom of these "desert fathers and mothers" was held in high reverence and formed the basis for later monastic life in both Western and Eastern Christian religious traditions.

Leading solitary lives in an extremely harsh environment led these spiritual practitioners to attain a high degree of introspection that resulted in many insights about impulse control. Believing that they could not attain spiritual perfection until they first conquered their bodily desires, many engaged in extreme practices of self-denial and deprivation of material needs. Although they do not represent role models for today, their reflections on self-regulation supplemented the ancient Greek synthesis in several ways. First, they filled out Aristotle's catalogue of virtues by including religious ones such as faith, hope, and love. Second, in their struggles with their own Dionysian impulses, they fleshed out a catalogue of the "deadly vices" that influences spirituality today. Interestingly, the original formulation was of eight vices, but pride and vainglory were collapsed into a single vice in later centuries. Like Eskimos who have many words for snow, the monk's sensitivity to the dangers of pride led to elaborating its depiction. Third, one scholar described their self-regulation strategies as seemingly developed by "a wise, experienced, compassionate cognitive behavioral therapist who also happens to be familiar with the depth psychologies" (Kurtz, 1999, p. 25). Specifically, they taught that for self-regulation "thoughts matter" (Funk, 1999). The very word for vice meant "a train of thought that engages the mind" (Tugwell, 1985, p. 25).

Two examples may suffice to illustrate how they anticipated cognitive therapy. At first glance, we might feel that the ancients were judgmental to include depression as a vice. However, one interpretation linked sadness to anger (anticipating Freud) and could also result from an "irrational turn of the mind" (Cassian, 2000, p. 214). Cognitive therapy not only addresses the "irrationality" of depression via negative automatic thoughts; it also works on the depressogenic schemas that create the disposition to view events negatively (Beck *et al.*, 1979). The desert fathers used many strategies similar to cognitive therapy. Evagrius Ponticus traced each of the vices to a specific schema. Using an approach that resembles the so-called "downward arrow" method to get at underlying schemas or irrational thoughts, Evagrius postulated that gluttony was related to fear of falling ill. Many other vices arose from "futile planning," that is, "the heart of the temptation is a train of thought leading us further and further away from our actual condition, making us solve problems which have not yet arisen and need not ever arise" (Tugwell, 1985, p. 26). One would be hard-pressed to find a more accurate definition of catastrophizing as used in cognitive-behavioral therapy (Barlow, 1988) 16 centuries later!

Fourth, in developing practices to control feelings and behavior, the desert monks uncovered various ineffective strategies. Relevant to our model of self-regulation are the ineffective ways to control thoughts and feelings. Monks learned that, despite desiring to spend all their time in spiritual reflection, they could not control their thoughts. The experience of the early spiritual master St. Anthony is a case in point. Having left mainstream society so that he could abandon his desires for wealth, sumptuous food, sex, honor, and so forth, he discovered in the desert to his horror that these seemed to be the *only* topics on his mind. Eventually, they discovered the worst strategy was to try to *control* unwanted thoughts, thereby triggering the "white bear" effect (see Chapter 9). Using agrarian images, they taught their followers to think of their mind as a wheat field that has both wheat and weeds growing in it. Using a biblical meta-phor, they advised people against uprooting the weeds (bothersome thoughts) lest they destroy the wheat (spiritual thoughts) as well. Finally, the desert monks advanced an understanding of virtue by seeing the root of all vice in excessive self-love (Tugwell, 1985). In this respect, their understanding dovetails with 12-step spirituality and its project of eliminating character flaws related to self-centeredness.

From a strategic view, then, the desert monks advocated two approaches to self-regulation that modern psychology independently systematized. The first is introspection (or guided discovery in cognitive-behavioral therapy language) to uncover the source of negative automatic thoughts that create emotional upset. To challenge your sadness when you've lost honor, wealth, or material goods, exam-ine your futile thoughts, the monks advised. Feeling desperately hungry? Stop and think whether depriving yourself right now will cause you to fall ill. Second, don't try to control the uncontrollable. The first strategy says you *can* challenge the last stop on your train of thoughts, for they usually represent unfounded fears. The second strategy says you cannot control their *initial appearance*, and if you try you make matters worse. You are better off being aware of these thoughts (e.g., mindfulness; Linehan, 1993) than trying to force them out. Disturbed by your anger at someone? Focus on the fact that you are annoyed rather than on the source of your annoyance (Tugwell, 1985), a strategy shared by Zen Buddhism (Hanh, 1991).

By now it should be evident that many of the self-regulation concepts discussed in this book were described in earlier philosophical and spiritual systems. Furthermore, what 12-step spirituality developed within its own tradition is greatly compatible with a virtue approach that attempts to overcome self-centeredness. We now need to take a look at self-regulation theory as it relates to virtue to finalize our clinical interventions.

Virtue and Self-Regulation

It is perhaps startling that psychologists today are proposing virtue as a serious variable for consideration in developing self-regulation. Psychology worked hard in its early history to distinguish itself from philosophy departments where it began and has placed great emphasis on the use of empirical methods and deterministic science. In the clinical realm it strives to remain value-free and nonjudgmental by eschewing positions that endorse religious-moral outlooks. Yet, a remarkable paper in a mainstream journal of personality suggests that self-regulation theory can make use of the ancient concept of virtue to make sense of important qualities required for adaptive human functioning (Baumeister & Exline, 1999). I will first summarize this position and then show how it brings together the entire range of clinical strategies we have discussed for treating pathological gambling. Further, we shall indicate how it legitimizes appropriate clinical interventions around moral conduct and harmonizes with traditional views related to addiction recovery.

Self-regulation theory views morality as "a cultural structure designed to enable people to live together in harmony" (Baumeister & Exline, 1999, p. 1166). Virtue represents internalization of the moral rules that facilitate living together. Without virtue, people would put their individual self-interests before that of the larger social good. To develop virtue, however, people require a key strength—namely, self-control. Universal moral codes such as the Ten Commandments represent the range of behaviors over which people need to exercise self-control for communal living. Similarly, the seven deadly sins represent failures of virtue that jeopardize community.

In the framework of self-regulation theory, then, self-control becomes the "master virtue" that allows people to keep their individual interests in check to accomplish the task of belonging to the larger social group. The authors highlight several implications of this view, some of which we have reviewed in Chapter 4. For instance, this master virtue is best viewed as a strength and a limited resource. If it does function like a muscle, it is possible to increase its skill with training. Furthermore, developing this master virtue requires three factors. People need standards; they need to self-monitor their behavior in relationship to those standards, and the self needs the "capacity to alter its own behavior so as to conform to standards" (Baumeister & Exline, 1999, p. 1177).

Virtue development is at odds with major social trends. The "reduced stability of social relationships" (Baumeister & Exline, 1999, p. 1184) has weakened the emotional glue that facilitated caring deeply about others. Guilt is what motivates us to care about and repair interpersonal damage. But with decreased social networks, the range of our guilt reactions becomes narrower and narrower. Second, capitalism orients people toward maximizing their own interests in the belief (hope) that others will benefit. Third, in the absence of a common religious-moral framework, the self has become the source of all moral value. Self-fulfillment or self-actualization now becomes the criterion for moral decisions. This is particularly troublesome from a self-control model. In the past, self-control was the foundation of morality, but now self-aggrandizement is accepted as our value-base. When maintaining self-esteem at all costs is the primary motivation, people engage in high-risk self-destructive behaviors. This brings us full circle to self-centeredness as central to addiction and other self-defeating behavioral patterns.

Gambling Treatment As Training in Virtue

Self-regulation theory, then, legitimately puts virtue within the scope of pathological gambling treatment. We did not set out, consciously at least, to create a treatment manual geared around training in virtue, but a good case could be made for that project. The following is a list of some connections between virtue and gambling treatment:

1. The emphasis on setting goals incompatible with pathological gambling relates to establishing alternate standards of virtue.
2. Motivational enhancement aims to examine value-bases other than the self to facilitate both appropriate guilt and awareness of falling short of one's standards.
3. Every specific intervention, whether behavioral or cognitive, emphasizes the crucial nature of self-awareness and self-monitoring.
4. Strategies to overcome procrastination could be described as overcoming sloth, one of the deadly vices.
5. Reevaluating the meaning of money through cognitive appraisal relates to avarice.
6. Interestingly, ancient spirituality viewed sadness as a vice, so that the cognitive therapy strategies described in this book work at this "irrational turn of mind" (Cassian, 2000, p. 214), lest it trigger gambling as an escape.

7. Strategies aimed at alleviating worry attempt to build courage, a model endorsed by an eminent authority in anxiety treatment (Rachman, 1990).

8. In concert with spiritual methods, we have advocated not trying to curtail gambling patient's thoughts or urges to gamble. We have suggested two strategies, however, to change pathological gamblers' *thinking*. The first is mindfulness to deal with the perceived overwhelming impulse triggered by desire or thought. The second is the cognitive processing strategies that attempt to change deeply rooted views of the world and self that fracture people's interpersonal relationships. If spirituality is "a way of viewing things" (Tugwell, 1985, p. viii), then changing "irrational" views through cognitive therapy is virtue-enhancing.

Pride the Ultimate Vice

We are left to discuss the vice that philosophers, spiritual masters, and 12-step traditions agree is central to immorality—pride or self-centeredness. Self-regulation theory, as reviewed in Chapter 4, quite intentionally identifies threatened egoism as the source of self-control failure and, therefore, as a threat to virtue. We have also noted that this theory is the only one that adequately accounts for the high preponderance of narcissistic patterns seen in pathological gambling. I have incorporated these views on threatened egoism into various treatment strategies. But the main point is that, unless clinicians recognize different strategies are required for high- versus low-self-esteem individuals, they will not understand the motivation of a sizeable number of pathological gamblers.

What approach should clinicians take regarding low- versus high-self-esteem pathological gambling patients? Self-centeredness takes two forms: one disposed towards self-enhancement, the other towards self-protection. These are both sins or vices because the former arises out of an excessively positive self-view and the latter out of an excessively negative self-view. They are extremes that meet in their degree of self-absorption. Biblical literature is replete with condemnations of both forms of self-centeredness. Self-protection due to low self-esteem is condemned. Jesus tells a parable about three servants given 5,000, 2,000, and 1,000 gold coins "according to his ability" (Matthew 25:16, American Bible Society, 1992, p. 1463). The first two doubled their respective amounts through wise investments and received greater awards. The third, who dug a hole and put the money there out of fear, received severe punishment. At the opposite end, biblical literature roundly despises egotism: "Pride goes before disaster, and a haughty spirit before a fall" (Proverbs 16:18, Benziger, 1988). The Psalms in the Hebrew Bible link egotism to violence, as does Baumeister: "So pride adorns them as a necklace; as a robe violence enwraps them" (Psalm 73:6). In the early Christian church Paul, had numerous warnings about excessive pride:

"For if anyone thinks he is something when he is nothing, he is deluding himself" (Galatians 6:3, Benziger, 1988). In the same letter he warns against odious comparisons: "You should each judge your own conduct. If it is good, then you can be proud of what you yourself have done, without having to compare it with what someone else has done" (Galatians 6:4, American Bible Society, 1992). One of the most precise links between threatened egotism and aggression occurs in the Hebrew Bible in the book of Genesis. Cain, insulted that God views his sacrifice as inferior to his brother's, murders Abel.

INTERVENTIONS FOR BUILDING CHARACTER–VIRTUE

This section describes an overall plan for developing individual character or virtue in pathological gambling patients. Therapists can avoid moralizing with these procedures in that the choices belong to the client, with goals and objectives representing a collaborative effort between client and therapist.

Character Defect Analysis

The worksheets below allow clients to nominate behaviors representing character development for them. The various themes revolve intentionally around virtue rather than vice to give the project a positive focus.

Each worksheet describes a single virtue with a general definition. In keeping with earlier definitions, they list two character defects (vices) that represent extremes on either side of the virtue. For example, under courage are the two extremes of rashness and timidity. I have selected worksheets that represent typical behaviors required for self-regulation in gambling recovery. Temperance is included because the high rate of comorbid addiction suggests that ignoring alcohol, drugs, sexual, and eating problems could lead to a gambling relapse. Some clients might choose other virtues that are not listed. For this reason, one form remains blank as a template for additional virtues and character defects. Each worksheet also lists "gambling traps" related to each character defect. In other words, each defect could lead to gambling for the unwatchful client. Under courage, we see that rashness could lead to foolish disregard of high-risk situations, for example, attending a business conference in Las Vegas. On the other hand, excessive fear of failure might result in missed opportunities for occupational advancement or intensifying personal relationships. As a result, dealing with low self-esteem, guilt, and loneliness could lead to escape-gambling. Each worksheet invites clients to provide examples of their character defects so that both client and therapist understand which behaviors to reduce or eliminate. Each sheet provides a definition of the virtue and asks for examples of how the person would know he or she is developing it.

Implementing Character Development Plans

Self-regulation theory maintains that self-control operates like a muscle, thereby meaning it can be overtaxed. Even though clients may have multiple character issues to deal with, careful discernment is required lest too much enthusiasm lead to attempting more than they can handle. This inevitably leads to avoiding the work altogether. Together client and therapist determine what is useful, necessary, and possible.

Having identified one virtue, the next step involves self-monitoring. Classic spiritual texts (e.g., Ganss, 1991) emphasize self-monitoring in virtue development to the same degree as control theory does. Borrowing from the notion of a "daily examination of conscience," Worksheets 15.7 and 15.8 organize character goals and invite the client to reflect on implementing them early in the day and again at night. In this way, clients attend to the standard, anticipate possible situations to try out virtuous behavior, and finally reflect on the experience. This endeavor ties together, therefore, the total therapeutic enterprise in gambling treatment. The client has identified character issues (personality traits) that facilitate gambling and those that could restrain it. Further, the client identifies the specific behaviors that counter the tendency to gamble. Finally, this daily "virtue diary" (Worksheet 15.8) keeps the standards front and center in the gambler's mind. Taken together, these steps represent a program to enhance self-regulation, the "moral muscle" that internalizes the community's interpersonal standards. In this way, therapists engage clients to consider "right action" from a purely psychological level and without coercion. At the same time, this is consistent for clients who desire incorporating moral strivings into a spiritual framework (Emmons, 1999).

This daily examination pulls it all together for clients. The reflective questions ask them to focus on recovery but at the same time aim for balance between enjoyable activities and duty. This borrows from relapse prevention models (Marlatt & Gordon, 1985) that advocate equilibrium between life's "wants" and "shoulds." When people with a history of addictive behavior feel overly taxed, relapse is tempting as an escape. With this program of daily reflection on a range of goals, our patients may learn that a full life is the opposite of an addicted one.

Truthfulness

Theme: **Truthfulness**—presenting myself to others as I really am

Extremes:
1. Boastful, *taking credit* for what I didn't do, wanting to appear as more than I am, lying to look good.
2. Putting myself down, *claiming less* about myself, lying so as to not look bad.

Gambling traps:
1. Need to boast leads to gambling to impress others; to look like a big-shot, or I need lots of money to keep up my image.
2. If I lie to protect myself, eventually I will feel guilty and desire to gamble.

Evidence for my lack of truthfulness:

Cost/benefit analysis:
    Benefit of truthfulness
    Cost of truthfulness
    Benefit of not being truthful
    Cost of not being truthful

If I were more truthful I would do or look like:

The first concrete steps in being more truthful are:

    1.
    2.
    3.
    4.

I will begin working on it (time, day) _____

In what way?

Responsible Conscience

Theme: **Responsible Conscience**—developing an appropriate sense of right and wrong about my behavior

Extremes:
1. Having no shame or guilt about the wrong things I have done to others.
2. Excessive shame and guilt about the wrong things I have done to others.

Gambling traps:

If I am indifferent to shame and guilt I could:
1. Ignore making amends and use the extra money to gamble.
2. Not care about hurting others with my gambling.
3. Commit illegal acts that lead to prosecution.

By excessive focusing on my guilt I could:
1. Avoid people who are supportive to recovery because of embarrassment.
2. Shrink from making amends.
3. Gamble to feel better.

Tips
1. For indifference: make a list of people injured by your gambling and imagine what it would feel like if the same had been done to you. What would you think and feel? How would it have effected your life? Your future? Your goals?
2. For excessive guilt, see the strategies in the section on guilt in Chapter 10.

Evidence for my lack of responsible consciousness:

Cost/Benefit analysis:
   Benefit of responsible conscience
   Cost of responsible conscience
   Benefit of not having a responsible conscience
   Cost of not having a responsible conscience

With a responsible conscience I would behave or look like:

The first concrete steps in having a responsible conscience are:
   1.
   2.
   3.
   4.

I will begin working on it (time, day) _____

In what way?

Humility

Theme: **Humility**—keeping my true talents in perspective through a grateful understanding of gifts I have received, and gratitude toward those who have nurtured these gifts [including God or higher power for believers]

Extremes:
1. Entitlement, taking excessive credit for accomplishments, exaggerating accomplishments, thinking that "it's all about me," caring only about how things effect me.
2. Putting myself down, minimizing my accomplishments, having no satisfaction in my gifts or what I do for others, lacking self-respect.

Gambling traps:
1. When my ego is threatened I could:
    a. Gamble to prove myself
    b. Become verbally or physically abusive
    c. Try to get the best of others
2. When I have no self-pride I could:
    a. Gamble to distract myself from feeling badly about myself or from loneliness
    b. Turn off friends by expecting them to fill up what I should give myself

Evidence for my lack of humility:

Cost/Benefit analysis:
  Benefit of humility
  Cost of humility
  Benefit of not being humble
  Cost of not being humble

If I were more humble, I would do or it would look like:

The first concrete steps in being more humble are:
  1.
  2.
  3.
  4.

I will begin working on it (time, day) _____

In what way?

Worksheet 15.4
Justice

Theme: **Justice**—giving or returning to people what is their due

Extremes:
1. Giving less than is due.
2. Giving more than is due.

Gambling traps:
1. Failure to pay back my debts (financial or social) including
   a. personal loans; institutional loans; items of others that were sold, stolen, defrauded, or conned; taxes.

2. Desire to pay off gambling-specific debts (bookies, casinos, track, loan-sharks, etc.) because
   a. The debts remind me of my gambling failures
   b. Getting debt-free allows me to get back into action

Evidence for my lack of justice:

Cost/Benefit analysis:
   Benefit of justice
   Cost of justice
   Benefit of not being just
   Cost of not being just

If I were more just, I would do or it would look like:

The first concrete steps in being more just are:
   1.
   2.
   3.
   4.

I will begin working on it (time, day) _____

In what way?

Courage

Theme: **Courage**—strength in the face of vulnerability

Extremes:
1. Rashness, overconfidence against barriers, not respecting one's limits.
2. Fearfulness, lack of confidence in actual ability, excessive worry about the future.

Gambling traps:
1. Becoming an "adrenaline-junkie," living life on the edge, gambling to create excitement.
2. Gambling to numb out, to forget my fears and anxieties.

Evidence for my lack of courage:

Cost/Benefit analysis:
   Benefit of courage
   Cost of courage
   Benefit of not being courageous
   Cost of not being courageous

If I were more courageous, I would do or it would look like:

The first concrete steps in being more courageous are:
1.
2.
3.
4.

I will begin working on it (time, day) _____

In what way?

Temperance

Theme: **Temperance**—moderation in physical pleasure

Extremes:
1. Excessive drinking or eating, use of illegal, non-prescribed drugs, inappropriate sex.
2. Lack of self-care, neglect of health, workaholism.

Gambling traps:
1. Substitute one addiction for another.
2. Use of alcohol or drugs causes loss of control and leads to gambling.
3. Excessive self-denial causes resentment and leads to gambling "because I deserve it."

Evidence for my lack of temperance:

Cost/Benefit analysis:
  Benefit of temperance
  Cost of temperance
  Benefit of not being temperate
  Cost of not being temperate

If I were more temperate, I would do or it would look like:

The first concrete steps in being more temperate are:
1.
2.
3.
4.

I will begin working on it (time, day) _____

In what way?

Worksheet 15.7
Implementing Goals Assessment

1. Make a list of your major activities for the past week. It should represent a reasonably typical week in your life. If it was unusual in the sense that you spent it recuperating from surgery or were away on vacation, do not evaluate it. If it was hectic and chaotic, but this is fairly typical, then include those events.

	9 a.m.–12 noon	12 noon–5 p.m.	5–9 p.m.	10 p.m.+
Monday				
Tuesday				
Wednesday				
Thursday				
Friday				
Saturday				
Sunday				

2. Now relate this typical week schedule to your Goal Summary Worksheet, asking yourself the following questions.

   Which of your goals are receiving too little attention?

   Which are receiving too much attention?

   Which are receiving about the right amount?

How is your shoulds/wants ratio? ["Shoulds": the things everyone *has* to do in life, e.g., wash dishes, pay bills, change diapers. "Wants": the things people enjoy, like, or find interesting, e.g., exercise, hobbies, vacations, eating out.]

   Too heavy toward the shoulds?   Wants/Likes?   Right Balance?

   If unbalanced, what needs to change?

   Change Plan:

Worksheet 15.8
Virtue Diary

Morning Reflection

Virtue to work on today:

What situations will provide a chance to achieve my goal?

Evening reflection:

Situation(s) that gave me a chance to work on this virtue:

What I should have done:

What I actually did:

If I was not successful doing what I should have, what could I have done differently?

How?

Strategies for tomorrow:

REFERENCES

AA World Services (1976). *Alcoholics Anonymous* (3rd ed.). New York: Author. (Original work published 1939.)

Abramson, L. Y., Seligman, M. E. P., & Teasdale, J. D. (1978). Learned helplessness in humans: Critique and reformulation. *Journal of Abnormal Psychology, 87,* 49–74.

Adkins, B. J., Kruedelbach, N. G., Toohig, T. M., & Rugle, L. J. (1988). The relationship of gaming preferences to MMPI personality variables. In W. R. Eadington (Ed.), *Gambling research: Proceedings of the Seventh International Conference on Gambling and Risk Taking* (pp. 180–192). Reno: University of Nevada-Reno.

Ahrons, S. (1989). *A comparison of the family environments and psychological distress of married pathological gamblers, alcoholics, psychiatric patients and their spouses with normal controls.* Unpublished doctoral dissertation, University of Maryland, College Park.

Alloy, L. B., & Abramson, L. Y. (1979). Judgment of contingency in depressed and nondepressed students: Sadder but wiser? *Journal of Experimental Psychology: General, 108,* 441–485.

American Bible Society (1992). *Good News Bible: With Deuterocanonicals and Apocrypha.* New York: Author.

American Psychiatric Association (1980). *Diagnostic and statistical manual of mental disorders* (3rd ed.). Washington, DC: Author.

American Psychiatric Association (1987). *Diagnostic and statistical manual of mental disorders* (3rd rev. ed.). Washington, DC: Author.

American Psychiatric Association (1994). *Diagnostic and statistical manual of mental disorders* (4th ed.). Washington, DC: Author.

American Psychiatric Association. (2000). *Diagnostic and statistical manual of mental disorders* (4th ed., text rev.). Washington, DC: Author.

Anderson, G., & Brown, R. I. F. (1984). Real and laboratory gambling, sensation-seeking and arousal. *British Journal of Psychology, 75*, 401–410.

Annas, J. (1993). *The morality of happiness.* New York: Oxford University Press.

Aristotle (1999). *Nicomachean ethics* (2nd ed.) (T. Irwin, Trans.). Indianapolis: Hackett.

Armstrong, K. (1993). *A history of God.* New York: Ballantine Books.

Bandura, A. (1969). *Principles of behavior modification.* New York: Holt, Rinehart & Winston.

Bandura, A. (1986). *Social foundations of thought and action.* Englewood Cliffs: Prentice-Hall.

Barlow, D. H. (1988). *Anxiety and its disorders: The nature and treatment of anxiety and panic.* New York: Guilford.

Barrone, D. F., Maddux, J. E., & Snyder, C. R. (1997). *Social cognitive psychology: History and current domains.* New York: Plenum.

Baumeister, R. F. (1991a). *Escaping the self: Alcoholism, spirituality, masochism, and other flights from the burden selfhood.* New York: Basic Books.

Baumeister, R. F. (1991b). *Meanings of life.* New York: Guilford.

Baumeister, R. F. (Ed.) (1993). *Self-esteem: The puzzle of low self-regard.* New York: Plenum.

Baumeister, R. F. (1997a). Esteem threat, self-regulatory breakdown, and emotional distress as factors in self-defeating behavior. *Review of General Psychology, 1*, 145–174.

Baumeister, R. F. (1997b). *Evil: Inside human violence and cruelty.* New York: W. H. Freeman.

Baumeister, R. F. (1998). The self. In D. T. Gilbert, S. T. Fiske, & G. Lindzey (Eds.), *Handbook of social psychology* (4th ed., pp. 680–740). New York: McGraw-Hill.

Baumeister, R. F., & Exline, J. J. (1999). Virtue, personality, and social relations: Self-control as the moral muscle. *Journal of Personality, 67*, 1165–1194.

Baumeister, R. F., & Scher, S. J. (1988). Self-defeating behavior patterns among normal individuals: Review and analysis of common self-destructive tendencies. *Psychological Bulletin, 104*, 3–22.

Baumeister, R. F., Heatherton, T. F., & Tice, D. M. (1993). When ego threats lead to self-regulation failure: Negative consequences of high self-esteem. *Journal of Personality and Social Psychology, 64*, 141–156.

Baumeister, R. F., Heatherton, T. F., & Tice, D. M. (1994). *Losing control: How and why people fail at self-regulation.* San Diego: Academic Press.

Baumeister, R. F., Smart, L., & Boden, J. M. (1996). Relation of threatened egotism to violence and aggression: The dark side of high self-esteem. *Psychological Review, 103*, 5–33.

Baumeister, R. F., Bratslavsky, E., Muraven, M., & Tice, D. M. (1998). Ego depletion: Is the active self a limited resource? *Journal of Personality and Social Psychology, 74,* 1252–1265.

Baumeister, R. F., Faber, J. E., & Wallace, H. M. (1999). Coping and ego depletion: Recovery after the coping process. In C. R. Synder (Ed.), *Coping: The psychology of what works* (pp. 50–69). New York: Oxford University Press.

Beach, S. R. H., Sandeen, E. E., & O'Leary, K. D. (1990). *Depression in marriage: A model for etiology and treatment.* New York: Guilford.

Beck, A. T., Rush, J., Shaw, B., & Emery, G. (1979). *Cognitive therapy of depression.* New York: Guilford.

Beck, A. T., Emery, G., & Greenberg, R. L. (1985). *Anxiety disorders and phobias: A cognitive perspective.* New York: Basic Books.

Benziger Publishing Company (1988). *The New American Bible.* Mission Hills, California: Author.

Bergin, A. E. (1991). Values and religious issues in psychotherapy and mental health. *American Psychologist, 46,* 394–403.

Bergler, E. (1970). *The psychology of gambling.* New York: International Universities Press. (Original work published 1957.)

Blaszczynski, A. P. (1988). *Clinical studies in pathological gambling; Is controlled gambling an acceptable treatment outcome?* Unpublished doctoral dissertation, University of New South Wales.

Blaszczynski, A. P., & McConaghy, N. (1994). Criminal offenses in Gamblers Anonymous and hospital treated pathological gamblers. *Journal of Gambling Studies, 10,* 99–127.

Blaszczynski, A. P., Wilson, A. C., & McConaghy, N. (1986). Sensation seeking and pathological gambling. *British Journal of Addiction, 81,* 113–117.

Blaszczynski, A., McConaghy, N., & Frankova, A. (1989). Crime, antisocial personality and pathological gambling. *Journal of Gambling Behavior, 5,* 137–152.

Blaszczynski, A. P., McConaghy, N., & Frankova, A. (1991). Control versus abstinence in the treatment of pathological gambling: A two to nine year follow-up. *British Journal of Addiction, 86,* 299–306.

Boyd, W. H., & Bolen, D. W. (1970). The compulsive gambler and spouse in group psychotherapy. *International Journal of Group Psychotherapy, 20,* 77–90.

Breen, R. B., & Frank, M. L. (1993). The effects of statistical fluctuations and perceived status of a competitor on the illusion of control in experienced gamblers. *Journal of Gambling Studies, 9,* 265–276.

Breen, R. B., & Zuckerman, M. (1999). 'Chasing' in gambling behavior: Personality and cognitive determinants. *Personality and Individual Differences, 27,* 1097–1111.

Breen, R. B., & Zuckerman, M. (2001). *Rapid onset of pathological gambling in machine gamblers.* Manuscript submitted for publication.

Brown, R. I. F. (1986). Arousal and sensation seeking components in the general explanation of gambling and gambling addictions. *International Journal of Addictions, 21,* 1001–1016.

Burns, D. D. (1989). *The feeling good handbook: Using the new mood therapy in everyday life.* New York: William-Morrow.

Butcher, J. N. (1990). *MMPI-2 in psychological treatment*. New York: Oxford University Press.

California Task Force to Promote Self-Esteem and Personal and Social Responsibility (1990). *Toward a state of self-esteem*. Sacramento: California State Department of Education.

Cannon, D. (1996). *Six ways of being religious: A framework for comparative studies of religion*. Belmont, CA: Wadsworth.

Cantor, N., & Sanderson, C. A. (1999). Life task participation and well-being: The importance of taking part in daily life. In D. Kahneman, E. Diener, & N. Schwarz (Eds.), *Well-being: The foundations of hedonic psychology* (pp. 230–243). New York: Russell Sage Foundation.

Carroll, D., & Huxley, J. A. A. (1994). Cognitive, dispositional, and psychophysiological correlates of dependent slot machine gambling in young people. *Journal of Applied Social Psychology, 24*, 1070–1083.

Carver, C. S., & Scheier, M. F. (1998). *On the self-regulation of behavior*. Cambridge: Cambridge University Press.

Cassian, J. (1997). *The conferences* (B. Ramsey, Trans.). New York: Paulist Press.

Cassian, J. (2000). *The institutes* (B. Ramsey, Trans.). New York: Paulist Press.

Castellani, B. (2000). *Pathological gambling: The making of a medical problem*. Albany: State University of New York Press.

Castellani, B., & Rugle, L. (1995). A comparison of pathological gamblers to alcoholics and cocaine misusers on impulsivity, sensation seeking, and craving. *The International Journal of Addictions, 30*, 275–289.

Ceci, S. J., & Liker, J. K. (1986). A day at the races: A study of IQ, expertise, and cognitive complexity. *Journal of Experimental Psychology: General, 115*, 255–266.

Chaplin, J. P. (1975). *Dictionary of psychology* (2nd ed.). New York: Dell.

Cheston, S. E. (2000). A new paradigm for teaching counseling theory and practice. *Counselor Education and Supervision, 39*, 254–269.

Christensen, A., & Jacobson, N. S. (2000). *Reconcilable differences*. New York: Guilford.

Ciarrocchi, J. W. (1987). Severity of impairment in dually addicted gamblers. *Journal of Gambling Behavior, 3*, 16–26.

Ciarrocchi, J. W. (1993). Rates of pathological gambling in publicly funded outpatient substance abuse treatment. *Journal of Gambling Studies, 9*, 289–294.

Ciarrocchi, J. W. (1995a). *The doubting disease: Help for scrupulosity and religious obsessions*. New York: Paulist Press.

Ciarrocchi, J. W. (1995b). *Why are you worrying?* New York: Paulist Press.

Ciarrocchi, J. W. (1998). Religion, scrupulosity, and obsessive-compulsive disorder. In M. A. Jenike, L. Baer, & W. E. Minichiello (Eds.), *Obsessive-compulsive disorders: Practical management* (3rd ed., pp. 555–569). St. Louis: Mosby.

Ciarrocchi, J. W. (1999). Spirituality for high and low rollers: The paradox of self-esteem in gambling recovery. In O. J. Morgan & M. R. Jordan (Eds.), *Addiction and spirituality* (pp. 173–191). St. Louis: Chalice.

Ciarrocchi, J. W., & Hohmann, A. (1989). The family environment of married pathological gamblers, alcoholics, and dually addicted gamblers. *Journal of Gambling Behavior, 5*, 283–289.

Ciarrocchi, J. W., & Reinert, D. F. (1993). Family environment and length of recovery for married male members of Gamblers Anonymous and female members of GamAnon. *Journal of Gambling Studies, 9,* 341–352.

Ciarrocchi, J. W., & Richardson, R. (1989). Profile of compulsive gamblers in treatment: Update and comparisons. *Journal of Gambling Behavior, 5,* 53–65.

Ciarrocchi, J. W., & Wicks, R. J. (2000). *Psychotherapy with priests, Protestant clergy, and Catholic religious.* Madison, Connecticut: Psychosocial Press.

Ciarrocchi, J. W., Kirschner, N., & Fallik, F. (1991). Personality dimensions of male pathological gamblers, alcoholics, and dually addicted gamblers. *Journal of Gambling Studies, 7,* 133–142.

Ciarrocchi, J. W., Peterson, S., & Moore, L. (1998). *Rates of pathological gambling in publicly funded and private substance abuse treatment programs.* Paper presented at the Twelfth National Conference on Problem Gambling, Las Vegas.

Cocco, N., Sharpe, L., & Blaszczynski, A. P. (1995). Differences in preferred level of arousal in two sub-groups of problem gamblers: A preliminary report. *Journal of Gambling Studies, 11,* 221–229.

Cole, B., & Pargament, K. I. (1999). Spiritual surrender: A paradoxical path to control. In W. R. Miller (Ed.), *Integrating spirituality into treatment: Resources for practitioners* (pp. 179–198). Washington, DC: American Psychological Association.

Comings, D. E., Rosenthal, R. J., Lesieur, H. R., Rugle, L. J., Muhleman, D., Chiu, C., Dietz, G., & Gade, R. (1996). A study of the D2 receptor gene in pathological gambling. *Pharmacogenetics, 6,* 223–234.

Corney, W. J., & Cummings, W. T. (1985). Gambling behavior and information processing biases. *Journal of Gambling Behavior, 1,* 111–118.

Costa Jr., P. T., & McCrae, R. R. (1992). *Revised NEO Personality Inventory: Professional manual.* Odessa, FL: Psychological Assessment Resources.

Coventry, K. R., & Brown, I. F. (1993). Sensation seeking, gambling and gambling addictions. *Addiction, 88,* 541–554.

Craske, M. G., Barlow, D. H., & O'Leary, T. (1992). *Mastery of your anxiety and worry.* Albany, NY: Graywind.

Crisp, B. R., Thomas, S. A., Jackson, A. C., Thomason, N., Smith, S., Borrell, J. Ho, W., & Holt, T. (2000). Sex differences in the treatment needs and outcomes of problem gamblers. *Research on Social Work Practice, 10,* 229–242.

Crockford, D. N., & el-Guebaly, N. (1998). Psychiatric comorbidity in pathological gambling: A critical review. *Canadian Journal of Psychiatry, 43,* 43–50.

Cunningham-Williams, R. M., Cottler, L. B., Compton, W. M., & Spitznagel, E. L. (1998). Taking chances: Problem gamblers and mental health disorders: Results from the St. Louis Epidemiologic Catchment Area Study. *American Journal of Public Health, 88,* 1093–1096.

Cunningham-Williams, R. M., Cottler, L. B., Comptom, W. M., Spitznagel, E. L., & Ben-Abdallah, A. (2000). Problem gambling and comorbid psychiatric and substance use disorders among drug users recruited from drug treatment and community settings. *Journal of Gambling Studies, 16,* 347–376.

Custer, R., & Milt, H. (1985). *When luck runs out.* New York: Facts on File.

Dale, K. L., & Baumeister, R. F. (1999). Self-regulation and psychopathology. In R. M. Kowalski & M. R. Leary (Eds.), *The social psychology of emotional and behavioral problems* (pp. 139–166). Washington, DC: American Psychological Association.

Darvas, S. (1981). *The spouse in treatment: Or, there is a woman (or women) behind every pathological gambler.* Paper presented at the Fifth Annual National Conference on Gambling and Risk-Taking, Reno, NV.

Derevensky, J. L., & Gupta, R. (2000). Prevalence estimates of adolescent gambling: A comparison of the SOGS-RA, DSM-IV-J, and the GA 20 Questions. *Journal of Gambling Studies, 16,* 227–252.

Dickerson, M. (1993). Internal and external determinants of persistent gambling: Problems in generalizing from one form of gambling to another. *Journal of Gambling Studies, 9,* 225–245.

Dickerson, M. G., & Adcock, S. G. (1987). Mood, arousal and cognitions in persistent gambling: Preliminary investigations of a theoretical model. *Journal of Gambling Behavior, 3,* 3–15.

Dickerson, M., Hinchy, J., & Fabre, J. (1987). Chasing, arousal and sensation seeking in off-course gamblers. *British Journal of Addiction, 82,* 673–680.

Dickerson, M., Hinchy, J., & England, S. L. (1990a). Minimal treatments and problem gamblers: A preliminary investigation. *Journal of Gambling Studies, 6,* 87–102.

Dickerson, M., Walker, M., England, S. L., & Hinchy, J. (1990b). Demographic, personality, cognitive and behavioral correlates of off-course betting involvement. *Journal of Gambling Studies, 6,* 165–182.

DiClemente, C. C., Story, M., & Murray, K. (2000). On a roll: The process of initiation and cessation of problem gambling among adolescents. *Journal of Gambling Studies, 16,* 289–314.

Dulles, A. (1994). *The assurances of things hoped for: A theology of Christian faith.* New York: Oxford University Press.

Echeburua, E., Fernandez-Montalvo, J., & Baez, C. (2000). Relapse prevention in the treatment of slot-machine pathological gambling: Long-term outcome. *Behavior Therapy, 31,* 351–364.

Ellis, A., & Harper, R. (1975). *A new guide to rational living.* North Hollywood, CA: Wilshire Books.

Emmons, R. A. (1999). *The psychology of ultimate concerns.* New York: Guilford.

Emmons, R. A., King, L. A., & Sheldon, K. (1993). Goal conflict and the self-regulation of action. In D. M. Wegner & J. W. Pennebaker (Eds.), *Handbook of mental control* (pp. 528–551). Englewood Cliffs: Prentice Hall.

Erikson, E. H. (1963). *Childhood and society* (Rev. ed.). New York: Norton. (Original work published 1950.)

Erikson, E. H. (1968). *Identity: Youth and crisis.* New York: Norton.

Exline, J. J., & Baumeister, R. F. (2000). Expressing forgiveness and repentance: Benefits and barriers. In M. E. McCullough, K. I. Pargament, & C. E. Thoresen (Eds.), *Forgiveness: Theory, research, and practice* (pp. 133–155). New York: Guilford.

Eysenck, S. B., & Eysenck, H. J. (1977). The place of impulsiveness in a dimensional system of personality description. *British Journal of Social and Clinical Psychology, 16*(3), 57–68.

Fisher, S. (2000). Developing the DSM-IV–DSM-IV criteria to identify adolescent problem gambling in non-clinical populations. *Journal of Gambling Studies, 16*, 253–274.

Fishman, D. (1999). *The case for pragmatic psychology*. New York: New York University Press.

Foa, E., & Kozak, M. J. (1986). Emotional processing of fear: Exposure to corrective information. *Psychological Bulletin, 99*, 20–35.

Frank, M. L., & Smith, C. (1989). Illusion of control and gambling in children. *Journal of Gambling Behavior, 5*, 127–136.

Franklin, J., & Ciarrocchi, J. (1987). The team approach: Developing an experiential knowledge base for the treatment of the pathological gambler. *Journal of Gambling Behavior, 3*, 60–67.

Franklin, J., & Richardson, R. (1988). A treatment outcome study with pathological gamblers: Preliminary findings and strategies. In W. R. Eadington (Ed.), *Proceedings of the Seventh International Conference on Gambling and Risk Taking* (pp. 392–407). Reno: University of Nevada-Reno.

Freud, S. (1974). Dostoevsky and parricide. In J. Halliday, & P. Fuller (Eds.), *The psychology of gambling*. London: Harper & Row.

Funk, M. M. (1999). *Thoughts matter: The practice of the spiritual life*. New York: Continuum.

Gaboury, A., & Ladouceur, R. (1989). Erroneous perceptions and gambling. *Journal of Social Behavior and Personality, 4*, 411–420.

Gallup Organization (1993). *GO LIFE Survey on Prayer*. Princeton, NJ: Author.

Ganss, G. E. (Ed.) (1991). *Ignatius of Loyola: The spiritual exercises and selected works*. New York: Paulist Press.

Gilovich, T. (1983). Biased evaluation and persistence in gambling. *Journal of Personality and Social Psychology, 44*, 1110–1126.

Gilovich, T., & Douglas, C. (1986). Biased evaluations of randomly determined gambling outcomes. *Journal of Experimental Social Psychology, 22*, 228–241.

Gilovich, T., Vallone, R., & Tversky, A. (1985). The hot hand in basketball: On the misperception of random sequences. *Cognitive Psychology, 17*, 295–314.

Goldfried, M. R., & Davison, G. C. (1996). *Clinical behavior therapy* (2nd ed.). New York: Wiley.

Goleman, D. (Ed.) (1997). *Healing emotions: Conversations with the Dalai Lama on mindfulness, emotions, and health*. Boston: Shambhala.

Gorski, T. T., & Miller, M. (1982). *Counseling for relapse prevention*. Independence, MO: Herald House-Independence Press.

Graham, T. T. (1990). *MMPI-2: Assessing personality and psychopathology*. New York: Oxford University Press.

Graham, J. R., & Lowenfeld, B. H. (1986). Personality dimensions of the pathological gambler. *Journal of Gambling Behavior, 2*, 58–67.

Greenberg, D., & Rankin, H. (1982). Compulsive gamblers in treatment. *British Journal of Psychiatry, 140*, 364–366.

Griffiths, M. D. (1990a). The acquisition, development, and maintenance of fruit machine gambling in adolescence. *Journal of Gambling Studies, 6*, 193–204.

Griffiths, M. D. (1990b). The cognitive psychology of gambling. *Journal of Gambling Studies, 6,* 31–42.

Griffiths, M. (1993). Factors in problem adolescent fruit machine gambling: Results of a small postal survey. *Journal of Gambling Studies, 9,* 31–45.

Griffiths, M., & Wood, R. T. A. (2000). Risk factors in adolescence; The case of gambling, videogame playing, and the internet. *Journal of Gambling Studies, 16,* 199–226.

Gupta, R., & Derevensky, J. (1997). Familial and social influences on juvenile gambling behavior. *Journal of Gambling Studies, 13,* 179–192.

Gupta, R., & Derevensky, J. L. (1998). An empirical examination of Jacobs' General Theory of Addictions: Do adolescent gamblers fit the theory? *Journal of Gambling Studies, 14,* 17–49.

Gupta, R., & Derevensky, J. L. (2000a). Adolescents with gambling problems: From research to treatment. *Journal of Gambling Studies, 16,* 315–342.

Gupta, R., & Derevensky, J. L. (2000b). Preface/editorial for the special issue. *Journal of Gambling Studies, 16,* 115–118.

Hanh, T. N. (1991). *Peace is every step: The path of mindfulness in everyday life.* New York: Bantam Books.

Hauerwas, S., & Pinches, C. (1997). *Christians among the virtues: Theological conversations with ancient and modern ethics.* Notre Dame, IN: University of Notre Dame Press.

Hayes, S. C., Jacobson, N. S., Follette, V. M., & Dougher, M. J. (Eds.) (1994). *Acceptance and change: Content and context in psychotherapy.* Reno, NV: Context.

Herman, C. P., & Mack, D. (1975). Restrained and unrestrained eating. *Journal of Personality, 43,* 647–660.

Hester, R. K., & Miller, W. R. (Eds.) (1995). *Handbook of alcoholism treatment approaches: Effective alternatives* (2nd ed.). Boston: Allyn & Bacon.

Hill, P. C., & Hood, R. W. (Eds.) (1999). *Measures of religiousness.* Birmingham, AL: Religious Education Press.

Hodgins, D. C., Currie, S., Makarchuk, K., & el-Guebaly, N. (2000). *Motivational enhancement and self-help workbooks as treatment for problem gamblers: Twelve-month outcome.* Paper presented at the annual convention of Association for Advancement of Behavior Therapy, New Orleans.

Hodgins, D. C., & el-Guebaly, N. (2000). Natural and treatment-assisted recovery from gambling problems: A comparison of resolved and active gamblers. *Addiction, 95,* 777–789.

Hollander, E., DeCaria, C. M., Finkell, J. N., Begaz, T., Wong, C. M., & Cartwright, C. (2000). A randomized double-blind fluvoxamine/placebo crossover trial in pathologic gambling. *Biological Psychiatry, 47,* 813–817.

Hood, R. W., Spilka, B., Hunsberger, B., & Gorsuch, R. (1996). *The psychology of religion: An empirical approach* (2nd ed.). New York: Guilford.

Hoolighan, M. (1991). *The rate and distribution of certain personality characteristics in Christian male clergy: A comparative study.* Unpublished doctoral dissertation, Loyola College in Maryland.

Hudak, C. J., Varghese, R., & Politzer, R. M. (1989). Family, marital, and occupational satisfaction for recovering pathological gamblers. *Journal of Gambling Behavior, 5,* 201–210.

Jacobs, D. F. (1986). A general theory of addictions: A new theoretical model. *Journal of Gambling Behavior, 2*, 15–31.

Jacobs, D. F. (1988). Evidence for a common dissociative-like reaction among addicts. *Journal of Gambling Behavior, 4*, 27–37.

Jacobs, D. F. (1989). Illegal and undocumented: A review of teenage gambling and the plight of children of problem gamblers in America. In H. J. Shaffer, S. A. Stein, B. Gambino, & T. N. Cummings (Eds.), *Compulsive gambling: Theory, research and practice* (pp. 249–292). Lexington, MA: Lexington Books.

Jacobs, D. F. (2000). Juvenile gambling in North America: An analysis of long term trends and future prospects. *Journal of Gambling Studies, 16*, 119–152.

Jacobson, N. S., & Christensen, A. (1996). *Acceptance and change in couple therapy: A therapist's guide to transforming relationships*. New York: Norton.

Jacobson, N. S., Christensen, A., Prince, S. E., Cordova, J., & Eldridge, K. (2000). Integrative behavioral couple therapy: An acceptance-based, promising new treatment for couple discord. *Journal of Consulting and Clinical Psychology, 68*, 351–355.

James, W. (1985). *The varieties of religious experience: A study in human nature*. Cambridge: Harvard University Press. (Original work published 1902.)

Jamison, K. R. (1993). *Touched with fire: Manic-depressive illness and the artistic temperament*. New York: The Free Press.

Janoff-Bulman, R. (1992). *Shattered Assumptions: Towards a new psychology of trauma*. New York: The Free Press.

Janoff-Bulman, R. (1999). Rebuilding shattered assumptions after traumatic life events. In C. R. Synder (Ed.), *Coping: The psychology of what works* (pp. 305–323). New York: Oxford University Press.

Johnson, E. E., Nora, R. M., & Bustos, N. (1992). The Rotter I–E Scale as a predictor of relapse in a population of compulsive gamblers. *Psychological Reports, 70*, 691–696.

Kabat-Zinn, J. (1990). *Full catastrophe living*. New York: Delacorte.

Kaufmann, W. (1973). *Without guilt and justice*. New York: Peter H. Wyden.

Kenny, A. (1998). *A brief history of Western philosophy*. Oxford: Blackwell.

Kuley, N. B., & Jacobs, D. F. (1988). The relationship between dissociative-like experiences and sensation seeking among social and problem gamblers. *Journal of Gambling Behavior, 4*, 197–207.

Kurtz, E. (1999). The historical context. In W. R. Miller (Ed.), *Integrating spirituality into treatment: Resources for practitioners* (pp. 19–46). Washington, DC: American Psychological Association.

Kusyszyn, I., & Rutter, R. (1985). Personality characteristics of heavy gamblers, light gamblers, non-gamblers, and lottery players. *Journal of Gambling Behavior, 1*, 59–63.

Kweitel, R., & Allen, F. C. L. (1998). Cognitive processes associated with gambling behaviour. *Psychological Reports, 82*, 147–153.

Ladouceur, R., & Walker, M. (1996). A cognitive perspective on gambling. In P. M. Salkovskis (Ed.), *Trends in cognitive therapy* (pp. 89-120). Oxford: Wiley.

Ladouceur, R., Arsenault, C., Dube, D., Freeston, M. H., & Jacques, C. (1997). Psychological characteristics of volunteers in studies on gambling. *Journal of Gambling Studies, 13*, 69–84.

Ladouceur, R., Sylvain, C., Letarte, H., Giroux, L., & Jacques, C. (1998). Cognitive treatment of pathological gamblers. *Behavior Research and Therapy*, *36*, 1111–1120.

Ladouceur, R., Bouchard, C., Rheaume, N., Jacques, C., Ferland, F., Leblond, J., & Walker, M. (2000). Is the SOGS an accurate measure of pathological gambling among children, adolescents and adults? *Journal of Gambling Studies*, *16*, 1–24.

Lakein, A. (1973). *How to get control of your time and your life*. New York: New American Library.

Langer, E. J. (1975). The illusion of control. *Journal of Personality and Social Psychology*, *32*, 311–328.

Langer, E. J., & Roth, J. (1975). Heads I win, tails it's chance: The illusion of control as a function of the sequence of outcomes in a purely chance task. *Journal of Personality and Social Psychology*, *32*, 951–955.

Langewisch, M. W. J., & Frisch, G. R. (1998). Gambling behavior and pathology in relation to impulsivity, sensation seeking, and risky behavior in male college students. *Journal of Gambling Studies*, *14*, 245–262.

Leary, K., & Dickerson, M. G. (1985). Levels of arousal in high and low frequency gamblers. *Behavioral Research and Therapy*, *23*, 635–640.

Leary, M. R. (1999). The social and psychological importance of self-esteem. In R. M. Kowalski & M. R. Leary (Eds.), *The social psychology of emotional and behavioral problems: Interfaces of social and clinical psychology* (pp. 197–222). Washington, DC: American Psychological Association.

Leith, K., & Baumeister, R. F. (1996). Why do bad moods increase self-defeating behavior, emotion, risk taking, and self-regulation? *Journal of Personality and Social Psychology*, *71*, 1250–1267.

Lesieur, H. R. (1984). *The chase: Career of the compulsive gambler*. Cambridge, MA: Schenkman.

Lesieur, H. R., & Blume, S. B. (1991). When Lady Luck loses: Women and compulsive gambling. In N. van den Bergh (Ed.), *Feminist perspectives on addiction* (pp. 181–197). New York: Springer.

Lesieur, H. R., & Blume, S. B. (1993). Revising the South Oaks Gambling Screen in different settings. *Journal of Gambling Studies*, *9*, 213–223.

Lesieur, H. R., & Klein, R. (1987). Pathological gambling among high school students. *Addictive Behaviors*, *12*, 129–135.

Lesieur, H. R., & Rosenthal, R. J. (1991). Pathological gambling: A review of the literature (prepared for the American Psychiatric Association Task Force on DSM-IV Committee on Disorders of Impulse Control Not Elsewhere Classified). *Journal of Gambling Studies*, *7*, 5–39.

Lesieur, H. R., Cross, J., Frank, M., Welch, M. White, C. M., Rubenstein, G., Mosely, K., & Mark, M. (1991). Gambling and pathological gambling among university students. *Addictive Behaviors*, *16*, 517–527.

Lewinsohn, P., & Gotlib, I. (1995). Behavioral theory and treatment of depression. In E. Becker & W. Leber (Eds.), *Handbook of depression* (pp. 352–375). New York: Guilford.

Lieberman, M., Yalom, I., & Miles, M. (1973). *Encounter groups: First facts*. New York: Basic Books.

Linehan, M. M. (1993). *Skills training manual for treating borderline personality disorder*. New York: Guilford.

Little, B. R. (1989). Personal projects analyses: Trivial pursuits, magnificent obsessions, and the search for coherence. In D. M. Buss & N. Cantor (Eds.), *Personality psychology*. New York: Springer-Verlag.

Lopez Viets, V. C., & Miller, W. R. (1997). Treatment approaches for pathological gamblers. *Clinical Psychology Review*, *17*, 689–702.

LoPiccolo, J. (1994). Acceptance and broad spectrum treatment of paraphilias. In S. C. Hayes, N. S. Jacobson, V. M. Follette, & M. J. Dougher (Eds.), *Acceptance and change: Content and context in psychotherapy* (pp. 149–170). Reno, NV: Context.

Lorenz, V. C., & Shuttlesworth, D. E. (1983). The impact of pathological gambling on the spouse of the gambler. *Journal of Community Psychology*, *11*, 67–76.

Lorenz, V. C., & Yaffee, R. A. (1986). Pathological gambling: Psychosomatic, emotional and marital difficulties as reported by the gambler. *Journal of Gambling Behavior*, *2*, 40–49.

Lorenz, V. C., & Yaffee, R. A. (1988). Pathological gambling: Psychosomatic, emotional and marital difficulties as reported by the spouse. *Journal of Gambling Behavior*, *4*, 13–26.

Lowenfeld, B. H. (1978). *Personality dimensions of the pathological gambler*. Unpublished doctoral dissertation, Kent State University.

MacIntryre, A. (1984). *After virtue: A study in moral theory* (2nd ed.). Notre Dame, IN: University of Notre Dame Press.

MacIntyre, A. (1998). *A short history of ethics: A history of moral philosophy from the Homeric age to the twentieth century* (2nd ed.). Notre Dame, IN: University of Notre Dame.

MacIntryre, A. (1999). *Dependent rational animals: Why human beings need the virtues*. Chicago: Open Court.

Marlatt, G. A. (1994). Addiction and acceptance. In S. C. Hayes, N. S. Jacobson, Follette, V. M., & Dougher, M. J. (Eds.), *Acceptance and change: Content and context in psychotherapy* (pp. 175–197). Reno, NV: Context.

Marlatt, G. A., & Gordon, J. R. (1985). *Relapse prevention: Maintenance strategies in the treatment of addictive behaviors*. New York: Guilford.

Marlatt, G. A., & Kristeller, J. L. (1999). Mindfulness and meditation. In W. R. Miller (Ed.), *Integrating spirituality into treatment: Resources for practitioners* (pp. 67–84). Washington, DC: American Psychological Association.

McCormick, R. A., Taber, J., Kruedelbach, N., & Russo, A. (1987). Personality profiles of hospitalized pathological gamblers: The California Personality Inventory. *Journal of Clinical Psychology*, *43*, 521–527.

McCown, W. G., & Chamberlain, L. L. (2000). *Best possible odds: Contemporary treatment strategies for gambling disorders*. New York: John Wiley.

McCrady, B. S. (1998). Some meditations on spirituality. *The Addictions Newsletter*, *6(1)*, 25–26.

McCullough, M. E., Pargament, K. I., & Thoresen, C. E. (Eds.) (2000). *Forgiveness: Theory, research, and practice*. New York: Guilford.

McNeilly, D. P., & Burke, W. J. (2000). Later life gambling: The attitudes and behaviors of older adults. *Journal of Gambling Studies, 16,* 393–416.

Meichenbaum, D., & Fong, G. T. (1993). How individuals control their own minds: A constructive narrative perspective. In D. M. Wegner, & J. W. Pennebaker (Eds.), *Handbook of mental control* (pp. 473–490). Englewood Cliffs: Prentice Hall.

Melville, C. L., Davis, C. S., & Matzenbacher, D. (2000). *Node-link mapping in group therapy for pathological gambling.* Paper presented at the 14th National Conference on Problem Gambling, Philadelphia.

Meyer, G., & Stadler, M. (1999). Criminal behavior associated with pathological gambling. *Journal of Gambling Studies, 15,* 29–42.

Miller, W. R. (1998). Can we study spirituality? *The Addictions Newsletter, 6(1),* 4–21.

Miller, W. R. (Ed.) (1999). *Integrating spirituality into treatment: Resources for practitioners.* Washington, DC: American Psychological Association.

Miller, W. R., & Heather, N. (Eds.) (1986). *Treating addictive behaviors; Processes of change.* New York: Plenum.

Miller, W. R., & Jackson, K. A. (1985). *Practical psychology for pastors.* Englewood Cliffs: Prentice-Hall.

Miller, W. R., & Rollnick, S. (1991). *Motivational interviewing: Preparing people to change addictive behavior.* New York: Guilford.

Miller, W. R., & Thoresen, C. E. (1999). Spirituality and health. In W. R. Miller (Ed.), *Integrating spirituality into treatment: Resources for practitioners* (pp. 3–18). Washington, DC: American Psychological Association.

Miller, W. R., Andrews, N. R., Wilbourne, P., & Bennett, M. E. (1998). A wealth of alternatives: Effective treatments for alcohol problems. In W. R. Miller, & N. Heather (Eds.), *Treating addictive behaviors* (2nd ed., pp. 203–216). New York: Plenum.

Millon, T. (1981). *Disorders of personality DSM-III: Axis II.* New York: John Wiley.

Mischel, W., Shoda, Y., & Peake, P. K. (1988). The nature of adolescent competencies predicted by preschool delay of gratification. *Journal of Personality and Social Psychology, 54,* 687–696.

Mok, W. P., & Hraba, J. (1991). Age and gambling behavior: A declining and shifting pattern of participation. *Journal of Gambling Studies, 7,* 313–336.

Moore, S. M., & Ohtsuka, K. (1999). Beliefs about control over gambling among young people, and their relation to problem gambling. *Psychology of Addictive Behaviors, 13,* 339–347.

Moos, R. H., & Moos, B. S. (1981). *Family Environment Scale manual.* Palo Alto, CA: Consulting Psychologists Press.

Moos, R. H., & Moos, B. S. (1984). The process of recovery from alcoholism, III: Comparing functioning in families of alcoholics and matched control families. *Journal of Studies on Alcohol, 45,* 111–118.

Moos, R., & Moos, B. (1990). *Alcoholism treatment: Context, process, and outcome.* New York: Oxford University Press.

Moos, R. H., Finney, J. W., & Cronkite, R. C. (1990). *Alcoholism treatment: Context, process, and outcome.* New York: Oxford University Press.

Moravec, J. D., & Munley, P. H. (1983). Psychological test findings on pathological gamblers in treatment. *The International Journal of the Addictions, 18,* 1003–1009.

Mundis, J. (1990). *How to get out of debt, stay out of debt and live prosperously*. New York: Bantam.

Muraven, M., Tice, D. M., & Baumeister, R. F. (1998). Self-control as limited resource: Regulatory depletion patterns. *Journal of Personality and Social Psychology, 74*, 774–789.

National Academy Press (1999). *Pathological Gambling: A critical review*. Washington, DC: Author.

National Endowment for Financial Education (2000). *Personal financial strategies for the loved ones of problem gamblers* [Brochure]. Denver: Author.

National Gambling Impact Study Commission (1999). *National Gambling Impact Study Commission Report to Congress*. Washington, DC: Author.

National Opinion Research Center (1999). *Gambling impact and behavior study: Report to the National Gambling Impact Study Commission*. Chicago: Author.

Nolen-Hoeksema, S. (1990). *Sex differences in depression*. Stanford: Stanford University Press.

Nussbaum, M. C. (1994). *The therapy of desire: Theory and practice in Hellenistic ethics*. Princeton: Princeton University Press.

Orford, J. (1985). *Excessive appetites: A psychological view of addictions*. Chichester: John Wiley.

Otto, R. (1950). *The idea of the holy* (2nd ed.). New York: Oxford University Press. (Original work published 1923.)

Paloutzian, R. F. (1996). *Invitation to the psychology of religion* (2nd ed.). Boston: Allyn & Bacon.

Pargament, K. I. (1997). *The psychology of religion and coping: Theory, research, practice*. New York: Guilford.

Pennebaker, J. W. (1990). *Opening up*. New York: Morrow.

Perls, F. S., Hefferline, R. F., & Goodman, P. (1951). *Gestalt therapy*. New York: Julian Press.

Piedmont, R. L. (1998). *The Revised NEO Personality Inventory: Clinical and research application*. New York: Plenum.

Piedmont, R. L. (1999). Does spirituality represent the sixth factor of personality? Spiritual transcendence and the five-factor model. *Journal of Personality, 67*, 985–1013.

Piedmont, R. L., & Ciarrocchi, J. W. (1999). The utility of the revised NEO Personality Inventory in an outpatient, drug rehabilitation context. *Psychology of Addictive Behaviors, 13*, 213–226.

Politzer, R. M., Morrow, J. S., & Leavey, S. B. (1985). Report on the cost-benefit/effectiveness of treatment at the Johns Hopkins Center for Pathological Gambling. *Journal of Gambling Behavior, 1*, 131–142.

Prochaska, J. O., & DiClemente, C. C. (1986). Toward a comprehensive model of change. In W. R. Miller & N. Heather (Eds.), *Treating addictive behaviors: Processes of change* (pp. 3–27). New York: Plenum.

Prochaska, J. O., DiClemente, C. C., & Norcross, J. C. (1992). In search of how people change: Applications to addictive behaviors. *American Psychologist, 47*, 1102–1114.

Prochaska, J. O., Norcross, J. C., & DiClemente, C. C. (1994). *Changing for good*. New York: Avon Books.

Project MATCH Research Group (1997). Matching alcoholism treatments to client heterogeneity. Project MATCH post treatment drinking outcomes. *Journal of Studies on Alcohol, 58,* 7–29.

Rachlin, H. (1990). Why do people gamble and keep gambling despite heavy losses? *Psychological Science, 1,* 294–297.

Rachman, S. (1990). *Fear and courage* (2nd ed.). New York: W. H. Freeman & Company.

Reinert, D. (1998). The act of surrender: Then and now. *The Addiction Newsletter, 6*(1), 7–22.

Reinert, D. F. (1999). Surrender and narcissism: Assessing change over alcohol treatment. *Alcoholism Treatment Quarterly, 17*(3), 1–12.

Reith, G. (1999). *Age of chance: Gambling in western culture.* London: Routledge.

Robinson, T. A. (1995). *Aristotle in outline.* Indianapolis: Hackett.

Rogers, C. R. (1951). *Client-centered therapy.* Boston: Houghton-Mifflin.

Rose, I. N. (1988). Compulsive gambling and the law; From sin to vice to disease. *Journal of Gambling Behavior, 4,* 240–260.

Rosenthal, R. J., & Rugle, L. J. (1994). A psychodynamic approach to the treatment of pathological gambling: Part I. Achieving abstinence. *Journal of Gambling Studies, 10,* 21–42.

Rugle, L. J., & Rosenthal, R. J. (1994). Transference and countertransference reactions in the psychotherapy of pathological gamblers. *Journal of Gambling Studies, 10,* 43–65.

Russo, A. M., Taber, J. I., McCormick, R. A., & Ramirez, L. F. (1984). An outcome study of an inpatient treatment program for pathological gamblers. *Hospital and Community Psychiatry, 35,* 823–827.

Sanderson, C., & Linehan, M. (1999). Acceptance and forgiveness. In W. R. Miller (Ed.), *Integrating spirituality into treatment: Resources for practitioners* (pp. 199–216). Washington, DC: American Psychological Association.

Schwarz, J., & Lindner, A. (1992). Inpatient treatment of male pathological gamblers in Germany. *Journal of Gambling Studies, 8,* 93–109.

Seligman, M. E. P. (1991). *Learned optimism.* New York: Knopf.

Shafranske, E. P. (Ed.) (1996). *Religion and the clinical practice of psychology.* Washington, DC: American Psychological Association.

Sharpe, L., Tarrier, N., Schotte, D., & Spence, S. H. (1995). The role of autonomic arousal in problem gambling. *Addiction, 90,* 1529–1540.

Sherman, N. (1997). *Making a necessity of virtue: Aristotle and Kant on virtue.* Cambridge: Cambridge University Press.

Shoda, Y., Mischel, W., & Peake, P. K. (1990). Predicting adolescent cognitive and self-regulatory competencies from preschool delay of gratification: Identifying diagnostic conditions. *Developmental Psychology, 26,* 978–986.

Sobell, L. C. (2000). Discussant. In E. Wulfert (Chair), *"Wanna bet?": Treating compulsive gamblers.* Symposium conducted at the annual convention of the Association for Advancement of Behavior Therapy.

Spilka, B., & McIntosh, D. N. (Eds.) (1997). *The psychology of religion: Theoretical approaches.* Boulder, CO: Westview.

Steel, Z., & Blaszczynski, A. (1998). Impulsivity, personality disorders and pathological gambling severity. *Addiction, 93,* 895–905.

Steele, C. M., & Josephs, R. A. (1990). Alcohol myopia: Its prized and dangerous effects. *American Psychologist, 45,* 921–933.

Stinchfield, R. (2000). Gambling and correlates of gambling among Minnesota public school students. *Journal of Gambling Studies, 16,* 153–174.

Sylvain, C., Ladouceur, R., & Boisvert, J. M. (1997). Cognitive and behavioral treatment of pathological gambling: A controlled study. *Journal of Consulting and Clinical Psychology, 65,* 727–732.

Taber, J. I., & Chaplin, M. P. (1988). Group psychotherapy with pathological gamblers. *Journal of Gambling Behavior, 4,* 183–196.

Taber, J. I., McCormick, R. A., Russo, A. M., Adkins, B. J., & Ramirez, L. F. (1987). Follow-up of pathological gamblers after treatment. *American Journal of Psychiatry, 144,* 757–761.

Tavris, C. (1989). *Anger: The misunderstood emotion.* New York: Simon & Shuster.

Taylor, S. E., Wayment, H. A., & Collins, M. A. (1993). Positive illusions and affect regulation. In D. M. Wegner & J. W. Pennebaker (Eds.), *Handbook of mental control* (pp. 325–343). Englewood Cliffs: Prentice Hall.

Taylor, S. E., Pham, L. B., Rivkin, I. D., & Armor, D. A. (1998). Harnessing the imagination: Mental simulation, self-regulation, and coping. *American Psychologist, 53,* 429–439.

Teasdale, J. D. (1999). Emotional processing, three modes of mind and the prevention of relapse in depression. *Behaviour Research and Therapy, 37*(Suppl. 1), S53–S78.

Tice, D. M., & Baumeister, R. E. (1993). Controlling anger: Self-induced emotion change. In D. M. Wegner & J. W. Pennebaker (Eds.), *Handbook of mental control* (pp. 393–409). Englewood Cliffs: Prentice Hall.

Toneatto, T. (1999). Cognitive psychopathology of problem gambling. *Substance Use and Misuse, 34,* 1593–1604.

Toneatto, T., Blitz-Miller, T., Calderwood, K., Dragonetti, R., & Tsanos, A. (1997). Cognitive distortions in heavy gambling. *Journal of Gambling Studies, 13,* 253–266.

Tonigan, J. S., Toscova, R. T., & Connors, G. J. (1999). Spirituality and the 12-step programs: A guide for clinicians. In W. R. Miller (Ed.), *Integrating spirituality into treatment: Resources for practitioners* (pp. 111–132). Washington, DC: American Psychological Association.

Tugwell, S. (1985). *Ways of imperfection: An exploration of Christian spirituality.* Springfield, IL: Templegate.

Vitaro, F., Arseneault, L., & Tremblay, R. E. (1997). Dispositional predictors of problem gambling in male adolescents. *American Journal of Psychiatry, 154,* 1769–1770.

Volberg, R. (2000). *Risks and correlates of pathological gambling among women.* Paper presented at the 14th National Conference on Problem Gambling, Philadelphia.

Volberg, R. A., & Abbot, M. W. (1997). Gambling and problem gambling among indigenous peoples. *Substance Use and Misuse, 32,* 1525–1538.

Wagenaar, W. A. (1988). *Paradoxes of gambling behaviour.* London: Lawrence Erlbaum Associates.

Walker, M. B. (1992). *The psychology of gambling.* Oxford: Pergamon.

Walsh, J. (2001). *Spirituality and recovery from pathological gambling.* Unpublished doctoral dissertation, Loyola College in Maryland.

Walters, G. D. (1997). Problem gambling in a federal prison population: Results from the South Oaks Gambling Screen. *Journal of Gambling Studies, 13*, 7–24.

Watson, D., & Clark, L. A. (1993). Behavioral disinhibition versus constraint: A dispositional perspective. In D. M. Wegner & J. W. Pennebaker (Eds.), *Handbook of mental control* (pp. 506–527). Englewood Cliffs: Prentice Hall.

Wegner, D. M. (1989). *White bears and other unwanted thoughts*. New York: Vintage.

Wegner, D. M. (1994). Ironic processes of mental control. *Psychological Review, 101*, 34–52.

Wegner, D. M., & Erber, R. (1992). The hyperaccessibility of suppressed thoughts. *Journal of Personality and Social Psychology, 63*, 903–912.

Wegner, D. M., & Erber, R. (1993). Social foundations of mental control. In D. M. Wegner & J. W. Pennebaker (Eds.), *Handbook of mental control* (pp. 36–56). Englewood Cliffs: Prentice Hall.

Wells, A. (1997). *Cognitive therapy of anxiety disorders: A practice manual and conceptual guide*. Chichester: Wiley.

Wells, A. (2000). *Emotional disorders and metacognition: Innovative cognitive therapy*. Chichester: Wiley.

Wells, K. B. (1999). Treatment research at the crossroads: The scientific interface of clinical trials and effectiveness research. *American Journal of Psychiatry, 156*, 5–10.

Wiebe, J. M. D., Cox, B. J., & Mehmel, B. G. (2000). The South Oaks Gambling Screen Revised for Adolescents (SOGS-RA): Further psychometric findings from a community sample. *Journal of Gambling Studies, 16*, 275–288.

Wiggins, J. S. (Ed.) (1996). *The five factor model of personality*. New York: Guilford.

Winters, K. C., & Anderson, N. (2000). Gambling involvement and drug use among adolescents. *Journal of Gambling Studies, 2000*, 175–198.

Winters, K. C., Bengston, P., Dorr, D., & Stinchfield, R. (1998). Prevalence and risk factors of problem gambling among college students. *Psychology of Addictive Behaviors, 12*, 127–135.

Wolfgang, A. K. (1988). Gambling as a function of gender and sensation seeking. *Journal of Gambling Behavior, 4*, 71–77.

Wood, G. (1992). Predicting outcomes: Sports and stocks. *Journal of Gambling Studies, 8*, 201–222.

Zitrow, D. (1996). Comparative study of problematic gambling behaviors between American indian and non-Indian adolescents within and near a norther plains reservation. *American Indian and Alaska Native Mental Health Research, 7*, 14–26.

Zuckerman, M. (1979). *Sensation seeking: Beyond the optimal level of arousal*. Hillsdale, NJ: Erlbaum.

Zuckerman, M. (1994). *Behavioral expressions and biosocial bases of sensation seeking*. New York: Cambridge University Press.

Zuckerman, M. (1999). *Vulnerability to psychopathology: A biosocial model*. Washington, DC: American Psychological Association.

National Council on Problem Gambling (NCPG) Affiliate List

National Council on Problem Gambling
208 G Street, NE
Washington, DC 20002
24-hour confidential helpline: 1-800-522-4700
http://www.ncpgambling.org

Arizona Council on Compulsive Gambling
Tel: 602.212.0278
Fax: 602.212.1725
Email: azccg@infinet-is.com
Helpline: 800.777.7207

Contact: Don Hulen, Executive Director
P.O. Box 23896
2922 N. 7th Avenue
Phoenix, AZ 85063
www.azccg.org

California Council on Problem Gambling
Tel: 760.320.0234
Fax: 760.416.1349
Email: onexbettor@aol.com
Helpline: 800.522.4700

Contact: Tom Tucker, Executive Director
121 S. Palm Canyon Drive
Suite 225
Palm Springs, CA 92262
www.calproblemgambling.org

Colorado Council on Compulsive Gambling
Tel: 303.400.3456
Fax: 303.400.3454
Email: commlink@worldnet.att.net
Helpline: 800.522.4700

Contact: Renee Rupe, Executive Director
P.O. Box 460625 (zip 80046-0625)
Aurora, CO 80015

Connecticut Council on Compulsive Gambling
Tel: 203.453.0138
Fax: 203.453.9142
Email: ccpg@ccpg.org
Helpline: 800.346.6238

Contact: Marvin Steinberg, Executive Director
47 Clapboard Hill Road
Suite 6
Guilford, CT 06437
www.ccpg.org

Delaware Council on Gambling Problems
Tel: 302.655.3261
Fax: 302.984.2269
Email: dcgp@dcgp.org
Helpline: 888.850.8888

Contact: Lisa Pertzoff, Executive Director
100 W. 10th Street
Suite 303
Wilmington, DE 19801-1677
www.dcgp.org

Florida Council on Compulsive Gambling
Tel: 407.865.6200
Fax: 407.865.6103
Email: flccg@aol.com
Helpline: 800.426.7711

Contact: Pat Fowler, Executive Director
P.O. Box 916187
145 Wekiwa Springs Road, Suite 105
Longwood, FL 32791-6187
www.gamblingproblem.org

Illinois Council on Problem and Compulsive Gambling
Tel: 847.296.2026
Fax: 773.589.2425
Email: seisenmd@aol.com
Helpline: 800.522.4700

Contact: Seth Eisenberg, President
8422 W. Sunnyside
Chicago, IL 60656

Indiana Council on Problem Gambling
Tel: 219.489.0506
Fax: 219.489.0506
Email: drwrphil@aol.com
Helpline: 800.994.8448

Contact: Ron Phillips, Ph.D., Executive Director
10104 Manhattan Circle
Fort Wayne, IN 46825

Kansas Coalition on Compulsive Gambling
Tel: 785.295.8361
Fax: 785.295.7977
Email: dxmd@srskansas.org
Helpline: 866.662.3800

Contact: Joyce Markham, President
St. Francis Hospital, Attn: Joyce Markham
1700 W. 7th
Topeka, KS 66606

Kentucky Council on Compulsive Gambling
Tel: 502.223.1823
Fax: 502.227.8082
Email: kmstone@mis.net
Helpline: 800.426.2537

Contact: Mike Stone, Executive Director
P.O. Box 4595
Frankfort, KY 40604-4595

Louisiana Association on Compulsive Gambling
Tel: 318.222.7657
Fax: 318.222.3273
Email: reece@councilonalcoholism.com
Helpline: 877.770.7867

Contact: Reece Middleton, Executive Dir.
2000 Fairfield Avenue
Shreveport, LA 71101-4581

www.laprobgamb.org

Maryland Council on Problem Gambling
    Tel: 410.788.8599
    Fax: 410.719.6298
    Email: jfranklin@trimeridian.com
    Helpline: 800.522.4700

Contact: Joanna Franklin, President
503 Maryland Avenue
Baltimore, MD 21228

Massachusetts Council on Compulsive Gambling
    Tel: 617.426.4554
    Fax: 617.426.4555
    Email: gambling@aol.com
    Helpline: 800.426.1234

Contact: Kathleen Scanlan, Executive Dir.
190 High Street
Suite 5
Boston, MA 02110
www.masscompulsivegambling.org

Michigan Council on Problem Gambling
    Tel: 313.396.0404
    Fax: 313.396.0407
    Email: casellink@aol.com
    Helpline: 800.270.7117

Contact: Warren Biller, Executive Director
18530 Mac Avenue
#552
Detroit, MI 48236

Minnesota Council on Compulsive Gambling
    Tel: 218.722.1503
    Fax: 218.722.0346
    Email: bgeorge@nati.org
    Helpline: 800.541.4557

Contact: Betty George, Executive Director
314 W. Superior Street
Suite 702
Duluth, MN 55802
www.nati.org

Missouri Council on Problem Gambling Concerns
    Tel: 816.531.7133
    Fax: 816.861.5087
    Email: moprobgamb@aol.com
    Helpline: 888.238.7633

Contact: Keith Spare, Executive Director
5128 Brookside Blvd.
Kansas City, MO 64112-2736

Mississippi Council on Problem and Compulsive Gambling
    Tel: 601.981.0878
    Fax: 601.981.0637
    Email: mcpcg@netdoor.com
    Helpline: 888.777.9696

Contact: Betty Greer, Executive Dir.
P.O. Box 12284 (zip 39236)
440 Bounds Street, Suite G
Jackson, MS 39206
www.msgambler.org

Montana Council on Problem Gambling
Tel: 406.256.1848
Fax: 406.256.1948
Email: mtcpg@mtcpg.org
Helpline: 888.900.9979

Contact: Gary Knopp, Executive Director
3300 2nd Avenue North
Suite 2
Billings, MT 59101
www.mtcpg.org

Nebraska Council on Compulsive Gambling
Tel: 402.292.0061
Fax: 402.291.4605
Email: exnccjb@aol.com
Helpline: 800.560.2126

Contact: Jerry Bauerkemper, Ex. Director
119 Mission Avenue, Suite G
Bellevue, NE 68005

www.nebraskacouncil.com

Nevada Council on Problem Gambling
Tel: 702.369.9740
Fax: 702.369.9765
Email: nevcouncil@aol.com
Helpline: 800.522.4700

Contact: Carol O'Hare, Executive Director
3006 S. Maryland Pkwy.
Suite 405
Las Vegas, NV 89109
www.nevadacouncil.org

New Hampshire Council on Problem Gambling
Tel: 603.256.6262
Fax: West Chesterfield, NH 03466
Email: vcpgjoym@sover.net
Helpline: 802.254.9800

Contact: Joy Mitchell, Executive Director
P.O. Box 13

New Mexico Council on Problem Gambling
Tel: 505.298.0165
Fax: 505.323.7765
Email: paceabq@aol.com
Helpline: 800.572.1142

Contact: Kandace Blanchard, Executive Director
5850 Eubank, NE B62
Albuquerque, NM 87111

New York Council on Problem Gambling
Tel: 518.427.1622
Fax: 518.427.6181
Email: jmoore@nyproblemgambling.org
Helpline: 800.437.1611

Contact: Jim Moore, Executive Director
119 Washington Avenue
The Dodge Building
Albany, NY 12210-2292
www.nyproblemgambling.org

Council on Compulsive Gambling of North Dakota
Tel: 701.255.2756
Fax: 701.255.2411
Email: bje@btigate.com
Helpline: 800.472.2911

Contact: Dick Elefson, Administrator
P.O. Box 7362 (zip 58507-7362)
418 E. Rosser, Suite C
Bismark, ND 58501

Ohio Council on Problem Gambling
Tel: 614.431.0887
Fax: 866.647.4700
Email: ahunter@columbus.rr.com
Helpline: 866.647.4700

Contact: Esther Hunter, Executive Director & President
6211 Linworth Road
Worthington, OH 43085

Council on Compulsive Gambling of Pennsylvania
Tel: 215.744.1880
Fax: 215.879.2443
Email: pa.council.cg@nni.com
Helpline: 800.848.1880

Contact: Tony Millilo, Executive Director
1002 Longspur Road
Audubon, PA 19403

Rhode Island Council on Problem Gambling
Tel: 401.727.2836
Fax: 401.727.2846
Email: tombroffman@worldnet.att.net
Helpline: 877.942.6253

Contact: Thomas Broffman, Vice President
P.O. Box 6551
Providence, RI 02940-6551

South Carolina Council on Problem Gambling
Tel: 407.647.3895
Fax: 407.647.3894
Email: paulrashe@cs.com
Helpline: 800.522.4700

Contact: Paul Ashe
941 N. Orlando Avenue
Winterpark, FL 32789

South Dakota Council on Problem Gambling
Tel: 605.987.3152
Fax: 605.987.3363
Email: notnac@dtgnet.com
Helpline: 888.781.4357

Contact: Larry Atwood, Executive Director
3818 S. Western Avenue
Suite 177

Texas Council on Problem and Compulsive Gambling
- Tel: 972.889.2331
- Fax: 972.889.2383
- Email: tcpcg@waymark.net
- Helpline: 800.522.4700

Contact: Sharon Lichtenstein, Deputy Director
P.O. Box 835895
Richardson, TX 75083

Vermont Council on Problem Gambling
- Tel: 802.254.9800
- Fax: 802.254.9888
- Email: vcpgjoym@sover.net
- Helpline: 888.882.8274

Contact: Joy Mitchell, Executive Director
P.O. Box 381
Brattleboro, VT 05302-0381

Washington State Council on Problem Gambling
- Tel: 206.546.6133
- Fax: 206.542.8981
- Email: ghanson@harbornet.com
- Helpline: 800.547.6133

Contact: Gary Hanson, Executive Director
P.O. Box 55272
Seattle, WA 98155-0272

www.wscpg.org

Wisconsin Council on Problem Gambling
- Tel: 920.437.8888
- Fax: 920.437.8995
- Email: wcpgamble5@itol.com
- Helpline: 800.426.2535

Contact: Rose Gruber, Executive Director
1825 Riverside Drive
Green Bay, WI 54301

www.wi-problemgamblers.org

Worksheets

Worksheet 7.1

Consequences of Gambling Checklist

Name: _____

Date: _____

Place a checkmark next to any item that occurred as a result of gambling.

For each item checked please rate how bothered you were by that consequence

0	1	2	3	4
not at all		somewhat		very much

	Occurred (checkmark)	Bothered (0–4)
Occupied too much time	_____	_____
Conflict at work	_____	_____
Felt out of control	_____	_____
Couldn't keep mind on job	_____	_____
Arguments with spouse/partner	_____	_____
Arguments with children	_____	_____
Arguments with other family members	_____	_____
Lost self-respect	_____	_____
Felt guilty	_____	_____
Spent less time at work	_____	_____
Time away from family activities	_____	_____
Spent less time with nongambling friends	_____	_____
Told lies	_____	_____
Didn't give others attention	_____	_____
Unpaid debts to friends	_____	_____
Unpaid debts on credit cards	_____	_____
Unpaid debts to banks/lending institutions	_____	_____
Late paying household bills	_____	_____
Late paying loans	_____	_____
Late paying credit cards	_____	_____
Illegal acts (other than gambling itself)	_____	_____
Unable to take vacations	_____	_____
Spouse/partner criticized you	_____	_____
Friends criticized you	_____	_____
Family members criticized you	_____	_____
Employer/co-workers criticized you	_____	_____
Violated your personal values	_____	_____
Unable to reach your career goals	_____	_____
Unable to reach your family goals	_____	_____
Unable to reach your financial goals	_____	_____
Unable to reach your spiritual goals	_____	_____
Kept secrets from people you're close to	_____	_____
Became violent	_____	_____
Thought about dying	_____	_____
Thought about hurting yourself	_____	_____
Tried to hurt yourself	_____	_____
Lost a job	_____	_____
Had things you purchased repossessed	_____	_____
Late paying rent	_____	_____

Worksheet 7.2
Decisional Balance

Continuing to gamble	Stopping gambling
Benefits	Benefits
Costs	Costs

Goal-Setting Worksheet

A. Developing *Abstinence/Recovery* Goals

    1. Goals for the next 10 years.

    2. Goals for the next 5 years.

    3. Goals for the next year.

    4. Goals if I died in six months.

B. Values Clarification

As I inspect these goals, do they appear to take into consideration my highest values? If not, add or adjust individual goals accordingly.

C. Finalized goal to work on immediately

Goal-Setting Worksheet

A. Developing *Occupational* Goals

   1. Goals for the next 10 years.

   2. Goals for the next 5 years.

   3. Goals for the next year.

   4. Goals if I died in six months.

B. Values Clarification

As I inspect these goals, do they appear to take into consideration my highest values? If not, add or adjust individual goals accordingly.

C. Finalized goal to work on immediately

Goal-Setting Worksheet

A. Developing *Family* Goals

   1. Goals for the next 10 years.

   2. Goals for the next 5 years.

   3. Goals for the next year.

   4. Goals if I died in six months.

B. Values Clarification

As I inspect these goals, do they appear to take into consideration my highest values? If not, add or adjust individual goals accordingly.

C. Finalized goal to work on immediately

Goal-Setting Worksheet

A. Developing *Relationship* Goals

   1. Goals for the next 10 years.

   2. Goals for the next 5 years.

   3. Goals for the next year.

   4. Goals if I died in six months.

B. Values Clarification

As I inspect these goals, do they appear to take into consideration my highest values? If not, add or adjust individual goals accordingly.

C. Finalized goal to work on immediately

Worksheet 7.7
Goal-Setting Worksheet

A. Developing *Health* Goals

   1. Goals for the next 10 years.

   2. Goals for the next 5 years.

   3. Goals for the next year.

   4. Goals if I died in six months.

B. Values Clarification

As I inspect these goals, do they appear to take into consideration my highest values? If not, add or adjust individual goals accordingly.

C. Finalized goal to work on immediately

A. Developing *Financial* Goals

   1. Goals for the next 10 years.

   2. Goals for the next 5 years.

   3. Goals for the next year.

   4. Goals if I died in six months.

B. Values Clarification

As I inspect these goals, do they appear to take into consideration my highest values? If not, add or adjust individual goals accordingly.

C. Finalized goal to work on immediately

Goal-Setting Worksheet

A. Developing *Recreational/Entertainment* Goals

1. Goals for the next 10 years.

2. Goals for the next 5 years.

3. Goals for the next year.

4. Goals if I died in six months.

B. Values Clarification

As I inspect these goals, do they appear to take into consideration my highest values? If not, add or adjust individual goals accordingly.

C. Finalized goal to work on immediately

Goal-Setting Worksheet

A. Developing *Spiritual/Religious/Personal Character* Goals

   1. Goals for the next 10 years.

   2. Goals for the next 5 years.

   3. Goals for the next year.

   4. Goals if I died in six months.

B. Values Clarification

As I inspect these goals, do they appear to take into consideration my highest values? If not, add or adjust individual goals accordingly.

C. Finalized goal to work on immediately

Goals-Summary Worksheet

Fill in from *item C* on the previous worksheets for *each of the content* areas.

Occupational:

Family:

Relationships:

Health:

Financial:

Recreational/Entertainment:

Spiritual/Religious/Personal Character

D. *To become aware of the potential conflicts among your goals, rate each one as to how important it is to you.* On a scale from 1 to 10, with 1 having little importance, and 10 having great importance. Put the number right next to the goal.

E. If any goals present a major conflict; problem-solve around them, and adjust accordingly.

F. **Now transfer your goals onto the Goal-Planning Worksheet, and add specific steps for accomplishing each one.**

Worksheet 7.12
Goal-Planning Worksheet

I. Using your Goals-Summary Worksheet, develop a plan for each content area.

II. Circle the content area for this plan.

Abstinence	Family	Relationship	Health
Financial	Recreational	Spiritual/Character	Occupation

III. Overall Goal:

IV. Steps necessary to attain goal

    1.   Date completed

    2.   Date completed

    3.   Date completed

V. Possible obstacle(s)

Specific steps to overcome obstacle(s)

1.

2.

3.

Resolving Goal Conflicts Worksheet

Strategy I. Decisional Balance

Benefits of achieving Goals A and B   Disadvantages of achieving Goals A and B

Benefits of *not* achieving Goals A and B   Disadvantages of *not* achieving Goals A and B

Strategy II. Setting Priorities, or Grandma's Rule

Some goals that appear to be in conflict can be resolved simply by setting priorities. For example, keeping a clean house vs. going fishing. Grandma's rule says, *Do the least appealing project **before** doing the more appealing one.* Grandma put it differently, "If you eat your spinach, you'll get your ice cream."

How could setting priorities resolve my goal conflicts?

Strategy III. Two-Chair Technique

1. Set up two chairs.
2. Identify one chair for Goal A, another for Goal B.
3. Argue the case aloud for Goal A in first chair.
4. Switch chairs. Argue the case for Goal B in second chair.
5. Do this until you notice a clear sense of direction toward one or the other.

Strategy IV. Visualization

1. Visualize conflict by changing it to a picture or metaphor, being handcuffed, being caught between two attractive entertainments, etc.
2. Visualize selecting Goal A.
3. Visualize all the consequences of this choice, feelings, behavior, what you think of yourself, what others will think, etc.
4. Visualize all consequences of Goal B in similar fashion.
5. Now which seems to be of more benefit?

Gambling Triggers Worksheet

1. **Describe a situation when I gambled recently**.
   What did I do earlier in the day?
   What did I do an hour before gambling?
   What did I do 30 minutes before gambling?
   What did I do 5 minutes before gambling?
   Feelings? Mood?

2. **Triggers Chart**.   Rate the intensity of urge to gamble at each stage.

   Urge Intensity Scale
   0–2   minimal
   3–4   moderate
   5–6   intense
   7–8   overwhelming

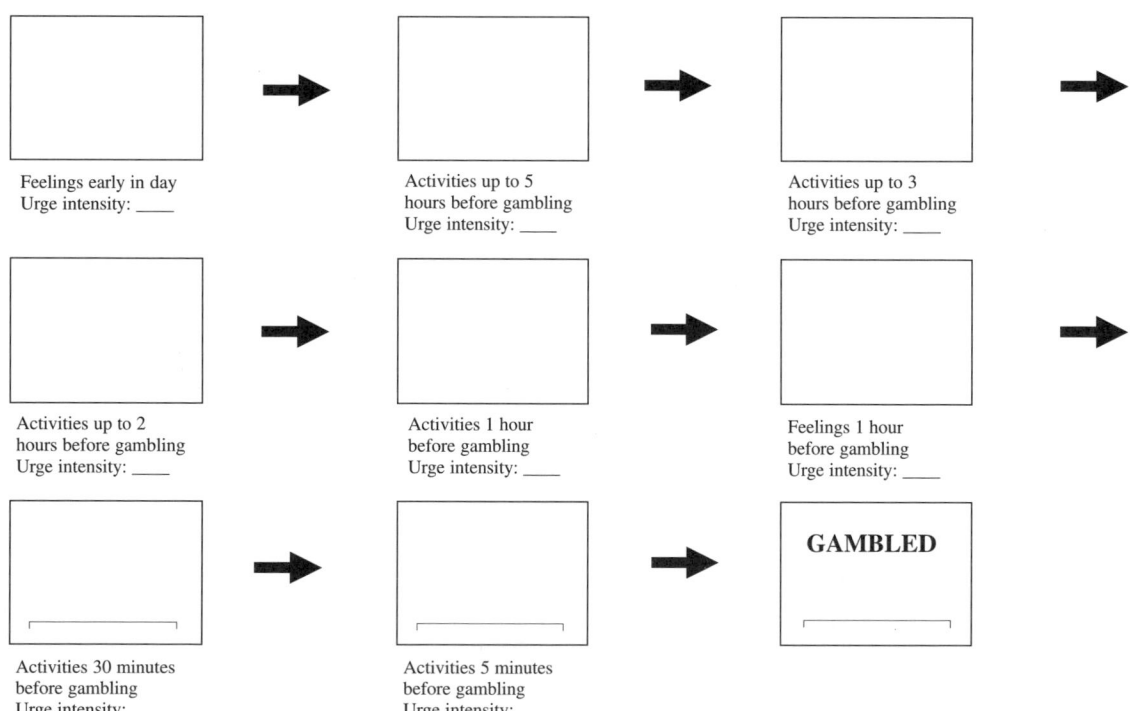

Feelings early in day
Urge intensity: _____

Activities up to 5
hours before gambling
Urge intensity: _____

Activities up to 3
hours before gambling
Urge intensity: _____

Activities up to 2
hours before gambling
Urge intensity: _____

Activities 1 hour
before gambling
Urge intensity: _____

Feelings 1 hour
before gambling
Urge intensity: _____

Activities 30 minutes
before gambling
Urge intensity: _____

Activities 5 minutes
before gambling
Urge intensity: _____

GAMBLED

Worksheet 8.2

Coping with Relapse
Lapse/Slip Analysis Worksheet

1. When a slip/lapse occurs, people often feel blindsided by the event. Yet they fail to see how they may have put the blinders on themselves. Slips usually occur when people take a step early in the slip process that makes resistance extremely difficult. Problem gamblers who were admitted to the addiction treatment hospital where I worked would sometimes decide to drive through Atlantic City. It was actually 200 hundred miles out of the way, but they wanted to take "the scenic route." Did they consciously intend to gamble? Some didn't. Was it sensible? What do you think?

2. The purpose of this worksheet is to dissect a recent slip/lapse to see whether you did things early in the process that made the slip more difficult to resist.

3. Use your Triggers Worksheet to analyze a recent slip/lapse.

4. Break down the event roughly into these stages:

   Preparatory:

   Middle:

   Ending:

5. What choice(s) did you make in the preparatory stage that you can now see set the stage for the slip/lapse?

   a. How did this/these choice(s) contribute to the slip/lapse?

   b. How aware were you *at the time* that this choice could be closely linked to a slip?

   c. How aware now?

   d. What do you need to do differently to keep the blinders off?

Gambling Behavior Warning Signs

Warning signs that I may be gambling or feeling urges to gamble

1.

2.

3.

4.

5.

6.

7.

8.

9.

10.

11.

12.

Coping with Relapse
Containing a Slip by Stopping Snowballing

1. Describe your slip/lapse.

2. Negative Thoughts about the Slip/lapse.

   A. Thoughts related to: *I messed up, might as well go all the way and do it right.*

   B. Thoughts related to: *It's no use, what's the point, I'm not strong enough anyway.*

3. Consequences of Negative Thoughts

   A. Negative Feelings.

   B. Effect on My Self-Esteem

   C. What I feel like doing right now.

4. Challenging the Negative Thoughts.

   A. Yes, I messed up—*but*, how worse will a binge make my situation?

   What resources do I have to get back on my feet?

   Who will support me even now if I sincerely try?

   Even though I made a mistake what personal qualities do I still have that are worthwhile?

   What evidence do I have that I still have some personal control?

   B. How can I use the slip as a learning experience?

   What would I do differently?

5. New Way of Thinking and Feeling

6. Plan for my Next Step.

   Who do I contact and share?

   What do I do next to get back in recovery?

Worksheet 9.1
Emotion Regulation
Introduction to Urge Surfing: Rehearsal Worksheet

1. **Rationale**. People often feel overwhelmed by their urges and cravings to engage in self-defeating behavior such as gambling, drinking alcohol, using drugs, overeating, and inappropriate sex. They more or less have the idea that strong urges/cravings *require* acting on them.

   In reality, we control the majority of our urges most of the time. Scientific proof of this statement comes from the fact that a great percentage of infants prone to screaming in the middle of the night reach their first birthday despite the homicidal urges of sleepy parents in the middle of the night.

2. In the following exercise, you are asked to *imagine* some aspect of your problem behavior, particularly situations that typically tend to trigger that urge in you. For a gambler, it might be reading about the point spread for football games in the newspaper or hearing a hot tip on a horse. For other problem behavior, it might be passing a bar or street corner where you did drugs.

3. Close your eyes and calmly visualize yourself in that setting. Imagine as clearly as you can its sights, sounds, colors, emotional feelings, energy, excitement, allure, and your own reactions. Play the scene out slowly as if you were watching it on video.
   A. As you begin, note the intensity of any urges to engage in your problem behavior that may perhaps arise. Describe its intensity on a scale of 0–9, with 0 being no intensity at all, and 9 being as intense as you could ever imagine.
   B. Continue to play the scene out in your head for 4–5 minutes, periodically jotting down the intensity level that you are experiencing.

4. Analysis
   A. What did you notice about your urge levels throughout the exercise?
      a. You may have noticed that it was not nearly as intense for you as the real situation, because it was only imaginary.
      b. If you are like most people, you may have also noticed *both* (a) your attention wandered a lot, making it difficult to keep thinking about the situation, and (b) your urge intensity fluctuated considerably over time.
   B. Assuming this was the case for you, what are the implications of how easy it is for our minds to wander, and how rapidly urges change their intensity over time?
      a. What does this suggest about your ability to maintain control over your urges?
      b. What would be a sensible emotional response to having these urges, instead of a sense of panic about being overwhelmed?

5. **Conclusions**. Thousands of years ago, spiritual masters discovered how to draw on the mind's power to control strong urges, and today psychologists are studying these methods scientifically. Spiritual masters call this practice "acceptance."
   A. Some psychologists who have applied these tools to recovery call this skill "urge surfing." The idea is not to fight the thoughts about gambling, drinking, using, etc., but to let the thoughts "surf" your mind in the same way that surfers handle strong waves—not by fighting or resisting, but by moving in harmony with them.
      a. Rather than being overwhelmed by this powerful force, people can learn how to let its energy work for them, and, most importantly, not to flee from them.
   B. If you would like to try out urge surfing, use the Acceptance–Urge Surfing Worksheet to see how it might work the next time you experience a notable urge or craving.

Worksheet 9.2

Emotion Regulation
Acceptance—Urge Surfing Worksheet

1. Describe the situation in which you currently are experiencing an urge to gamble.

2. Rate its intensity level (0 very low; 9 extreme).

3. Resisting the idea creates "The White Bear Effect." The novelist Leo Tolstoy's older brother told Leo when he was a child that they could play together as soon as Leo would go in a corner and truthfully say he was not thinking about white bears. Naturally, his brother's suggestion meant Leo could never get the idea out of his, so his brother was never bothered by Leo.

4. Instead of fighting the thought/urge, consider urge surfing it or accepting it.

5. Process:

   A. Observe, describe, but do not evaluate the goodness or badness of the urge/craving. Be aware that it simply *is*.

   B. You will note, perhaps, that the urge/craving fades somewhat at times, increases at other times, and may altogether disappear.

   C. Can you think of yourself surfing the urge the way a swimmer surfs a wave?

   D. Or, perhaps, observing the urge is like watching a fish in a large aquarium. It moves around, sometimes stopping in the middle to stare back at the spectator, sometimes moving left to right, sometimes disappearing altogether behind the sea plants.

   E. Every so often write down the intensity of the urge.

   Observation   Intensity Level

6. Continue the process until you notice you are feeling much more in control—not of the urge (after all, the urge *is* not-you) but in control of yourself existing side by side with the urge or craving.

7. Conclusions you have drawn from this experience?

Challenging Beliefs Leading to Negative Feelings

Situation: Describe the situation around the time you were feeling anxious, depressed, guilty, or angry.

Beliefs: What negative *beliefs* or *expectations* automatically went through you mind when you were in that situation?

Feelings: What painful feelings did these beliefs or expectations lead to?

Challenging the Beliefs or Expectations: Is there any evidence that those beliefs or expectations are not totally accurate? Describe the contrary evidence.

Coping with the Situation: Even if the situation can't change, what evidence do you have that you could manage it? Based on your talents? Your past experience? Support persons? Resources?

New Perspective: What is a different way to now look at the situation?

Changed Feeling: How did your feelings change after you looked at the situation differently?

List of Beliefs about Gambling
and Reasons for Gambling

Check all that apply.

- ❐ I have a system that works.
- ❐ I'm a lucky person.
- ❐ I'm a positive thinker.
- ❐ Fate is on my side.
- ❐ I'm a more knowledgeable gambler than most.
- ❐ My system can beat the odds.
- ❐ I've won before.
- ❐ I'm at my lucky place.
- ❐ I deserve to win.
- ❐ Others can't keep up with me.
- ❐ The time is right.
- ❐ I have this special feeling.
- ❐ I can influence the outcome.
- ❐ I am confident in myself.
- ❐ I have prayed.
- ❐ I have my lucky object.
- ❐ After so many losses, it's the time to win.
- ❐ I am very experienced.
- ❐ My luck has changed.
- ❐ Today is lucky.
- ❐ Gambling will solve my problems.
- ❐ Gambling will make me feel better.

Other: _____

_____

_____

_____

Gambling Beliefs and Reasons Worksheet

I gambled, desire to gamble, or will gamble because
(select most important reasons from checklist)

1. _____
2. _____
3. _____
4. _____
5. _____

Evidence for these ideas: _____
_____
_____

Evidence against these ideas: _____
_____
_____

Positive consequences if I gamble   **Negative consequences if I gamble**

Negative consequences if I don't gamble   **Positive consequences if I don't gamble**

Decision: _____

Why: _____

Strategies for not gambling: _____

Worksheet 11.3
Gambling Timeline

Name: _____

Date: _____

Part A: Select the most recent week in which you gambled.

Days gambled	Amount gambled	Net loss	Net win
_____	_____	_____	_____

Part B: Think about the three months prior to this most recent week.

First month

	Days gambled	Amount gambled	Net loss/net win
Week 1	_____	_____	_____
Week 2	_____	_____	_____
Week 3	_____	_____	_____
Week 4	_____	_____	_____
Total:	_____	_____	_____

Second Month

	Days gambled	Amount gambled	Net loss/net win
Week 1	_____	_____	_____
Week 2	_____	_____	_____
Week 3	_____	_____	_____
Week 4	_____	_____	_____
Total:	_____	_____	_____

Third Month

	Days gambled	Amount gambled	Net loss/net win
Week 1	_____	_____	_____
Week 2	_____	_____	_____
Week 3	_____	_____	_____
Week 4	_____	_____	_____
Total:	_____	_____	_____

Problem-Solving Worksheet

I. **Description of current problem**

1. Define the problem.

2. How does it interfere with important goals in your life?

3. Is the problem related to any of the following:

   a. aimlessness, i.e., lack of a goal?
   b. too rigid of a goal?
   c. incompatible goals?
   d. overextending; biting off more than I can chew?

4. If yes to any of these, first identify what is the most important goal—the primary goal and purpose in wanting to solve this problem.

II. **Motivation for solving the problem**

Benefits of solving it   Benefits of not solving it

Negatives of solving it   Negatives of not solving it

III. **Final problem definition**

IV. **List as many solutions as possible**. Quantity, not quality of solutions is important. Do not censor or evaluate solutions, yet.

V. **Place a + or – next to solutions as to their effectiveness**

VI. **Select solution(s)**

VIII. **Identify specifics of implementing the solution**

Who?

What?

When?

Where?

How?

Date completed:

VIII. **Evaluate the solution**

Adjustments?

Changing Behavior
Procrastination Analysis Worksheet

1. People usually procrastinate for one of two reasons.

   A. *Fear or worry about being criticized* about the task, or not doing it as well as it should be done. The criticism can be from others, or from within me.

   B. The task itself is *boring, uninteresting, or unimportant* to them.

2. Describe the task(s) you are currently procrastinating on.

   A. What part, if any, relates to concern about doing it well?

   B. What part, if any, relates to being boring, uninteresting, or unimportant to you?

3. Describe the negative automatic thoughts behind each part.

   A. Worry concern, e.g., I might not do it well enough

   B. Not important, e.g., I'm wasting my time, it's not important, I should only do things that are interesting and engaging.

4. Consequences of these negative beliefs.

   A. *Emotional* Consequences: As a result of procrastinating what do I end up feeling?

   B. *Behavioral* Consequences: What are the *effects* of procrastinating on my occupation, relationships, health, finances, self-worth, recovery, spiritual/personal development? (Reply to all that are relevant.)

5. Challenging these negative automatic thoughts.

   A. What are alternatives to my *anxiety-related* concerns? What is the evidence I *can* do this adequately?

   B. How might I be over-predicting a bad outcome, thinking in all-or-none terms, fortune-telling what others think or feel, etc.?

   C. Even if I didn't do it perfectly well, or had to admit that I messed up, how could I cope with that?

6. New way of viewing the situation

Procrastination Change Worksheet

1. Describe the task that you are procrastinating on.

2. Break it down into three parts.

    Beginning/Preparation

    Middle

    Ending

3. *Visualize each sequence slowly*, as if watching yourself doing the task on video.

    Make sure you see yourself doing even the smallest part of each step, e.g., filing individual pages into a folder; opening the paint can with a screwdriver; deciding which space to place the clutter.

    Rate your feelings on a scale of 1–9, with 1 being very negative, 5 neither positive nor negative, and 9 being very positive.

4. *Repeat the visualization* of yourself doing the task for a period of about 5 to 10 minutes. Rate your feelings after the last visualization in the same manner that you did after the first one.

5. *Action Steps*

    A. Set aside a period of time for the task.

    B. Once you are actually in that time period, examine the component parts that you listed under #2 above.

    C. Take the very first step and *break it down even further* into 2–4 smaller steps. For example, if the task is clear clutter off the desk:

        a. decide where the items are to go
        b. decide on what type of containers to put them in
        c. gather the actual containers

D. Begin by doing just the first step in this smaller sequence; then the second, third, and so forth, completing all the tasks in the Beginning/Preparatory stage.

    a.   now rate your feelings from negative to positive.

E. Be aware of how, perhaps, you have gained some momentum and can just keep going.

F. Keep a record of what got accomplished and when.

        Finished   When

_____

_____

_____

_____

_____

_____

_____

_____

_____

_____

G. If stuck, identify the next step, and break it down into 2–4 smaller parts.

H. Continue as in previous section. Visualize again, if necessary.

Truthfulness

Theme: **Truthfulness**—presenting myself to others as I really am

Extremes:

1. Boastful, *taking credit* for what I didn't do, wanting to appear as more than I am, lying to look good.
2. Putting myself down, *claiming less* about myself, lying so as to not look bad.

Gambling traps:

1. Need to boast leads to gambling to impress others; to look like a big-shot, or I need lots of money to keep up my image.
2. If I lie to protect myself, eventually I will feel guilty and desire to gamble.

Evidence for my lack of truthfulness:

Cost/benefit analysis:
   Benefit of truthfulness
   Cost of truthfulness
   Benefit of not being truthful
   Cost of not being truthful

If I were more truthful I would do or look like:

The first concrete steps in being more truthful are:

   1.
   2.
   3.
   4.

I will begin working on it (time, day) _____

In what way?

Worksheet 15.2
Responsible Conscience

Theme: **Responsible Conscience**—developing an appropriate sense of right and wrong about my behavior

Extremes:
1. Having no shame or guilt about the wrong things I have done to others.
2. Excessive shame and guilt about the wrong things I have done to others.

Gambling traps:

If I am indifferent to shame and guilt I could:
1. Ignore making amends and use the extra money to gamble.
2. Not care about hurting others with my gambling.
3. Commit illegal acts that lead to prosecution.

By excessive focusing on my guilt I could:
1. Avoid people who are supportive to recovery because of embarrassment.
2. Shrink from making amends.
3. Gamble to feel better.

Tips
1. For indifference: make a list of people injured by your gambling and imagine what it would feel like if the same had been done to you. What would you think and feel? How would it have effected your life? Your future? Your goals?
2. For excessive guilt, see the strategies in the section on guilt in Chapter 10.

Evidence for my lack of responsible consciousness:

Cost/Benefit analysis:
   Benefit of responsible conscience
   Cost of responsible conscience
   Benefit of not having a responsible conscience
   Cost of not having a responsible conscience

With a responsible conscience I would behave or look like:

The first concrete steps in having a responsible conscience are:
1.
2.
3.
4.

I will begin working on it (time, day) _____

In what way?

Humility

Theme: **Humility**—keeping my true talents in perspective through a grateful understanding of gifts I have received, and gratitude toward those who have nurtured these gifts [including God or higher power for believers]

Extremes:
1. Entitlement, taking excessive credit for accomplishments, exaggerating accomplishments, thinking that "it's all about me," caring only about how things effect me.
2. Putting myself down, minimizing my accomplishments, having no satisfaction in my gifts or what I do for others, lacking self-respect.

Gambling traps:
1. When my ego is threatened I could:
   a. Gamble to prove myself
   b. Become verbally or physically abusive
   c. Try to get the best of others
2. When I have no self-pride I could:
   a. Gamble to distract myself from feeling badly about myself or from loneliness
   b. Turn off friends by expecting them to fill up what I should give myself

Evidence for my lack of humility:

Cost/Benefit analysis:
   Benefit of humility
   Cost of humility
   Benefit of not being humble
   Cost of not being humble

If I were more humble, I would do or it would look like:

The first concrete steps in being more humble are:
   1.
   2.
   3.
   4.

I will begin working on it (time, day) _____

In what way?

Justice

Theme: **Justice**—giving or returning to people what is their due

Extremes:
1. Giving less than is due.
2. Giving more than is due.

Gambling traps:
1. Failure to pay back my debts (financial or social) including
   a. personal loans; institutional loans; items of others that were sold, stolen, defrauded, or conned; taxes.

2. Desire to pay off gambling-specific debts (bookies, casinos, track, loan-sharks, etc.) because
   a. The debts remind me of my gambling failures
   b. Getting debt-free allows me to get back into action

Evidence for my lack of justice:

Cost/Benefit analysis:
   Benefit of justice
   Cost of justice
   Benefit of not being just
   Cost of not being just

If I were more just, I would do or it would look like:

The first concrete steps in being more just are:
   1.
   2.
   3.
   4.

I will begin working on it (time, day) _____

In what way?

Courage

Theme: **Courage**—strength in the face of vulnerability

Extremes:
1. Rashness, overconfidence against barriers, not respecting one's limits.
2. Fearfulness, lack of confidence in actual ability, excessive worry about the future.

Gambling traps:
1. Becoming an "adrenaline-junkie," living life on the edge, gambling to create excitement.
2. Gambling to numb out, to forget my fears and anxieties.

Evidence for my lack of courage:

Cost/Benefit analysis:
   Benefit of courage
   Cost of courage
   Benefit of not being courageous
   Cost of not being courageous

If I were more courageous, I would do or it would look like:

The first concrete steps in being more courageous are:
1.
2.
3.
4.

I will begin working on it (time, day) _____

In what way?

Temperance

Theme: **Temperance**—moderation in physical pleasure

Extremes:
1. Excessive drinking or eating, use of illegal, non-prescribed drugs, inappropriate sex.
2. Lack of self-care, neglect of health, workaholism.

Gambling traps:
1. Substitute one addiction for another.
2. Use of alcohol or drugs causes loss of control and leads to gambling.
3. Excessive self-denial causes resentment and leads to gambling "because I deserve it."

Evidence for my lack of temperance:

Cost/Benefit analysis:
Benefit of temperance
Cost of temperance
Benefit of not being temperate
Cost of not being temperate

If I were more temperate, I would do or it would look like:

The first concrete steps in being more temperate are:
1.
2.
3.
4.

I will begin working on it (time, day) _____

In what way?

Worksheet 15.7
Implementing Goals Assessment

1. Make a list of your major activities for the past week. It should represent a reasonably typical week in your life. If it was unusual in the sense that you spent it recuperating from surgery or were away on vacation, do not evaluate it. If it was hectic and chaotic, but this is fairly typical, then include those events.

	9 a.m.–12 noon	12 noon–5 p.m.	5–9 p.m.	10 p.m.+
Monday				
Tuesday				
Wednesday				
Thursday				
Friday				
Saturday				
Sunday				

2. Now relate this typical week schedule to your Goal Summary Worksheet, asking yourself the following questions.

Which of your goals are receiving too little attention?

Which are receiving too much attention?

Which are receiving about the right amount?

How is your shoulds/wants ratio? ["Shoulds": the things everyone *has* to do in life, e.g., wash dishes, pay bills, change diapers. "Wants": the things people enjoy, like, or find interesting, e.g., exercise, hobbies, vacations, eating out.]

Too heavy toward the shoulds?   Wants/Likes?   Right Balance?

If unbalanced, what needs to change?

Change Plan:

Worksheet 15.8
Virtue Diary

Morning Reflection

Virtue to work on today:

What situations will provide a chance to achieve my goal?

Evening reflection:

Situation(s) that gave me a chance to work on this virtue:

What I should have done:

What I actually did:

If I was not successful doing what I should have, what could I have done differently?

How?

Strategies for tomorrow: